Fishing Update No. I

Edited by Parker Bauer

PARKER BAUER has worked as a fishing guide, a newspaper environmental columnist, and a scriptwriter of documentary films on outdoor sports and natural history. He has edited numerous books for The Hunting & Fishing Library and other publishers.

CY DECOSSE INCORPORATED
Chairman: Cy DeCosse
President: James B. Maus
Executive Vice President: William B. Jones

FISHING UPDATE No. I
Editor and Project Director: Parker Bauer
Hunting & Fishing Library Director: Dick Sternberg
Project Managers: Jan Baron, Melissa Erickson, Tracy Holte
Art Directors: Bradley Springer, William B. Jones, Jim Schletty
Principal Photographer: William Lindner
Technical Photo Director: Joseph Cella
Staff Photographers: Rex Irmen, John Lauenstein
Contributing Photographers: Erwin & Peggy Bauer (pages 76-77, 78, 85, 87, 90, 93, 94, 99, 102, 105, 106, 118, 142-143, 152-153); Ken Darwin, Michigan Fisherman (115); Fred Dole (82); Bill Eppridge, Sports Illustrated (137); Daniel Halsey (24); Tom Huggler (60, 116); The In-Fisherman (45); Jack Parry (47); Steve Price (101); Bruce D. Rosenlund/U.S. Fish and Wildlife Service (132); William Roston (131, 133)
Illustrators: Joe Greenwald (138-139), Greg Hargreaves (148-149), Bob Millea (46, 48, 49), Todd Treadway (156-157, 158), Jon Q. Wright (61, 73, 128, 135)
Researchers: Rob Merila, Mike Hehner, Dave McCormack
Production Manager: Jim Bindas
Assistant Production Managers: Julie Churchill, Jacquie Marx
Typesetting: Jennie Smith, Linda Schloegel
Production Staff: Janice Cauley, Joe Fahey, Carol Kevan, Yelena Konrardy, David Schelitzche, Nik Wogstad

Cooperating Individuals and Agencies: Joel Anderson; Ron Blanchett; Wade Bourne; Richard W. Bowles; Tim Bozorth, Idaho Bureau of Land Management; Barry & Janet Brown, Clearwater West Resort; Ted Capra & Associates; Homer Circle; Soc Clay; Bob Clouser; Don Coffey Company; Ed Corkum; Mike Crowley; Robert E. David, U.S. Fish & Wildlife Service; Bump Elliot; Mark Emery; Kelly Ferguson; Butch Furtman; Leonard Holt; Paul C. Johnson; Glenn Lau; George Laycock; Andy Lessin; Nick Lyons; Minnesota Dept. of Natural Resources; Dennis Pixton; Joe Robinson; Max Robinson & Associates; Bruce Rosenlund, U.S. Fish & Wildlife Service; Johnny Slack; Neil Soderstrom; Gary Soucie; Dick Sternberg; The Tommy Thompson Company; Brad Weakley
Cooperating Manufacturers: AJ Custom Canvas; Alumacraft Boat Company; Angler's Pride; Fred Arbogast Company, Inc.; Arctic Cat Snowmobiles; Jim Bagley Bait Company, Inc.; Berkley, Inc.; Big Jon, Inc.; Blue Fox Tackle Company; Bomber Bait Company; E. F. Brewer Company; Brother's Bait Company; Browning; Bumble Bee Bait Company; Burke Fishing Lures; Bob Campfield Tip-Ups; Cannon/S & K Products, Inc.; Lew Childre & Sons, Inc.; Citation Tackle Company, Inc.; Classic Manufacturing Company; Cordell Tackle; Daiwa Corporation; Depth Talker, Inc.; Dri-Rind, Inc.; Du Pont Company; Evinrude Outboards; Feldmann Eng. & Mfg. Co., Inc. (Jiffy Ice Augers); Fenwick/Woodstream; Fish World Lures; Fishtec, Inc.; Furuno USA, Inc.; The Gaines Company; Glide-Rite, Inc.; Grumman Boats; Gudebrod, Inc.; HT Enterprises; Hankie Lure Company; Hart Tackle Company; James Heddon's Sons, Inc.; Hydra-Sports, Inc.; Impulse Manufacturing; Incoe Corporation (Speedtrol Downriggers); Ins-Tent Manufacturing; Johnson Fishing, Inc. (Minn Kota Trolling Motors); Johnson Outboards; Keeper Bait Company; King Marine Electronics, Inc.; Koden International, Inc.; Kwikfish Lures, Ltd.; L & S Bait Company of Florida; LC's Lures; Lamiglas, Inc.; Lazer Tail; Bill Lewis Lures; Lit'l Buffalo Bait Company; G. Loomis, Inc.; Lowrance Electronics, Inc.; Lund American, Inc.; Lunker Lure Products; Mann's Bait Company; Mariner Outboards; Martin Reel Company; Mercury Marine; Micronar Products/Si-Tex Marine Electronics; Mitchell, Inc.; Nordic Crestliner Boat Company; Norman Mfg. Company, Inc.; Northland Tackle Co.; The Orvis Company; Ozark Mountain Tackle Company; Penn Fishing Tackle Mfg. Co.; Pflueger Fishing Tackle; Poe's Lures; Proos Manufacturing Company; Rabble Rouser Lures; Rebel/Plastics Res. & Dev. Corp.; Ross Reels; Ryobi America Corporation; Sage; Scientific Anglers/3M; Shadow Lake Lures; Shakespeare Company; Shimano American Corporation; Skeeter Products; Specialists In Sports, Ltd.; Sports Specialties of Milwaukee; Storm Manufacturing Company; Strike Master, Inc.; Sunline Company, Ltd.; Suzuki America Corporation; TV Tackle, Inc.; Tru-Turn, Inc.; Vortex Lures; Walker Downriggers; The Weller Company; R. L. Winston Rod Co.; Wood Manufacturing Co., Inc. (Ranger Boats); Yamaha Motor Corporation; Zebco/MotorGuide; Zetabait, Inc.
Color Separations: La Cromolito
Printing: R. R. Donnelley & Sons Co.(0188)

Cover: Steelhead fishing on Ward Creek, Alaska (photo by Erwin & Peggy Bauer)

Also available from the publisher: *The Art of Freshwater Fishing, Cleaning & Cooking Fish, Fishing With Live Bait, Largemouth Bass, Panfish, The Art of Hunting, Fishing With Artificial Lures, Walleye, Smallmouth Bass, Dressing & Cooking Wild Game, Freshwater Gamefish of North America*

Library of Congress Catalog Card Number 87-27285
ISBN 0-86573-025-3

Distributed by Prentice Hall Press
A Division of Simon & Schuster, Inc., New York, NY
ISBN 0-13-319229-6

Contents

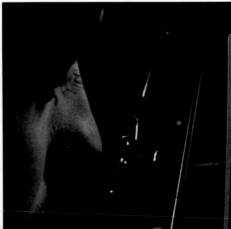
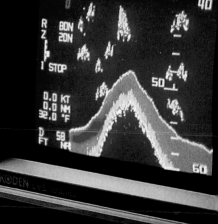

Introduction

Today, for the first time ever, you can buy a baitcasting reel with a built-in computer designed to prevent back-lashes, a setup that renders your thumb superfluous. Does it work? And, if it does, is such a device a servant or a thief?

Even curiouser, perhaps, than the computer invasion is the arrival of genetic engineering on the fisheries scene. A growing number of state fish and game agencies are stocking salmon, trout, and bass whose chromosomal counts have been altered by workers in white lab jackets; the chief rationale is to supply anglers with trophy fish of a size never met in nature. Again a question: Is this progressive fish management, or science running amuck and cutting perilously close to the heart of the sport?

The aim of this book is to report, from the vantage of 1988, what's happened recently in the world of angling—including topics like those just suggested. What's happened, in fact, is a very great deal, much of it complex, some of it controversial. Never is angling completely insular. Other worlds impinge on it, no matter how insistently we've viewed it as a refuge, a realm apart.

The first section of the book, on new fishing equipment, can help you decide whether your days on the water could be made more pleasant and productive by one of the latest rods, reels, lures, lines, boats, motors, down-riggers, or ice-fishing shelters—or whether, in truth, you might be as well off without it. Gear from more than ninety manufacturers is included. Our writers and staff have field-tested nearly all of this equipment, and offer expert appraisals of performance and usefulness. These opinions are unaffected by any fears of losing advertisers, since we have none to lose.

Angling techniques have become highly specialized. Downrigger trolling for lake trout in twilight waters 150 feet down is worlds away from curve-casting a speck of nymph over a rainbow so close you can almost count its spots. The largemouth bass angler, from the perspective of the north-woods walleye and pike nut, seems to speak a mysterious tribal language occluded by grits and to-bacco. So our section on new techniques brings you the experience of a select group of experts in various special-ties. The article on fishing for muskies, as an example, is written by a genial fanatic who not only fishes tire-lessly for the species but also works as a muskie guide, designs and sells muskie lures, and even conducts an annual muskie-fishing school. Regardless of species, all the techniques in the book are new in the past couple of seasons or somewhat less recent but still not widely known.

We also submit our pick of the most productive fishing spots in North America for 1988 and beyond. We do so with an eye out for the glowering spirit of Aldo Leopold, who once wrote that "knowledge of the whereabouts of good hunting or fishing is a very personal form of prop-erty" and regarded where-to-go writing as an "organized promiscuity." If what he had in mind was the revelation of a particular covert or pool that descending hordes could decimate in a morning, a week, or a month, then of course we agree. But if he was talking about bigger territory—a vast forest or reservoir, say—we'd point out that anglers are going to go somewhere and it seems use-ful to direct them to waters that can comfortably handle more pressure than they're getting, which is precisely what we do. Some of these are newly formed reservoirs; others are polluted waters that have been rehabilitated; still others are lakes or streams where special regula-tions insure good fishing even though pressure may not be light.

What will angling be like in the year 2000 and after? The fourth section of the book deals with the intriguing field of fisheries science, where, to a great degree, the future of angling is now being determined. Anglers must inform themselves and make their opinions known on public policy, because science, by definition, is dispas-sionate. It's clear enough that scientific discovery, by itself, is not going to neutralize the airborne witches' brew of acid rain; after all, science made acid rain pos-sible to begin with. Science now offers a cure, but so far it hasn't been bought. Understanding what's at stake in such matters is the vital first step—which is why this section is included.

Finally, we present a brief album of fishing adven-tures and misadventures—the recollections of anglers who have, above all, learned to *pay attention*. These pieces confirm one of our early assertions: that angling is not insular, but is linked in innumerable ways, some visible and some not so visible, to everything else in life. Here we enter a zone not only of the timely, but also of the timeless. The essential question these writ-ers pose—and attempt to answer—is, to state it simply: Why fish?

A word about authority: Throughout the book, our re-searchers have made every effort to insure factuality. The interpretation of facts, however, has been left to the various authors, all of whom are qualified interpret-ers. Not all the equipment evaluations are assignable to the writers; some have been supplied by numerous other experts.

New Equipment

Rods & Reels

C. Boyd Pfeiffer

Reduced to their essence, rods are nothing more than levers; reels nothing more than winches. Today's levers and winches are a treat to use, however, offering better materials (lighter, stronger, more sensitive) and more useful features (not mere gimmicks) than ever before.

In rods, the greatest improvements of the past year or so are the new forms of graphite, IM6 and IMX, with higher modulus than previous types. The higher the modulus, the stiffer the material—which means more powerful rods can now be built with no increase in blank thickness or weight.

Changes in design are apparent, too. More and more rods are made especially to detect whatever goes on, or whatever doesn't, at the far end of the line: the wobble or vibration of a plug, the flutter of a spinner, and at last the twitch (or, conversely, the cutoff of all sensation) that signals a strike. Openings are fashioned in the rod grip so fingers can rest on the graphite blank; or the grip itself is shaped of graphite, a better conductor of all those faint vibes than cork or foam.

One major rod-making trend of recent years is dying out fast: the use of boron and boron-graphite composites. True, boron does have a higher modulus than graphite— so why have nearly all the manufacturers dropped it? At first, when the hype for boron was heaviest and anglers everywhere wanted it bad, the raw material proved difficult to get. Later, when there was loads of the stuff, the proud new owners of boron rods didn't take long to discover that boron was heavier than graphite, but only slightly stiffer and more sensitive. Yet the prices were generally 30 to 40 percent steeper. A better question might be: How did boron last as long as it did?

Reels may have started out as simple winches, but in recent years many have become so encrusted and impacted with gadgets, the winch itself is pretty tough to locate. Have you had a look under the hood of your car lately? The reel builders seem to be taking their cues from GM and Toyota. Nowadays there are automatic bail openers,

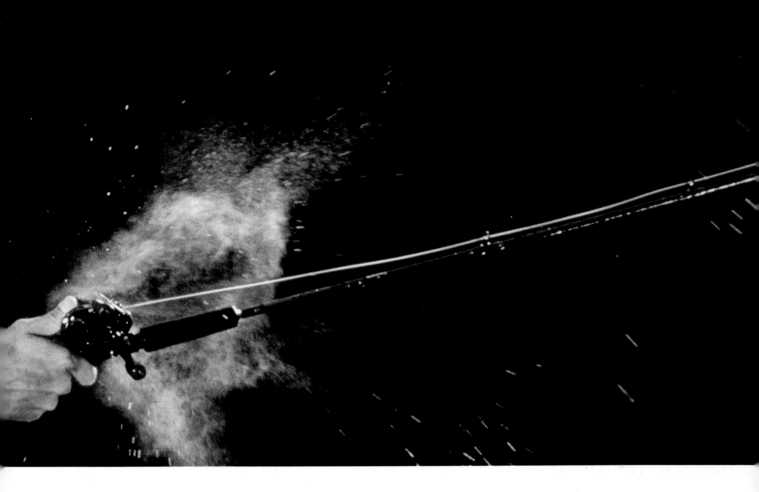

flipping switches, supplementary drags for live-bait fishing, mechanical and computerized line counters, automatic transmissions, even a built-in computer designed to control backlashes.

In at least one case, though, the reel makers are returning us to the old way of doing things. Front-drag spinning reels, abandoned by most manufacturers for several years, are making a comeback. Except in some saltwater regions, notably Florida, it's been difficult or impossible to find a front-drag reel in any tackle store. Rear-drag models took over the market for more than a decade— a clear-cut case of an inferior product selling like hotcakes solely on the merits of glossy ad campaigns.

The problem with rear drags is plain enough. In a rear type, the surfaces where the drag slippage occurs are necessarily smaller than those in a front drag. Also, more heat builds up in a rear drag, since the gear housing has no openings like those around the line spool. Because of the smaller surfaces and the heat which makes them expand, rear drags are more likely to stutter and snap your line at some critical moment. The sales pitches emphasized their ease of adjustment during the fight: the rear knob was supposed to be simpler to grab. Whether this is true is debatable; even if it is, the tradeoff isn't worth it.

So it's welcome news that front-drag reels are coming back strong. Not surprisingly, the models now available are generally even smoother than their fondly remembered forerunners of many years ago. The reels to look for are the Ryobi D series, Zebco/Quantum QSS series, Quantum QMD, and Daiwa Ultralight and Black Gold.

In both spinning and baitcasting reels, the trend to high-speed gearing goes on. A pair of new spinning models from different manufacturers feature 6.3:1 ratios—the fastest ever for spinning. For baitcasting, the high end is 7.1:1 in a single new model. In fresh water these reels come in most handy for reeling buzzbaits (and sometimes spinnerbaits) like crazy to keep them up on top. At the other extreme, one of this year's baitcasting reels has a ratio of only 3.8:1. The aim is to give a slower retrieve which is best for taking the new extra-deep crankbaits to maximum depth, and to offer more reeling power for playing big fish.

Not unpredictably, one company has introduced a casting reel that attempts to have things both ways. It retrieves at a 6:1 ratio, then shifts to 2:1 for the fight. Two-speed spinning and trolling reels have been around for some time, but remain a minority enthusiasm.

Can fly outfits possibly get any lighter? Not without adding some new weight classes (with negative numbers!) to the industry-standard system. Until a couple of years ago, the lightest fly rods and lines you could lay your hands on were 3-weights. These seemed adequately delicate and unimpeachably sporting for anything down to stunted bluegills and brook sticklebacks. Then came the 2-weights, big sellers, and this year Orvis has brought out the first 1-weight rod and line. How well do they work? Read on.

Spinning Reels

If we set out to design our own spinning reel, our three main goals would be maximum casting distance, a smooth drag, and avoidance of tight coils in the line as it comes off the spool. The Daiwa *TG1300H Tournament Gold* reaches two of these goals admirably and does fairly well on the third, which is two or three more than most other reels manage.

To maximize casting distance, this reel has a spool much longer than usual: that is, the front flange and the rear skirted flange are farther apart. The extra length means there's more line in big coils near the perimeter of the spool. A cast, even a long heave, will peel line mainly from this perimeter area, rather than emptying the perimeter quickly and pulling line from the smaller coils near the core, as would happen with a shorter spool. The line comes off the long spool far more easily, because friction is kept to a minimum. The big outer coils rub the front flange much less than the inner ones would. We threw a ⅜-ounce plug with 14-pound line, and got casts as long as we'd expect using 6- or 8-pound with other reels.

The TG1300H features a butter-smooth front drag instead of the fickle rear type which is still the standard in the industry. And even here the long spool helps out: because of it, there's virtually no change in effective drag tension from the beginning of a fight to the end. With a shorter spool, the drag effect is considerably greater when lots of line is out than it is when most of the line is on the spool, unless you continually readjust the setting to compensate.

The only way to our third goal—no tight coils in the line as it peels off—is to build a spool with a larger diameter. Like combat boots, spools of this type don't look especially chic, and even if the engineers were to give one a try the marketing types would instantly shoot it down. So this Daiwa doesn't have quite the diameter it might—if it did, the spool wouldn't need to be quite so long—but it does spurn the comic shrink-spools you see on most others.

The Shimano *Magnumlite GT-X 2200SQ* is generally a fine reel, though it suffers from a spool smaller than it really should be. This model features the auto-opening QuickFire II bail for one-hand casting; it's easier to operate than auto bails on other brands and on older Shimanos. The drag system, the Fightin' Drag II, allows you to set the proper tension for hooking fish and then to override it as necessary during the fight. Before starting to fish, you set a lever at a detent position and adjust the drag knob for the hooking tension you want; later, when you're struggling with a fish, moving the lever one way or the other from the detent position will decrease or increase the tension.

Just be sure to test the increased-tension setting *before* you ever hook a fish, so you'll be sure it isn't so tight your line might snap. The drag is a rear type, unfortunately, but it's about as smooth as rear drags ever get. We tested it by tying our line to the bumper of a car, then driving away: a workout as rigorous as it's likely to receive in most any inland fishing. The smoothness was surprising, though not really as good as you'd get with a first-rate front drag.

The Browning *810H* and *812H* reels boast the highest gear ratios available—6.3:1. (In this regard they're tied, actually, with the Quantum Express X3, X4, and X5.) Though ultrahigh ratios do have their uses—say, for a long day of hell-bent cranking to keep a buzzbait up on top—what likely sells most reels of this kind is just the indissoluble old American romance with speed, apart from any practical considerations.

The truth is that for most angling a lower ratio might be better. It tends to slow your retrieve, and undoubtedly more anglers fish too fast than too slow. (See, for example, the discussion of extra-deep crankbaits on pages 18 and 19.) And the lower gearing definitely gives you more power, often critical for playing those long-awaited trophy fish. In situations when high speed is a help, though, the new Brownings are a good choice. The drag is on the rear, but the spool is a bit larger than most and the gear train is smooth and silent.

Daiwa TG1300H Tournament Gold   *Shimano Magnumlite GT-X 2200SQ*   *Browning 810H*

Lew Childre BB-1LG *Quantum 381* *Daiwa PT33SH*

Penn Speed Shifter 2000 *Shimano Bantam Magnumlite BSM-2200FS* *Ryobi E1*

Baitcasting Reels

The Lew Childre *BB-1LG* is a sturdy reel with no magnetic anti-backlash mechanism, no flipping switch, nothing but lightweight, dependable performance. We think the flat, paddle-type handles—which first appeared on the Childre BB-1 about fifteen years ago—are still the most comfortable to use for any sort of fishing. Another first-rate feature is the unusually rapid level-wind, which lays the line down on the spool in crisscross fashion rather than in almost parallel turns as on most other reels. This keeps the incoming line from digging into the turns that lie beneath it, so it will peel off the spool far more smoothly on the following cast. The BB-1LG is just the right size for light to medium freshwater fishing. It's compact, but not a case of the extreme shrinking that in past years rendered such curiosities as the Ryobi VM3G, Ryobi V-MAG 3, and Childre BB-XLM.

Another new no-nonsense reel is the Quantum *381*, so named because it has a low 3.8:1 gear ratio. It's specifically designed for crankbait fishing, where maximum reeling power and medium-slow retrieves are desirable. Nonetheless, it's a good general-purpose casting reel, suitable for everything but those occasional situations where ordinary subsonic reeling won't do. The gears run very smoothly; and this reel, unlike the Childre above, does have a magnetic anti-backlash system. On the inside of the sideframe there's a sliding freespool control, called Q-Cast, which operates like a thumb bar for one-hand casting.

At the other end of the spectrum is the Daiwa *PT33SH*, whose 7.1:1 ratio is the highest on any casting reel. It's good for fishing buzzbaits or bulging the surface with

spinnerbaits. The paddle handles are easy to get a grip on, and the pronounced snap of the switch when you change from flipping to casting is reassuring. Using other reels, we've sometimes thought we had the switch firmly set where we wanted it, but were rudely corrected when we tried to launch our lure.

For those tormented souls who can't make up their minds, the Penn *Speed Shifter 2000* is a two-speed model with both a 6:1 and a 2:1 ratio. It's the first baitcasting reel built to shift gears, and the shifting is automatic. The higher ratio is for retrieving, the lower for playing your fish, but you don't have to throw a lever in the heat of battle to make the downshift. Instead, the reel senses the additional resistance after the hookup and makes the switch itself. A little spooky, if it works. Unfortunately, we weren't able to get a reel to test, so we can't say how well the theory works out in practice.

The Shimano *Bantam Magnumlite BSM-2200FS* is worth noting mainly because of its new Fightin' Star drag system. This allows you to set the drag tension you want to fish with, then reduce or increase it as necessary while fighting a fish, and return it at any time to the original setting with certainty rather than guesswork. The original setting is made with a knurled dial on the reel-handle shaft; the adjustments during the fight are accomplished easily with a star-drag wheel also on the shaft. The star rotates only 160 degrees, so you don't need to screw it around and around simply to make a minor adjustment. In the middle of this turning range is a detent which marks your original setting. The drag performs well, but we found the setting procedure recommended by Shimano unnecessarily difficult.

11

Loomis Spin Jig

Lew Childre Spin Pistol Cajun Style

Fenwick Crankshaft

Daiwa Procaster

Loomis Mag Bass

Daiwa Power Mesh

Browning Spiral Plus

Shimano BeastMaster

Shakespeare Ugly Stik Tournament Class

Look, Ma, no thumbs: the Ryobi *E1* is the first reel ever with an anti-backlash system controlled by computer. This is a rather big reel, and it's definitely on the heavy side, what with the built-in computer chip, battery pack, and any other crypto-components the company's whiz kids may have managed to slip in. Throughout a cast, the computer monitors how fast the spool is revolving, and determines the position of the magnets that keep it from overrunning. The battery pack will operate for up to eight hours of casting and can be recharged with the 12-volt cigarette-lighter adaptor, or with an optional 110-volt AC version.

You can fish the E1 in any of four different computer modes, depending on how much control you want to surrender. (For that matter, the computer can be shut off completely and you're left with a standard magnetic system—though it's hard to see why anyone who forks over the astounding price for this model would want to do that.) Mode 1 has the least braking effect, mode 4 the most. The mode setting determines how many RPMs the spool is allowed to reach before the magnetic braking cuts in. An indicator on the sideframe flicks back and forth so you can actually—and continually—view how much effect you're getting: we tried it and would say it's roughly as interesting as reruns of *The Love Boat*. The computer turns on at the beginning of each cast when you press the thumb bar; it gives you a conspiratorial little beep.

For the most part, the anti-backlash device does work. We definitely preferred the lightest setting, mode 1. This is the only one that allows distance casting, and even so you can't reach out quite as far as you could with a good non-computer reel—Ryobi's own V-Mag or T1, for instance. The other modes are better suited to short, accurate shots at particular targets. The reel takes some getting used to: you have to put a little more force in your casts or the lure will fall short.

The E1 is a bit of a flop, however, when it comes to casting against the wind, bouncing a bait off a log or

piling, or slamming out a long shot with two hands on the rod. Under this sort of duress, it pays you back with a bird's nest every time. We question whether a really experienced baitcaster will want to swallow the limitations: the callused, educated thumb can still do a better job than anyone's silicon chip. For those who are only occasional anglers—spouses and youngsters—it may be a different story.

Spinning and Baitcasting Rods

There's nothing fancy about the Loomis *Spin Jig* rods— just good basic construction in the superb, sensitive IM6 graphite material. We used the 5-foot 10-inch model SJR700, which performed very well with jigs and other light lures on 6-pound test. The grip is plenty thick enough for comfort and has a sliding-ring reel seat; the rod action is medium. Five models are available from 5 feet 10 inches to 6 feet, all spinning.

The Lew Childre *Spin Pistol Cajun Style* spinning rods have a swollen butt grip that really lets you grab hold. When making a long cast, you don't get the feeling you're going to launch your rod right across the lake, as you do with some others. The grip is molded of firm plastic. Available in four models from 6½ to 7 feet.

The *Vectra* baitcasting rods from Berkley feature a straight handle of textured graphite. The grip is harder than a foam or cork type, but gives you greater sensitivity to lure action and strikes. The graphite blank runs all the way down through the handle, and the spacers between the blank and grip are also made of graphite. Anglers who still prefer short grips are out of luck here: all the Vectras have the popular long handles, which do allow you to brace the rod better under your forearm. Four models from 5½ to 7 feet.

In the *Crankshaft* baitcasting series from Fenwick, the butt is graphite but the tip is fiberglass. As the name suggests, these rods are intended for crankbait fishing; they have power in the butt and a slow, soft action in the tip. The theory behind the design is that the slowness allows a bass more time to engulf a crankbait, giving you deeper, surer hooking. In tests this was impossible to prove or disprove; but to us, at least, the premise sounds a little fishy. We do like the butt grip, which is swollen just behind the reel seat for better palming of the reel. Three models, two of them telescoping, from 6 to 7 feet.

A good workhorse series is the Daiwa line of *Procaster Power Rods*. These are straight-handle baitcasting rods; we tested the 6-foot PR51T-2, which has a fast action ideal for most bass and walleye fishing. Twelve models from 6 to 7 feet.

The Loomis *Mag Bass* is a fine telescoping rod designed for pitching. The material is IM6 graphite; we used this rod for pitching, flipping, and ordinary casting, all with good results. The Mag Bass comes in three models, all 6 feet 8 inches long.

The Daiwa *Power Mesh* series has a crisscross layer of graphite fibers on the outside of the blank. This new kind of wrapping is supposed to give the rod added strength and protection from breaking when you're fighting that trophy of a lifetime. We didn't stress the rod all the way to the breaking point, but we did put a tremendous bend in it that would have broken many other rods. Five spinning models from 5½ to 7 feet, and three casting models from 5½ to 6 feet.

A similar series, also with reinforcement wraps, is the Browning *Spiral Plus* line. The material is IM6 graphite; we used a 7-foot casting version that was light but powerful. Six spinning models from 5 to 6½ feet, and fourteen casting models from 5½ to 7½ feet.

The Shimano *BeastMaster Fightin' Rods* have thick butt sections that flare to form the reel seat. The construction is all graphite, so this is another series of rods with excellent sensitivity. On the spinning and straight-handle casting models, we like the long sliding collar that completely covers the rear threads of the reel seat: it spares your casting hand all the irritating rubs. BeastMaster rods come in three spinning and four casting models, from 5½ to 6½ feet.

The Shakespeare *Ugly Stik Tournament Class* rods are similar to past Ugly Stiks, except that the finish is sanded smooth. The tip is still clear—and ugly—and the rod has lots of power in the butt. The reel seat has two extra-large openings under the reel seat for direct blank-to-hand contact. Six spinning models from 5 to 7 feet; three casting models, all 5½ feet.

Trolling Reels

The Mitchell *782*, designed for downrigger trolling, looks like an oversize fly reel. It's strictly heavy-duty; the drag, with its large surfaces, is exceptionally smooth. The drawback is that it's a single-action reel and retrieves more slowly than a multiplier. Still, the huge spool holds 500 yards of 20-pound test, and with only 50 yards or so out it will recover about 12 inches with each turn of the handle. A multiplying version of this reel, though certain to be more costly, is something we'd like to see. The 782 is designed to be used with the Mitchell Signature rods (see rod section following).

The big feature on the Daiwa *Great Lakes System 47LC* is a line counter. It measures the amount of line you let out, and does so with considerable accuracy, provided you start with a full spool. There's a small button for resetting the counter to zero. Otherwise, the 47LC works like almost any other trolling reel, though its 5.1:1 gear ratio is faster than most.

Trolling Rods

The Mitchell *Signature* rods are specially designed for use with the 782 trolling reel. The guides on these rods are mounted on the underside of the blank, as on a spinning rod, but are much smaller than spinning guides.

A good match for the Daiwa trolling reel described above is the 7-foot 783GL in the *Great Lakes System* series. An excellent feature of all these rods is the unusual foregrip, which is triangular in cross-section. This shape helps to prevent twisting of the rod in your hands during a fight. Six rods in the series, from 7 to 10½ feet.

Mitchell 782 and Mitchell Signature Rod (left), Daiwa 47LC and Great Lakes 783 (right).

Ross Gunnison   *Martin MG8SS*   *Scientific Anglers System Two-L*   *Sage 700 Series*

Fly Reels

The Ross *Gunnison* is a classically designed, well-built reel with a skeletal frame and ventilated pop-off spool. All the parts are machined, not stamped, and the finish is matte black. The drag has a wide range, and we found it quite smooth. The reel converts to right-hand winding if you prefer, but you have to disassemble and reassemble the drag. That's the only shortcoming of this reel, though, and it's minor; once you get the handle where you want it, you're fixed for life. The Gunnison comes in three models, for lines ranging from 4 to 10 weight.

The Martin *MG8SS* doesn't look flashy, but it's a rugged, well-thought-out design that holds plenty of line for heavy freshwater fishing. The spool is large enough for a WF9F and 150 yards of 20-pound Dacron backing. We like the unusual reel foot, which is offset to one side to balance the reel properly on the rod. On fly reels one side is generally a little heavier than the other, so the rod grip tends to twist in your hand—definitely a source of finger and wrist fatigue after several hours of casting. We'd suggest, though, that the drag knob be improved: the small, pyramidal shape is tough to get a grip on with wet hands.

Scientific Anglers had a bit of a sticky drag with some of their early System Two fly reels, but the problem seems to be solved with the new *System Two-L*. The drag is a caliper type, similar to the old one but very smooth. The new reels are available in four sizes for lines from 4 to 8 weight. They have the same black finish and pop-off spool as on the earlier models, but the weight is now lighter.

The Sage *700 Series* reels offer a unique way to avoid the tight coils of fly line that develop on those small, precision, imported reels. The 700 models have a large, cage-type spool that rides on three separate axles and completely lacks the usual sort of core. There's very little difference between the inside and outside diameters of the spool. The major result is lessened coiling of the line, which means less of the old pulling-and-stretching routine preparatory to casting. Another benefit is a faster retrieve speed than is possible with other single-action fly reels; this helps when you're reeling in a long line to move to a different spot, or trying to keep tension on a fish running toward you.

For many anglers, one drawback of the 700 reels will be the lack of a drag mechanism. To apply pressure to a fish, you palm the rim of the spool. Most fly reels today have spools designed for palming, but they also have mechanical drags. Curiously, Sage catalogs state that "the line tension on conventional reels can increase up to five times from the leader to the end of the backing," whereas with the 700 reels "it increases only 1.3 times, so you can fish with lighter leaders." Without a drag, the minimal increase in "line tension" becomes a moot point. These reels do have a knob to provide what a company spokesman calls "spool overrun tension": at most, this is enough to keep the line from unwinding onto the water by its own weight. The series includes three models, all of them quite expensive, for lines from 4 to 10 weight.

Fly Rods

This year, for the first time ever, a 1-weight fly rod has appeared on the market. According to reports, anglers at first were ordering the Orvis *One Weight* several times faster than the company could turn it out. The main impetus behind those early sales of this 7½-foot, 1⅜-ounce stick was probably its novelty. Even while careening to the phone with Visa card in hand, all but the most ingenuous buyers must surely have wondered if such an attenuated wand wouldn't end up gathering dust in the closet after the first couple of trips. Could it possibly cast farther than a couple of rod lengths? Would a 1-weight line have the momentum to deliver any fly other than the microscopic sort you can't get tied on in the first place? And what about the wind? The slightest puff would put you out of business, wouldn't it?

Our tests determined the One Weight is ideal for any trout situations where the ultimate in delicacy is required: spring creeks in the Alleghenies or the Rockies, late-summer low water on hard-fished eastern rivers. And it's enjoyable to use even in some cases where heavier tackle would do the job as well—farm-pond angling for blue-gills, for instance. A reasonably skilled caster can throw about 50 feet of line with it, all that's necessary in these pocket situations. The biggest flies we could turn over comfortably were size 12 dries, size 10 nymphs, and the tiniest rubber-legged panfish poppers. Again, that's about all you'll ever need.

We found that casting is really a pleasure with a rod this light. Even after a long day of fishing you won't have a tired wrist, which is the principal cause of sloppiness in fly casting. The action is typical of most Orvis rods—somewhat slower than that of graphite models from the other top manufacturers. About the only design flaw is the grip, which, at only 5 inches long, is far too short for optimum comfort. The heel of any adult angler's hand will overlap well onto the reel seat, rubbing against one of the knurled sliding rings. The scaled-down grip *looks* right in proportion to the rest of the rod, but it's not truly functional.

The only line available for the rod is a 1-weight floating double-taper, also sold by Orvis. Most anglers may prefer double-tapers when fishing very light rods, but undoubtedly there are some, including us, who would like the option of a weight-forward. Though more difficult to "mend" on the water, a weight-forward definitely shoots better and casts farther.

Many of the very best fly rods are manufactured by small specialty companies rather than the big outfits that turn out spinning and baitcasting equipment. One of the finest of these smaller builders is Winston, which this year has a new 7½-foot *Light Trout Rod* for 2-weight lines. This rod serves all the purposes mentioned in connection with the Orvis rod above, and can handle somewhat larger flies and longer casts as well. Throwing half a fly line with this model is no problem at all.

In its *Steelhead, Salmon, Bass, and Saltwater* series, Winston has a new 9-footer for 10-weight line. It casts well, turns the heavy line over crisply, and has ample power in the butt for lifting fish alongside a boat or levering them into the shoreline shallows. The extra-large stripper guides, size 16 and 12, allow the line to flow freely when you're shooting for maximum distance. It might flow even better, we think, if the first stripper guide were moved another 2 or 3 inches up the rod from the handle.

In its *IMX* series, Loomis is offering a new kind of graphite, IMX, with the highest modulus yet; that is, it's stiffer and more powerful than any other graphite available. We've been fishing with a 9-foot, 6-weight model and found it a superb casting instrument. We were able to cast a full fly line plus 10 or 15 feet of backing with scarcely any effort: long shoots and good loop control, no huff and puff. This definitely is a different material, not just another chimera from the ad men. The IMX series includes two-piece models ranging from a 7-foot 9-inch rod for 2-weight lines to a 10-footer for 8-weights; and four-piece travel rods ranging from a 9-foot 4-weight to a 9½-foot 8-weight.

Another new high-modulus rod is the 9-foot 6-weight in the Sage *LL (Lightline Lightweight)* series. It's made of the powerful Graphite II material and features a beautifully finished up-locking teak reel seat. It's a rod that's designed to give you the best of both worlds: delicacy on the one hand, and casting distance on the other. The 6-weight is a good compromise in this regard, and the 9-foot length gives you casting power as well as line control on the water. We do have one criticism: the grip, particularly toward its front, is about the skinniest imaginable. A rod of this length and weight surely needs a grip that fills up the hand better. As it is, your hand continually slides forward on the cork, and it's tougher to punch out a long cast. By the end of a long day, you'll begin to feel some cramping in your fingers.

A unique new rod with two tip sections comes from Lamiglas, the *Esprit Graphite F 865-8*. Though it's not a pack rod, we think it's a good choice for traveling to an area where more than one line weight is necessary, or to a new place where you're not sure what weight would be most suitable. It's 8 feet 6 inches long; one tip takes a 5- or 6-weight line, the other a 7- or 8-weight. We fished both tips with weight-forward lines and got good loop control, distance, and accuracy. One problem: the threads on the reel seat have a tendency to bind.

C. Boyd Pfeiffer is the editor of Fishing Tackle Trade News. *He's written eight books, including* Tackle Care *and* The Orvis Guide to Outdoor Photography. *His articles have appeared in dozens of national magazines and won numerous outdoor-writing awards.*

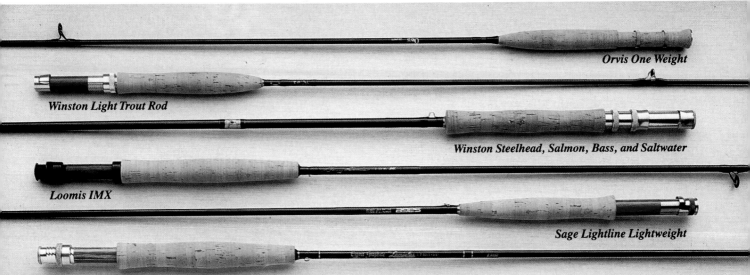

Orvis One Weight

Winston Light Trout Rod

Winston Steelhead, Salmon, Bass, and Saltwater

Loomis IMX

Sage Lightline Lightweight

Lamiglas Esprit Graphite F 865-8

Lures

C. Boyd Pfeiffer

Lures have come a long way since the day when James Heddon was whittling on a chunk of wood and tossed it into Michigan's Dowagiac River, only to have a largemouth roll out and engulf it; and since the day when Julio T. Buel dropped a tablespoon during a rowboat picnic in northern New York, and a "big fish" materialized and promptly made a slash at it.

Neither of these innovators could have foreseen where their unwitting discoveries would eventually lead: namely, to our present-day battery of baits molded of polysyllabic synthetic substances, lures that glow seductively in the dark and emit chemical smells and come-on noises all claimed to be irresistible to any normal, healthy, American gamefish.

One recent development that's gotten plenty of fanfare—and one that definitely helps catch fish—is the extra-deep-diving crankbait. Several manufacturers had lures of this type in their 1987 lineups, all designed to plunge to the 20-foot level. This year, one company has gone well beyond that barrier, introducing a futuristic-looking diver rated for 30 feet. Almost certainly we'll be seeing more of these extra-deep crankbaits from other manufacturers. Numerous improvements are still possible, including steeper diving angles and lower buoyancy.

Another trend is to lures combining hard and soft plastics: plugs sporting curly worms or other soft-plastic tail dressings. These lures are highly effective, since the wiggling of the plug gives the worm an enticing action you couldn't impart simply by rigging the worm Texas-style and twitching it with your rod tip. The problem with such combination lures is that hard and soft plastics don't mix. When the two materials are nestled together in your tackle kit, the soft stuff turns the hard into a ghastly marmalade. One lure—Storm's Deep Tubby Eel—beats the problem with a tail of harmless, harder "soft" plastic; for the rest, though, the only solution is to store the plugs and tails separately.

This year the bait makers have also brought out a number of plugs with bodies designed to slide up and down your line. To rig up, you thread the line through the body from top to bottom, then through a bead and bullet weight, and finish by tying it to the hook eye. The design serves at least two purposes. When a hooked fish jumps or shakes its head, the body just slides up the line; its weight won't help tear the hook loose. The weight may be considerable, since some of these lures—the sinking models—have metal pellets inside for rattling. The other advantage, with the models designed to float, is that you can dangle the hook (which comes with a fur dressing) under the body and twitch it to draw fish from below.

Last year saw the introduction of spinnerbaits with blade arms of flexible cable, rather than stiff wire. The flexibility seems to give the lure more action, but the big plus is a better hooking percentage. When a fish hits from certain angles the cable gives way, instead of deflecting the strike from the hook as stiff wire often will. More of these cable baits have appeared this year, and one manufacturer has a new model using cable not just for the blade arm, but also for the short lower arm leading to the body.

The most interesting new finish for lures is the "guanine" reflective type available on some models from Rebel, Heddon, and Cordell. The strobelike flashing you see when baitfish dart and turn in the light is thought to be reflected by the amino acid guanine in their scales, and this new finish simulates the effect surprisingly well.

Surface Plugs

The new Arbogast *Jitter-Tail* is basically a Jitterbug with an upturned weedless hook, and also a swivel-attached worm hook which you rig with any plastic worm you want. The Jitter-tail floats horizontally, with the worm hanging down at an angle. We found this combination bass lure can be fished effectively at least two different ways: by reeling slowly, so only the worm wiggles; or faster, so the plug wobbles too. It comes in ⅜- and ⅝-ounce sizes.

The *Great Snake* is an enlarged version of last year's Snake Bait from Burke. This 10-inch model really looks like a snake on the water, its curly tail swimming realistically and leaving a wide wake. Eight color patterns are available; some of these verge on the bizarre (there's one with a powder-blue head and white tail), and we prefer the more realistic schemes.

The *Teeny Pop-R* by Rebel is a ⅛-ounce version of the Pop-R, a plug that's recently become popular among tournament fishermen for largemouths (see "Largemouth Bass," page 55). In our tests the small edition proved excellent for eastern stream smallmouths. We fished it with the same skipping and diving technique generally used with the bigger bait. The fur tail seems to direct strikes to the rear treble, a definite advantage. Use 4- to 6-pound line and a loop knot; heavier line and clinch knots will impede the action.

Another spinoff of the Pop-R is the ¼-ounce *Drop Pop-R*, one of the various new baits designed to slide on the line. The lure has a fur-dressed treble, which you can drop below it and jiggle to tease fish into striking. With the ¼-ounce weight supplied and a 6- to 8-pound line, it works great.

MirrOlure, known for its fine saltwater plugs, has introduced the *StickUp*, a cigar-shaped walk-the-dog lure that stands almost vertical when at rest. It looks much like the Heddon Zara Spook, and comes in sizes from ⅓ to ⅝ ounce.

Another good walk-the-dog bait is the ¾-ounce *Woodwalker* from Ozark Mountain. Shaped like a large cigar plug on a diet—the midsection is slender—it splashes and spits as it zigzags across the surface. We found it also works well if fished with a straight darting retrieve or just quietly swum across the surface. Realize, however, that if you slam this painted wooden lure into rocks or otherwise knock it around, it won't hold up as well as a plastic bait.

The Heddon *Zara Puppy*, a new pint-sized Zara Spook, is easier to throw than many other small lures because of its bullet shape. This ¼-ounce Zara is designed for walking the dog, but requires a lighter line and more delicate touch than the familiar big version. Like the Teeny Pop-R, it's great for stream smallmouths.

Heddon has also introduced the *Drop-Zara*, a ¾-ounce sliding type, with all the usefulness of the original Zara plus the special sliding advantages already described.

Poe is a new company turning out well-made wooden plugs. The vee-cut face of its ¼-ounce *Blurpee* popper produces small pops and gurgles, or a large ga-blub when you want to wake up the bass in the suburbs. You can also work it walk-the-dog fashion, or under the surface for short bursts.

A chunky lure with a long skirt, the ⅜-ounce Bagley *Pop'N B2* pops and gurgles like the Blurpee, but also dives when pulled sharply. It floats upright in the water, so with slight twitches you can make it nod and send rings across the water while it stays in one place—a good way to tease a reluctant bass when you know where he's holed up. The lure does have a couple of drawbacks, however. The hooks occasionally hang up with one another on a cast, and the skirt is so long it caused short strikes that cost us fish; we recommend cutting about a third of it off.

The ½-ounce *Pop'N B3* is a longer bait that floats horizontally. It has a chugging action and doesn't dive. In addition, both this lure and the B2 can be used for walking the dog. And both come either with or without rear propellers: we tried each type, with good success.

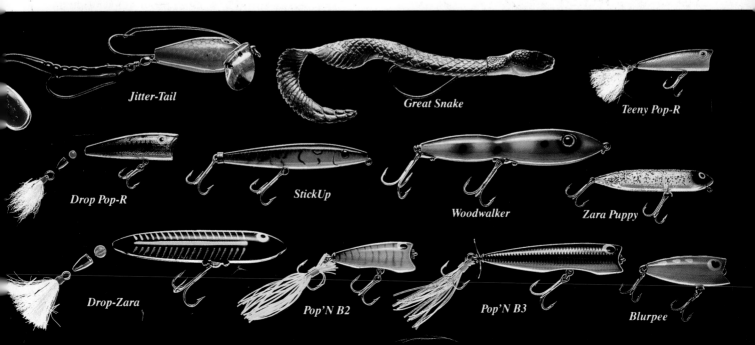

Jitter-Tail   *Great Snake*   *Teeny Pop-R*

Drop Pop-R   *StickUp*   *Woodwalker*   *Zara Puppy*

Drop-Zara   *Pop'N B2*   *Pop'N B3*   *Blurpee*

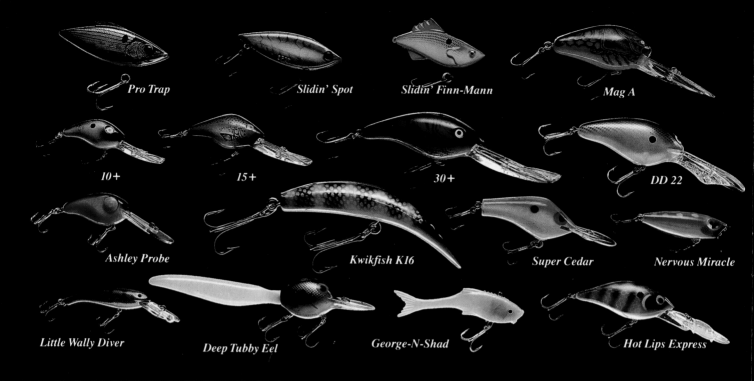

Pro Trap   Slidin' Spot   Slidin' Finn-Mann   Mag A

10+   15+   30+   DD 22

Ashley Probe   Kwikfish K16   Super Cedar   Nervous Miracle

Little Wally Diver   Deep Tubby Eel   George-N-Shad   Hot Lips Express

Subsurface Plugs

The big news in this category is the variety of vibrating plugs designed to slide on the line: the Bill Lewis *Pro Trap* in both ⅜- and ⅝-ounce sizes, the ½-ounce Cordell *Slidin' Spot*, and the ¼-ounce Mann *Slidin' Finn-Mann*. All these have rattle chambers with pellets, and all can be cast long distances with ease. As already mentioned, they slide up the line when you're fighting a fish, so the weight of the body doesn't help dislodge the hook. In our tests we found this new feature a definite advantage.

Something the lure companies don't tell you is that you can rig the Pro Trap and Slidin' Spot upside down, running your line through from bottom to top, for a countershading effect. Light on the back and dark on the belly, the lure becomes more visible against any natural background. In many cases, this will get you more strikes. You'll notice a difference in the action, but not enough to affect your success one way or the other. The Slidin' Finn-Mann, however, does lose most of its vibration if rigged this way.

Last year's extra-deep-diving crankbaits were a big success for the manufacturers who brought them out, so the bandwagon is a bit more crowded in 1988.

The Bomber *Mag A*, one of the early 20-foot types, is available this year in a new crayfish finish—something we really like, since the bait itself was designed to dig right down to the rocks where crayfish live. The Mag A, ¾ ounce, has a rapid, tight wiggle.

Mann's 20+ is joined this year by the ⅛-ounce *10+* and ¼-ounce *15+*, both of which run shallower, and also by the huge-lipped *30+*, designed to dive an unprecedented 30 feet. The 30+ is less buoyant than the 20+, so it's easier to keep down where you want it. To fish this 3-inch, ¾-ounce bait, you need to make lob

casts with a long rod; snappy casts with a shorter rod would break the light (about 10-pound test) lines required for maximum depth. The 30+ has a wider wiggle than most of the other deep divers.

In the 20-foot class, the new Bill Norman *DD 22* has a moderate wiggle, somewhere between those of the Bomber and Mann's lures. Like the 30+, it has low buoyancy. We like the unusually steep angle of descent, which gets the lure down to the fish quickly. It weighs ⅝ ounce.

The ¼-ounce *Ashley Probe* from Rabble Rouser, another new 20-footer, features a loud rattle chamber for additional attraction. Low buoyancy on this one, too.

Of course, the big question is this: Do these extra-deep divers really get down as far as the manufacturers claim? We're talking about casting, not trolling, under typical fishing conditions.

The answer: Well, maybe.

The lures will plunge reasonably close to the advertised depths, but only if careful attention is paid to tackle and technique. Light lines are required, and long rods definitely help; long casts and a medium-slow retrieve with the rod tip held low are absolute musts.

In tests, various bottom depths were read with a high-quality depth finder, buoys were placed to mark the depths, and the lures were cast and retrieved to determine whether they would bump the bottom. The tackle consisted of 6-pound mono and a 6½-foot double-handed rod. Throughout the retrieves, the rod tip was touching the water but not dipping beneath. The 20-foot lures generally reached depths somewhat greater than 17 feet; the Mann's 20+ got down slightly deeper than the others.

With 14-pound mono, the maximum depth is much less—14 feet, or not even that. Whatever the lure and line, the depth can be increased by using the kneel-and-reel technique, pointing the rod tip as far down in the water as possible while retrieving. All the manufacturers of extra-deep crankbaits emphasize a medium-slow retrieve; it's a myth that rapid reeling delivers the most depth. A slower retrieve gives a steeper dive and gets the lure down faster.

Another new plug, the Kwikfish *K16*, is a 5½-incher for Great Lakes trolling. It has a slow, undulating wobble, and heavy-duty hooks for holding the biggest kings. Be careful when dropping it over the side, though, because the two hooks are close together and can easily hang up.

In its *Super Cedar* line, Poe has several new, well-built wooden plugs with lips of clear, tough Lexan. There are shallow, medium, and deep runners, ranging from ½ to ¾ ounce, all with a tight wiggle. The ¼-ounce *Nervous Miracle*, a shallow runner, has a metal lip. All these are well-built plugs of unexceptional design: they do catch their share of fish.

The slim *Little Wally Diver* by Cordell is designed as a walleye lure, but worked equally well for bass in our tests. The wiggle is tight, and the lure travels deep despite the small lip. The fluorescent colors are ideal for walleyes. Weight is 1/5 ounce.

The Storm *Deep Tubby Eel* floats horizontally, its eel-like straight tail hanging down slightly. It's a diving bait with low buoyancy, so you can fish it slowly at a constant depth. That, and the lifelike plastic skirt, make it good for cold-weather casting or trolling. A thinner tail would be better, for livelier action on these slow retrieves. Storm sells soft curly tails for use on this lure, and these definitely are better than the thick, straight tail that comes with it. The lure weighs ⅝ ounce.

The fast-sinking Mann's *George-N-Shad* is a durable soft plastic lure over a weighted core, with a single treble hook. It runs almost like a vibrating plug, but we also like it for vertical jigging. When jigged, it dives head down and rises head up, so the body has lots of action. The tail doesn't do much, however, and could stand some redesigning. Weights range from ¼ to 1 ounce.

Here's a really different way of adjusting lure depth: all you need is a cigarette lighter and an Angler's Pride *Hot Lips Express*. This ½-ounce plug has a wide lip which can be bent along two transverse lines when you apply heat. You bend one line for medium depths, or both for deeper diving. Unfortunately, the lip will take only six to twelve bends before it breaks. Some anglers may wonder, as we did, whether this isn't a concept whose time hasn't come yet.

Soft Plastics

The *Kangaroo* soft-plastic series by Fish World has been expanded with a new lizard, frog, and snake. Each has the Kangaroo pocket (arrow) into which you can put split-shot, a ⅛-ounce bullet weight, solid or jell scent, a cork for surface fishing, cut bait, anything you want. This is a useful idea; we particularly like the larger pockets on the snake and lizard.

The Zetabait *Bubba* is the first rattle-eye worm on the market. The big doll eyes do seem to get more strikes; some studies have suggested that large eyes trigger strikes from predatory fish. The Bubba has a thick body that makes it easy to rig any way you want. This lure definitely catches fish, but it does have a problem: the eyes fell off several of our Bubbas even before we fished them.

We like the pronounced flapping action of the *Paddle Tail* worm by Culprit. It's excellent for fishing Texas-style, and its 5-inch size also makes it ideal for use as a tail on spinnerbaits or on any of the combination plug-and-soft-plastic lures described earlier.

The Culprit *Captivator* is a bullet weight with a live-rubber skirt tied to a neck at the rear. The skirt adds action to any worm, and we believe it added some bass to our catch. Twelve different colors are available, and three sizes: ¼, ⅜, and ½ ounce.

LazerTail, the company with the glow-in-the-dark soft plastics, has a new four-legged *Crawfish*. It's phosphorescent, with a slim body. The theory is that the glow makes a lure look fatter than it really is, so the body is slimmed down for greater realism. It wasn't available in time for testing, but we think it should be excellent for deep water.

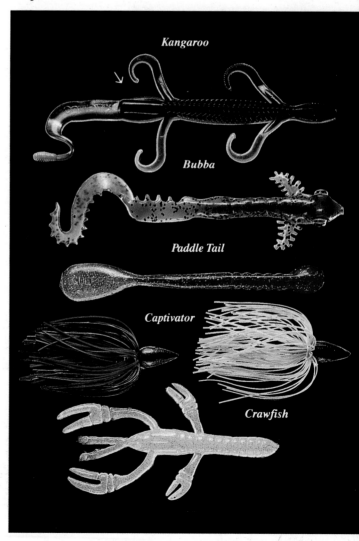

Kangaroo

Bubba

Paddle Tail

Captivator

Crawfish

Fireball Jig

Limberneck Jointed Jig

Swivel Jig

Dance's Craw

Marsh Invader

Jig N Eel

Crankjig

'Poxy Jig

Jigs

Peterson's new *Fire-Ball* has a short-shank hook, so you can tip it with a minnow and still have a compact lure. It gave us a better hooking percentage than ordinary jigs, with fewer short strikes. The stinger wire that comes with it is a bit heavy, so we substituted a length of stiff 12-pound mono when a stinger was needed. Sizes: ⅛, ¼, and ⅜ ounce.

The *Limberneck Jointed Jig* by Brother's has the head and hook design of the Short Arm spinnerbait described above. The tapered head, swinging hook, and Y-shaped weedguard make it ideal for working through brush. In shoreline fishing, we found the lure difficult to hang up. A Brother's split-tail grub (not included) or an Uncle Josh Pork Frog will give the lure more action: the head can rest intermittently on the bottom, the tail and skirt waving above. Weights from ⅛ to ½ ounce.

A similiar lure is the Hart *Swivel Jig*. It has a loosely attached Tru-Turn hook, on which you rig whatever soft-plastic worm you like. Sizes range from ⅛ to ½ ounce.

The ⅜-ounce *Dance's Craw* by Fish Formula is a realistic-looking imitation designed to be hopped and darted along the bottom. The tail and claws are much too stiff, though, and don't produce any lifelike action in the water.

A flat, spoonlike lead body on the ⅜-ounce Hankie *Marsh Invader* allowed it to swim over and through most weeds in our tests. The live-rubber skirt also gives it an attractive fluttering action when twitched or hopped with the rod tip.

Like the Shimi-Spin described earlier, the new *Jig N Eel* from Dri Rind has a fluttering chamois-type tail that

won't go bad like pork rind or attack hard lures like soft-plastics. The slightest rod movement makes the lure dance, and it practically turns somersaults when fished with a straight up-and-down jigging action. It comes in sizes from ¼ to ½ ounce.

The Lit'l Buffalo *Crankjig* has a vibrating soft-plastic shad tail, and a diving lip on the head. We liked the way the lip helped keep the lure down at the desired depth when trolling. In ⅜- and ¾-ounce sizes.

Sometimes we want lures that have a good jigging action but are very lightweight—for fly casting, for example, or for fishing over the tops of shallow weeds. The new Gaines *'Poxy Jigs* have epoxy heads available in several different shapes, including ball, bullet, and slider types. The hooks come in sizes 6 to 3/0, either bare, feathered, or skirted. The small sizes with bare hooks are ideal for flyrodders who want to tie wet or streamer patterns for panfish or trout, and the larger sizes for bass anglers working the shallows. The light epoxy material makes these lures more difficult to cast than lead-head jigs, but they hop in the water remarkably well.

Spoons

The Specialists in Sports *Weedless Demon* has a good wobbling action, but the big single hook, advertised as "Lazer-sharp," has lots of paint on it which in effect dulls the point. Size is ³⁄₁₆ ounce.

The *Klipr* spoon by Vortex comes with a set of vinyl slip-over covers called "Trims." There are five of these, each a different color. The idea, of course, is to switch these until you find which one the fish will take at a given time. The Trims fit very snugly; when removing them, use pliers to hold the hook and avoid any possible accidents. No snap-swivel comes with the spoon, so you'll need to add one—not only for better action but also to eliminate retying your line every time you change colors. The Klipr works for most spoon techniques other than vertical jigging; in trying to jig it, we discovered that the hook tends to fold along the blade of the spoon on the drops, making it tough to hook fish. The lure comes in weights of ⅛ to ¾ ounce.

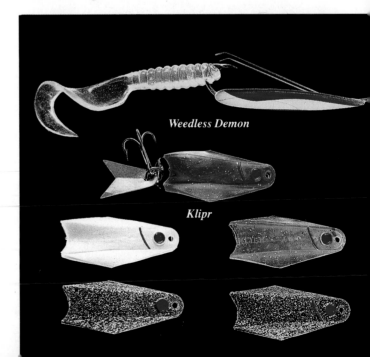

Weedless Demon

Klipr

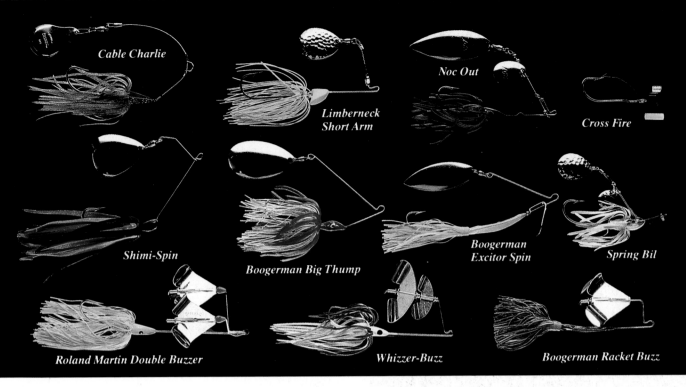

Cable Charlie

Limberneck Short Arm

Noc Out

Cross Fire

Shimi-Spin

Boogerman Big Thump

Boogerman Excitor Spin

Spring Bil

Roland Martin Double Buzzer

Whizzer-Buzz

Boogerman Racket Buzz

Spinner-Type Lures

The *Cable Charlie* spinnerbaits from Bumble Bee come in both single- and tandem-blade models, with a choice of blade shapes: willowleaf and the company's own Alabama and Chopper Bee styles. The flexible cable connecting the body and blades has a constant pulsating action. And it does seem to make hooking surer, at least in our experience with some tough-to-hook fish in brush-piles. Despite the flexibility, the lure rides in the water just as well as a regular spinnerbait and is just as weed-less. Weights from ³/₁₆ to ³/₈ ounce.

The popular Limberneck spinnerbaits by Brother's have cable running from the blades to the line eye, but not from the eye to the body as in the Cable Charlie series. Hooking is still much better than with ordinary spinner-baits, however. A new version, the *Limberneck Short Arm*, is available this year. The body is jointed: that is, the hook swings from it loosely rather than being rigidly attached. Our tests proved this an excellent bait for flip-ping: the joint lets the hook cock upward, so the lure can sink in an upright position rather than tipping for-ward; the single blade helicopters perfectly. The joint also permits lots of tail action when the lure is jigged, a real advantage in flipping. Sizes from ⅛ to ½ ounce.

LC's Lures has come up with a different way to improve hooking. The new *Noc Out* is a traditional-looking tan-dem spinnerbait, but it features a blade arm that knocks forward 60 degrees when a bass hits it, leaving the hook more exposed. Available in ³/₈- and ½-ounce sizes.

Still another route to better hooking is to add a stinger hook to your spinnerbait, and the new Tru-Turn *Cross Fire* hook is an excellent choice. It comes with several sizes and types of rubber tubing to hold it in place be-hind the spinnerbait hook. There's also a removable wire weedguard with a diamond-shaped bend at the tip to fully shield the hook point.

The *Shimi-Spin* by Dri Rind has a very large Indiana blade that swings wide and slow for lots of flash in off-colored water. It has a bulky skirt of an imitation-chamois material, which develops an enticing action like a pork strip but can be reused indefinitely. An ideal bait for slow, twitching retrieves and helicoptering. Weights range from ¼ to ½ ounce.

The ³/₈-ounce *Boogerman Big Thump* from Shadow Lake Lures has a thin, flat body that slides easily over struc-ture, a large blade, and reversed live-rubber skirts under a vinyl plastic skirt. The *Boogerman Excitor Spin* has the same body, but a long willowleaf blade (a current fa-vorite for largemouths in weeds; see "Largemouth Bass" on page 55) and a small roto blade. The Excitor Spin comes in ³/₈- and ½-ounce sizes; we prefer to reverse the skirt for more bulk and action.

The ³/₈-ounce *Spring Bil* from Lunker Lure is a cross be-tween a spinnerbait and a jig. It's available with either single or twin blade arms, and has a small metal lip molded into the lead body. The lip gives it an attractive wobbling and adds more flash. You can fish it deep or work it with your rod high, swimming it along or just under the surface; it makes a snakelike wake.

The Blue Fox *Roland Martin Double Buzzer* puts out plenty of noise, the blades clicking together as it buzzes across the surface. It's an effective buzzbait, but the double blades will occasionally lock together. There's a simple solution, though: just halt your retrieve for a split second and they'll separate. Sizes: ¼, ³/₈, and ½ ounce.

The *Whizzer-Buzz* from Citation is an in-line buzzbait with counter-rotating blades. This ¼-ouncer requires a very fast retrieve to stay on the surface; for best results, start reeling even before it hits the water.

For maximum noise, the single blade of the *Boogerman Racket Buzz* clicks against the long sledlike body. We re-versed the skirt to give the lure more bulk. Weights are ³/₈ and ½ ounce.

New Equipment:

Line

C. Boyd Pfeiffer

It's amazing that almost fifty years after the introduction of nylon fishing lines there are still improvements being made. Today, lines are no longer just "line"; instead, a variety of types are designed and manufactured for different purposes.

Prime Plus is the latest version of cofilament line from DuPont. The previous type, which was simply called Prime, got a bad rap from most anglers who tried it. It often broke very easily, even though it apparently had suffered no excessive abrasion, nicks, or other damage. Cofilament is a two-part line—it has a polyester core and a nylon sheath—and the bonding of these was sometimes inadequate. When Prime would snap, internal slippage was usually obvious: the core would stick out noticeably past the end of the sheath.

The theory behind cofilament line is an attractive one. The low-stretch polyester core should give excellent sensitivity to lure action and strikes, and also make for positive hook-sets. The nylon sheath should provide abrasion resistance and good knot strength. And it appears, on the basis of our early tests, that the new Prime Plus will finally make good on the promises. Prime Plus is still more likely than monofilament to break under sudden shock, because it doesn't stretch as much; but the maddening pop-offs under light pressure appear to have ended. When this new line is stressed beyond its limit, the core and sheath break off cleanly and evenly. In addition, it seems thinner than Prime for any given pound-test, and considerably limper.

To check out the limpness, we wound some 14-pound Prime Plus on a Daiwa TG1300 spinning reel; the smallish spool of this model is actually rated for 6- to 10-pound line. Even at first, when still dry, the Prime Plus cast smoothly off the spool and gave us very good distance. It's definitely reduced the wiriness that was one of the hallmarks of the earlier stuff.

The newest monofilament from Berkley, the other giant of the line business, is *TriMax*. It's advertised as a "tri-polymer," a type that incorporates three different kinds of nylon in a single strand. Here too, the intent is to combine in one product the best properties of the different materials. Berkley's claims for the line include low stretch, great strength for any given diameter, and exceptional wet strength. There's no doubt that it stretches

less than most other lines, Berkley's own Trilene XL among them; but Prime Plus has even less stretch.

To test diameter and strength, we used a micrometer and an Ametex L-30 force gauge—the same gauge that manufacturers use to demonstrate line strength at consumer sport shows. We found that TriMax labeled 10-pound test and Prime Plus labeled 12-pound test had virtually the same diameter: .012 inch for the TriMax, .0125 inch for the Prime Plus. In actual strength, ironically, the TriMax came out well ahead: 14.4 pounds, versus 12.5 for the Prime Plus. These were tests with dry lines. But nylon definitely loses strength when it absorbs water, so line makers work to develop products as water-resistant as possible, with varying degrees of success. According to our gauge, the TriMax dropped to 13.2 pounds after an overnight soaking, a loss of only 8.8 percent. Prime Plus, by comparison, dropped to 11.3 pounds, a 10.2 percent loss.

One drawback we should mention is the stiffness of TriMax. Though it casts well enough, it does tend to spring off the spool in coils, especially in cold weather.

Siglon V is a new imported monofilament from Sunline, manufactured to IGFA line-class specifications. Sunline claims that its strength is unaffected by exposure to ultraviolet in the atmosphere, and that special resins help keep water out. On our instruments, Siglon sold as 10-pound test measured .010 inch and tested 10.2 pounds dry, 9.2 pounds wet; the loss was only 8.8 percent, equivalent to that of TriMax. This is a good slick line for long casts, and it's limper than most. The tint is grayish.

Another slick mono—even slicker, in fact—is *Silver Thread* from Bagley. It flies through the guides with amazing speed, but its extraordinary slipperiness also causes a problem. When you reel in, the line tends to dig into the coils already on the spool. With a baitcasting outfit, this is likely to cause a record-class backlash on the following cast: not just a few unruly loops, but the kind of miserable killer snarl that can only be redeemed with your sharpest fillet knife. Still, there are virtuoso thumbers who prefer Silver Thread over others for its extra casting distance, even using it in tournaments. The spooling problems seem less pronounced with line tests over 10 pounds. And with spinning tackle, the difficulties don't exist.

When dry, Silver Thread labeled 16-pound test measured .0135 inch, slightly thicker than the TriMax sample discussed above; it actually tested 14.2 pounds, just under the TriMax. When wet, however, it dropped to 12.0 pounds, a significant 15.3 percent loss. A newer Bagley line has been introduced, but too late for us to test: Silver Thread II.

Ewell Parker's imported *TC* monofilament has an unusual camouflage pattern: alternating 3-foot bands, red and clear. The idea here is that red is highly visible to the angler above water, but is lost—that is, turns a nondescript dark color—when fished several feet underwater. In most cases, of course, you would tie your lure to a clear segment of the line. In our tests, TC

showed very good casting qualities, average dry strength, and a 12.9 percent strength loss when wet.

Anglers looking for a very low-priced mono that performs well should consider *Viking* line, which also is imported. It's strong for its diameter and has good abrasion resistance. While fishing for walleyes in the rocks, we've bent plenty of jig hooks before snapping this line. It's not as limp as many premium lines, though, and the limpness decreases after you've fished with it for a while.

The *Wet Cel Mono Core* fly lines by Scientific Anglers resemble the clear Shakespeare lines produced many years ago. They're completely translucent, an advantage for casting over saltwater flats species which spook very easily at the sight of a fly line sailing above them; and also for trout and smallmouths in clear, low-water conditions. How well do Mono Cores cast? Anglers impressed by the way they shoot have taken to calling them "slime lines." They're intermediate in weight, sinking slowly. One skilled angler we know adds his own special camouflage to these lines, inking in dark-colored bands with a waterproof marking pen. The only notable shortcoming of Mono Core is its "memory": it has a greater tendency to come off the reel in coils than ordinary fly lines. But stretching it before fishing is a quick cure for the problem.

FishTec has introduced its *SB AirFlo*, the first fly line with a Kevlar core. According to the advertising, it has virtually no stretch and very little tendency to coil, casts and shoots better than other lines, and has a finish "more abrasion-resistant than steel," one that won't crack with age and exposure to ultraviolet light. Our tests verified the low stretch, and certainly this is the greatest feature of the line, making far better hook-sets possible. Sinking big stout-wire hooks in tough-jawed fish like trophy largemouth bass has long been a problem for fly anglers, since the rod is so flexible and ordinary fly lines stretch so much.

It's also true that the AirFlo comes off the reel with minimal coiling. On other points, however, our testers had some doubts. One found it difficult to form tight loops when casting, and said the line seemed to drag in the guides rather than whistling on through. Another got tight loops readily and felt the line would shoot as well as any other, though perhaps not any better. These contrary assessments may result from different styles of casting.

The AirFlo has an exceptionally smooth finish, with none of the bubbles apparent in other brands. But the claim that it resists abrasion better than steel is clearly absurd: in fact, if you snag the line on your reel while double-hauling, the coating rips away from the core rather easily. We do like the nonstretch quality, a real asset for such fish as bass and pike; but an ordinary line will give better shock absorption for trout fishing with light, fragile tippets.

Ice-Fishing Gear

Steven A. Griffin

"There must be a better way," ice anglers have muttered while fighting cold and wind and trying to tempt sluggish fish. And over the years, better equipment to help them enjoy ice fishing has indeed been developed—much of it in the past season or two.

Shelters You Can Carry

Consider, for example, the windbreak manufactured by AJ Custom Canvas. The *Fish 'n' Shelter* is a corner-shaped outfit of aluminum tubing and canvas. It's light—7 pounds 5 ounces—and folds flat for carrying with a shoulder strap. Once you've selected a fishing spot, you drill an extra hole upwind, then anchor the windbreak with a short rod placed below the ice. The windbreak locks open with Velcro straps and aluminum arms that form seat supports.

The Fish 'n' Shelter is a good compromise, since many anglers long for protection from the wind but hate to give up mobility by huddling inside a wooden shanty. I've tested it in 30-mph winds, and it's worked admirably. Be sure to secure the tie-down rod beneath the ice first, because the unfolded windbreak acts like a sail.

Another alternative is a full, portable shanty, such as the *Ins-Tent* from Ins-Tent Manufacturing. Easy set-up is a goal of fishing-shelter makers, so I tested this one with my wife timing me. I opened the box, then read the instructions and got the shelter set up, all in the space of three minutes. Spikes secure the shelter to the ice. The black fabric walls have vents to release condensation and provide fresh air.

Ins-Tents come in sizes for one, two, or four persons. The one-person model, which I tested, weighs about 15 pounds. Ins-Tents also are available in "solar" versions, with a white-coated polyester exterior and a black nylon liner. On clear days these capture the heat of the sun, boosting the inside temperature by as much as 60 degrees.

Graphite Jigging Rods

Panfish bite lightly in winter, and in the past the only reliable way to detect strikes was to watch a float or a wire strike indicator attached to the rod tip. These days, if you fish bare-handed, graphite ice rods are making it possible to actually feel those delicate strikes.

For several seasons I've used a custom-built graphite rod to jig through the ice for bluegills and crappies. Now, commercially built *jigging rods by Cabela's and HT Enterprises* are available to do the same job. These light rods have performed well in my tests with 2- and 4-pound line. They work without a float or wire, but I still like a small float for times when the rod is resting on the ice.

The revolutionary *Indi* ultralight jigging rod, from Sports Specialties of Milwaukee, will handle line even lighter than 1-pound test. Its thin graphite tip is as sensitive as the wire indicators I've used, and offers the bonus of touch for bare-handed angling. Make sure your hooks are sharp, since the Indi sweeps gracefully into a fight, leaving you a little short of hook-setting power.

High-Tech Tip-Ups

For taking on the real fighters—lake and brown trout, pike, and walleyes—anglers have long debated which tackle works best. A rod and reel offers the most exciting fights, but tip-ups work on their own—a real plus if your state or province allows fishing with more than one line.

That debate may have been settled. Bob Campfield, who makes *Camp-n-Field tip-ups*, has a new design incorporating an 18-inch fiberglass rod. When the flag waves, you lift the tip-up from the water, fold the arms, then fight your fish with the rod and plastic reel. The spool is large, for deep fishing. The new Camp-n-Field tip-up is a little awkward to carry, though a ferrule does allow you to remove the rod from the base. But it's well worth the extra weight and bulk, when that flag waves and a rod-and-reel battle awaits.

HT Enterprises uses ABS plastic in its many rugged models. The HT *Polar tip-up* has a tripping device adjustable for sensitivity, and a shaft that turns to alert you to a running fish. Deep-water trout fans like the new *TU-5*, with its 500-foot-capacity spool. The *Windlass*, which jigs by wind power, now comes with a heavy, quick-change spring for bobbing heavier baits or lures.

HT has also introduced its *Fisherman* tip-ups. The Deep Lake Fisherman holds 1500 feet of line, an advantage for deep water. An adjustable drag keeps your bait from setting off the flag, but allows smooth line take-off when a wary brown or laker hits. My only beef is the plastic locking lugs on the arms. Wing nuts must be loosened to set the rig up, a tough operation with cold hands. But I do like the V-shaped frame that's easy to remove from the ice.

Best New Baits and Lures

You might not expect advances in live bait, but then along come *EuroLarvae* from Wazp. These grub baits, developed in England, are dyed red, yellow, or blue-green, to add a touch of color on days when panfish are finicky. EuroLarvae are tough: even when threaded on a hook

they keep wiggling, and a single EuroLarva will often catch several panfish.

In the repertory of ice-fishing lures, the Air-Plane Jig, by Northland, is well-established. A new version is the *Mini Air-Plane Jig*, in compact ¼- and ⅜-ounce sizes.

Don't imagine this smaller jig is just for small fish. It's effective in any light-tackle ice fishing with 6- to 10-pound line. A test trip convinced me of that, when a 9-pound lake trout slammed a chartreuse-and-green Mini bounced on a light jigging rod strung with 6-pound mono. After a ten-minute battle the exhausted fish lay atop the ice, the sharp hook still firmly buried in its jaw.

The Mini is also an excellent lure for walleyes—which the bigger Air-Plane wasn't.

Since the Mini has a spiral action, it's a good idea to use a swivel about 2 feet up the line. It comes with a trailing treble hook dressed with bucktail, or with a plain jig hook to which you add bait.

Specialty Ice Lines

New fishing lines have been developed with the ice angler in mind. Weller has a black, vinyl-coated Dacron line called *Flag* that won't absorb water, kink, or coil. At 20-pound test, it's a great hand line for big fish, and is well-suited to tip-up fishing for pike and other big species.

Gudebrod's new *Ice Line* is coated with Teflon, so it won't absorb water and stiffen. It looks and feels like the braided black line that's been a tip-up standard, but the Teflon should do away with some of the freeze-up headaches we've suffered.

I've also tried DuPont *Prime* line, the new nylon cofilament. It stretches very little, an advantage to heavy-tackle anglers trying to set big hooks. But in the lighter weights for panfish and small trout, the brittle cofilament breaks too easily. For ice fishing, I use it only in 8-pound test or heavier.

Top-Rated Power Augers

Big changes in power augers have been rare in recent years, but makers keep fine-tuning their designs.

One of our experienced testers rates the *Jiffy Model 30* the best he's ever lugged onto the ice. "There's just something about the way the Jiffy cuts. A lot of augers get caught at the bottom of the ice hole. This one punches right through."

StrikeMaster has introduced its *Magnum III Plus*, a 49cc machine. This one has benefitted from a boost in power; the former model displaced 33cc.

And E. F. Brewer makes the *Nordic Star*, which resembles the Jiffy. Our testers say this machine is built well, but the blade design requires you to apply more pressure to bore the hole.

Steven A. Griffin is the author of Ice Fishing Methods and Magic, *one of only four books ever written on ice fishing. His outdoor articles appear in* Great Lakes Fisherman *and other magazines.*

Downriggers

Terry R. Walsh

Since the invention of the rod and reel, few things have revolutionized fishing like the downrigger. Born on the Great Lakes twenty years ago to catch the newly introduced Pacific salmon, this unique device has been adopted for many other kinds of fishing that demand precise depth control.

Consisting of a frame that mounts on the boat, a large spool of wire cable, a boom with a pulley at the end, and an 8- to 14-pound weight which takes the lure to any desired depth, the downrigger allows the angler to present a lure at the exact level where the fish are holding. When a fish strikes, the fishing line pulls free of a line release just above the weight, and the angler then fights the fish with his rod and reel.

The early downriggers were crude at best, but today's models have entered the computer age. Here's a rundown on the best for 1988:

Big Jon, entering its nineteenth year of production, continues to improve the *Big Jon Junior,* its most popular unit among amateurs and professionals alike. The frame is anodized aluminum, the cable spool and pulley are G.E. Lexan plastic, and the boom is ⅝-inch, flexible aircraft aluminum available in lengths from 2 to 5 feet. The motor will retrieve a 10-pound weight at 100 feet per minute with only 4 amps draw. The multidisk clutch is very smooth. A spring-drive counter keeps track of the depth. Rod holders and swivel bases are optional.

The flexible boom serves two purposes: adding erratic, enticing action to your lures when the boat rolls on choppy water, and reducing the chance of boom damage with bottom hangups. I've had these booms bend all the way to the water when the weight snagged, and they've returned to their normal position once the tension was released.

I also like the unique tip-up boom feature, which makes line setting on the long booms a cinch. An automatic motor shutoff is available in 1988, eliminating repeated resetting of circuit breakers. I do have a criticism of the spring counter: it needs frequent rezeroing and occasionally breaks.

Cannon dropped its cast-aluminum frames last year, opting for lighter, stronger ones made of Lexan. The new streamlined *Magnum 10A II* electric and *Uni-Troll 6* manual have stainless-steel booms in lengths from 18 to 66 inches. The gear-driven depth counters are accurate. Both units come with an adjustable rod holder and carry

a limited lifetime warranty. Accessories available include dual rod holders and swivel bases. Conversion kits can upgrade the manual units to electric, or the electric units to Digi-Troll computer operation.

A unique feature on the manual model is the clutch brake that lets you lower the weight at any speed you desire by turning the handle back slightly (it doesn't turn as the weight is lowered). Turning it forward stops the weight. Crank the weight up, and it stays right where it is whenever you stop—a highly innovative feature.

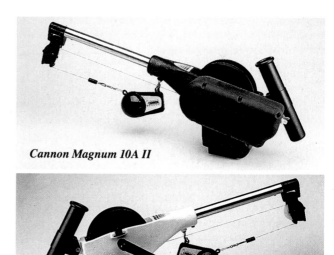

Cannon Magnum 10A II

Cannon Uni-Troll 6

Cannon downriggers definitely offer features that others don't. There's a convenient weight-holder hook right on the back of the boom. A nice feature on all the bases is a shear pin which prevents expensive downrigger damage in docking mishaps. An eared switch guard prevents accidentally starting the motor.

On the Digi-Troll models, a computer allows you to preset the trolling depth of the weight, and it will unfailingly return to that depth until reset—a nice feature when you forget to check the depth of a hot line before bringing up the weight. Digi-Trolls also shut off automatically when the weight reaches the surface, and will shift the weight up and down at programmed intervals to get more strikes. These are excellent downriggers, though some anglers object to their bulk: they're a nuisance to work around when netting fish.

The most recent models from Penn are the *Fathom-Master 800* electric series, complementing the popular 600 manual series. The 800 comes with a 24-inch boom and a fixed base, while the 820 features a 48-inch boom and a five-position swivel base. The motor and circuitry are completely housed in a streamlined polymer housing, which features an internal fan to dissipate heat. A handy carrying handle is part of the housing.

Penn Fathom-Master 800

The on-off switch is just behind the cable spool on the right side of the housing, where it's not likely to be bumped accidentally. The 800 series downriggers are easy to install and remove, thanks to a convenient, oversized lock-down knob. They have the same smooth clutch system used in the manual 600s. The booms on all Penn downriggers are of gold anodized aluminum. Dual rod holders are a new option this year.

In a word, Proos downriggers are rugged. Practically every part is thick, solid aluminum—the frames, the cable spools, the 18-inch to 6-foot booms. The standard electric *26M* has a lethargic weight-retrieve speed of only 70 feet per minute, which many anglers have objected to. But this complaint has been answered by the new *XF Turbo*, which is twice as fast.

Both units feature conveniently located on-off and circuit-breaker switches on the rear of the motor housings. An automatic shutoff is another nice feature. The XF Turbo and the deluxe *26MB* electric feature slip clutches. Rod holders and swivel bases are optional. Like the Cannon models, Proos downriggers are massive units that occupy considerable space on a transom.

Speedtrol enters its third year with a much-improved product. Its compact, low-profile, *Electric* unit features an anodized frame and an ABS motor housing. The inch-thick tubular boom is made of stainless steel in lengths from 16 to 54 inches. An added tip-up feature gets the long booms up and out of the way for docking convenience, and an improved swivel-head assembly has eliminated the cable-jam problems once common with Speedtrol units. A new high-speed motor with automatic shutoff has significantly increased weight retrieve to 105 feet per minute. An eight-position swivel base is avail-able, as are dual rod holders. The company also markets a manual model.

The new electric is available in both right- and left-hand versions for user convenience, a feature I wish more companies offered. The motor switch, poorly located on top of the unit in previous years, has now been moved to the side. The rod holder, however, still is poorly positioned, ahead of the motor housing on the boom—a long reach on boats with a high freeboard.

Walker electrics are available in two models, a standard gray *EDR-234* and a deluxe chrome *EDRC-234*. These compact units have completely enclosed motors and circuitry; slip clutches; ABS plastic cable spools; 2- to 4-foot booms of inch-thick, solid, anodized aluminum; and belt-driven counters. These are well-made units that carry a lifetime warranty.

The on-off switch has been moved from the top of the units to the back, where it's less prone to accidental start-ups, but I'd like a larger switch. The dual rod holders, a standard feature, are positioned for easy access, and the weight-retrieve rate is a crisp 100 feet per minute with a 10-pound ball. The optional Duo Temp-Sense monitor, giving water-temperature readings on the surface and down at the weight, was new for 1987.

On the negative side, the color of the ABS plastic housings has shown a tendency to fade with time. And the glitter of the new chrome finish seems out of place on this well-established downrigger.

Terry R. Walsh has been a Great Lakes charter captain for twelve years, and writes articles for Outdoor Life, Field & Stream, *and* Fishing Tackle Trade News.

Boats

Frank Sargeant

When it comes to boat selection, fishermen have never had it so good. This year they can choose from a host of specialized boats designed for different kinds of fishing, with features to solve just about any problem they're ever likely to encounter.

And a trend toward package rigs—complete with boat, motor, trailer, and accessories—now makes it easier to get the boat you need, usually at a lower price than you'd pay by selecting all the components individually. Some of the outboard manufacturers, in fact, have jumped into the boat-building business themselves. OMC and Brunswick, the parent companies of Johnson-Evinrude and Mercury-Mariner, have bought out several major producers of outboard hulls in the past two years.

"Nobody buys a car without an engine," one company executive told us. "We think the entry-level boater will find it easier to get into the sport if he's offered a turn-key rig, ready to take to the ramp the day he signs the papers. A delay of a week or so while the motor is mounted, the trolling motor is installed, and all the electronics are put in place is enough to chill a lot of sales."

There are hundreds of different bass boats in fiberglass, aluminum, and Kevlar. Lighter weights and improved bottom designs are giving more speed this year without increases in horsepower or fuel consumption. And some really significant changes in interior design have popped up, too: the way bass boats are defined may well be changed with the arrival of the first center console from a major manufacturer this year.

In recent years, bass boats have evolved in two different directions. One is toward greater size, luxury and speed: 20-foot fiberglass dream machines equipped with motors generating better than 200 horses and capable of eye-watering speeds—with prices to match. The other is toward lightness and fuel efficiency: aluminum models of more limited dimensions, but rigged with all the vital fishing amenities. They're no match for deep-vee fiberglass hulls in rough, open water, but are excellent for most bass fishing and far less costly.

During the past few seasons, cold-water fishermen have finally started getting the attention they deserve. This year many manufacturers are offering boats designed specifically for northern anglers in pursuit of walleyes, perch, northern pike, and Great Lakes salmon and trout.

These "pike boats" have lots of freeboard for rough water, and semi-vee bottoms to soften the ride. Some are especially designed for backtrolling, and all have the special amenities that have made bass boats so popular—live wells, rod boxes, lots of other enclosed storage, and more.

In short, whatever your boating and fishing interest, you're likely to find something that suits you perfectly in the 1988 crop of boats.

Bass Boats

The most intriguing new bass boat is the 20½-foot fiberglass *SK-2000* from Skeeter. It's the first center-console bass boat; but, having fished from it, we'd be willing to bet it won't be the last. The high seat behind the swept-back console allows great visibility. More important, its location close to the centerline greatly improves the balance and handling of the boat when it's operated with only one person aboard. The seat is far easier to get into and out of than the conventional type, and is less likely to get you wet in rough water.

Even more interesting than the interior is the bottom design. Skeeter invested over half a million dollars in developing this hull, and it shows in the performance as well as the appearance. The big difference is apparent when you drop the hammer—this is perhaps the only high-performance bass boat in the business that doesn't have a "hole-shot" problem. Instead of wallowing with the stern down and the bow pointed at the clouds, the 2000 just shoots off, almost flat, with an acceleration that takes your breath away. Powered by a 220 Excel Yamaha without any prop-doctoring, our test boat ran 73 mph.

Other things to like in this new Skeeter were the automotive-type dash with all instruments in a single factory-installed pod, and a large, lockable electronics box, eliminating the need to remove depth finders overnight.

Add to all this the fact that the boat looks as if it just landed from Jupiter, and it's sure to be the most talked-about model of the year. In price it will run about the same as other luxury bass boats in the 20-foot category.

Skeeter SK-2000

Hydra-Sports Striper

Hydra-Sports' new fiberglass *Striper*, 17½ feet, is an enhanced version of the earlier model 1800. It's ideal for fishermen in search of striped bass on the big reservoirs of the South, or for those after trout and salmon on the Great Lakes. Add a trolling motor at the bow (with the built-in wiring harness, the job is easy) and it makes a good big-water boat for largemouths.

The Striper has a pocket hull, common on bass boats but not on center-console boats. There's a hollow, or pocket, in the bottom near the transom, which allows higher engine-mounting. The advantages include blinding speed—over 55 mph with the 150 Pro-V Yahama we tested—and excellent performance in rough water. At 1400 pounds, the Striper weighs about the same as a large fiberglass bass boat, but with its deep bow it handles big waves far better. It has an extremely solid feel, with none of the tin-can sounds you hear in thinner hulls running rough water. The hull does have a slight tendency to get "horsy" in rollers at speed, owing to the high buoyancy and the rocker (upcurved bottom) aft, but this is controllable with motor trim.

All hardware is corrosion-proof, and the fittings and finish are of a quality not expected on small boats. It's self-bailing, a comfort when you leave it in the water overnight. A removable pedestal seat on the bow deck is part of the package. Small enough to fish by yourself, big enough to carry a crew of four, the Striper is a great all-around boat.

The fiberglass Ranger *680C*, just under 17 feet, is the ideal combination boat for the angler who likes to sneak into those tiny outback ponds and rivers after work, but also enjoys occasional trips to the big lakes for bass or

pike. At 875 pounds, it's light enough to be trailered just about anywhere, even up a muddy river bank with four-wheel drive. Yet, at 16 feet 11 inches down the centerline, it's big enough to handle rough water when it has to. The hull is also one of the roomiest in its size range, because the console is tiny and located along the side.

It lacks the aft casting platform that most bass boats have, so there's more deck space to walk around in, plus greater security for those who don't like a high aft seat. Even the bow platform is lowered enough to give the feeling you're fishing "in" the 680 rather than "on" it. The light weight also means good speed with minimal horsepower: a 75-horse is adequate, a 90 all you'd ever need. The same hull is also available in a tiller-steering model without the console, ideal for backtrolling.

Ranger 680C

Grumman Outlaw SX

Grumman's new all-welded version of the popular 17-foot *Outlaw SX* should be one of the leaders in aluminum bass boats this year. The Outlaw SX is much more solid than riveted boats, is made of heavier-gauge aluminum, and should last forever without danger of leaks—which usually are the big problem in riveted boats as they age. It weighs just 635 pounds (25 more than the riveted Outlaw) and is rated for 80 horses, though it will run just fine with 50.

The boat leaps out of the hole, runs shallow water beautifully, and is exceptionally easy to handle at the launching ramp. A forward battery-storage box reduces the length of wire running to the trolling motor—thus minimizing voltage drop. The bottom has 6 degrees of vee all the way to the stern—a lot less than fiberglass vees, but a lot more than most flat-bottomed aluminums. In rough water, it definitely helps.

The Outlaw SX is available as a complete package including motor, trailer, and electronics from most Grumman dealers, as are eleven other models by the company this year.

Pike Boats

The 16½-foot Lund *Pro-V* may have the sturdiest aluminum hull in its class; in fact, some say it's overbuilt. It's made of .100-inch aluminum, some 28 percent thicker than lesser boats, and weighs in at a whopping 970 pounds. Our testers say it should last forever. They also point out the sizeable locking rod boxes, long enough to handle 8-foot salmon rods, and the locking electronics box near the stern in the tiller-steering model. The seating is comfortable both for running and backtrolling. A 24-gallon tank gives all the range anyone is ever likely to want in a boat this size—in fact, the testers were able to fish three days with a 60-horse on a single tankful.

The only thing they don't like is the somewhat bow-heavy weight distribution: in rough seas the bow tended to drop low and allow lots of spray in unless the motor was trimmed very high. They advise using nothing less than a 60-horse outboard on the boat because of its unusual weight.

Lund Pro-V

Crestliner Viking Deluxe

The Crestliner *Viking Deluxe*, 16½ feet, draws praise from our test users for its smooth, welded construction that rivals fiberglass, and its heavy, baked-on enamel paint that's far tougher to scratch than the finish on most other aluminum hulls. Testers also like the exceptional stability resulting from the 78-inch beam and from the 22-gallon fuel tank located at the boat's center of gravity. "It just doesn't rock like you expect an aluminum to do when you walk around in it," one fisherman notes. The tank location also minimizes weight on the trailer tongue—a blessing for the lone angler when hitching and unhitching.

Another plus is the steady tracking of the boat in back-trolling—"the deep vee all the way to the transom acts like a keel, which keeps the boat going straight even in side winds." The vee gives a soft ride, and the high bow keeps water out of the cockpit and off the passengers in windy weather. The boat runs about 30 mph with a 60-horse outboard, and uses a miserly 1 gallon per hour in backtrolling. The weight is just 710 pounds, but the bottom is built of durable .090-inch aluminum. There's ample storage for long rods, and locking boxes for electronics.

Our anglers particularly like the instrument location, on the left side at the stern, exactly where a tiller operator normally looks when he's in the most comfortable steering position. Splash guards are needed, though, to keep water from coming over the transom during backtrolling in rough weather.

The Alumacraft *Competitor*, also 16½ feet, is a semi-vee riveted-aluminum backtroller. According to our testers, it does a good job of tracking in reverse, and it's exceptionally dry at speed going forward, because of a bow-high running attitude. With a 60-horse outboard, the test boat exceeded 30 mph. It felt exceptionally solid in large waves, with none of the flexing common in thin

metal boats, and the ride was soft. The storage boxes under the bow deck are unusually dry, and there's locking storage throughout.

Alumacraft Competitor

A couple of suggested improvements would be to move the live well from the side of the boat to the center, where it wouldn't create an imbalance when full, and to open up the battery storage area at the stern with a larger lid, so that the batteries would be easier to lift in and out for off-the-boat charging. One user said that the locking electronics box next to the stern seat is a good idea, but that the box should be larger to accommodate the pair of sounders that many serious anglers prefer these days.

The fuse panel for all the electronics is located in the locking box, where it's easy to see and reach. The boat's wiring is well protected, of adequate gauge, and generally easy to get to.

Frank Sargeant is the outdoor editor of the Tampa Tribune, *and boating editor of* Bassmaster *and* Saltwater *magazines. His articles on fishing and on fishing equipment have appeared in many national outdoor publications.*

31

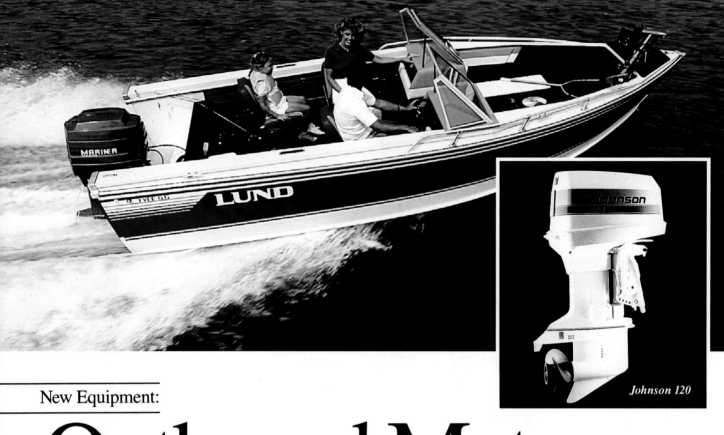
Johnson 120

Outboard Motors

Frank Sargeant

Any complacency that might have existed in the board rooms of U.S. outboard manufacturers has evaporated since the invasion of quality Japanese motors about five years ago. American builders found the going tough for a while, but soon responded to the challenge with new factories, state-of-the-art building techniques, and new designs. The competition has been hard on profits but great for the consumer, who now has a wider choice among better products built both at home and abroad.

Evinrude's four-cylinder *140* has a boost in cubic inches, up to 122 from 110, which helps particularly in low-end torque, lifting a bass boat out of the hole. We used this motor on a full-sized bass rig and found performance close to that of much larger, six-cylinder engines, but gas consumption considerably lower. The 140 has an automatic slow-down device to prevent damage if overheated, and a new Quickstart ignition that advances the spark on cold starts to prevent stalling. Like all outboards these days it starts at high revs, annoying but better than restarting repeatedly until the engine warms.

Johnson has upgraded its *120* with more displacement—equal to the Evinrude and Johnson 140s'—but the decrease in carburetion should make for an exceptionally long-lived engine. Our test motor showed no tendency to stall at low speeds, perhaps because of the spark-advance system shared with Evinrude. Planing was quick, and the motor was very easy on fuel for the power available. The low profile is a plus for trollers who don't want anything to obstruct their view aft. One question buyers might ask, though: Since the 120 has the same displacement and weight as the Johnson and Evinrude 140s, why not go with the extra power?

The new Mariner four-cylinder *100* offers exceptional smoothness, yet plenty of low-end torque. A new reed valve keeps fuel atomized even at idle, preventing the carbon-loading common in many outboards. The 105-cubic-inch block is bigger than the six-cylinder 115's, and uses the same bearings as the six; the minimal horsepower demand should make for excellent longevity. The window on the cowling for checking the oil level in the injection system is a nice touch.

Mariner's new *8* has a unique manual trim you can adjust to six positions just by pushing down the tiller; our test model required only a firm push with one hand. This is a big improvement, allowing the same trim control on small boats as on big rigs with power trim. Also very nice in a manual start is the fuel primer—a pull or two will squirt just enough fuel to the twin cylinders for easy starts. The exhaust is underwater, through the prop hub, as quiet as on any small twin you'll find. A knob on the cowling lets you adjust trolling speeds as low as 650 rpm. The motor weighs 69 pounds.

The big news from Mercury is an updated high-performance bass-fishing motor, the 150-hp *XR4*. Its greater displacement—142.2 cubic inches, compared to the 121 of the predecessor XR2—has reduced the wide-open throttle range to 5000-5500, down from the screaming 6000s of Mercury models gone by. The result should be less maintenance and fewer blown engines. The gear ratio of the new engine has been lowered to 1.78:1, from the 2:1 of the XR2. We didn't have a matched pair of old and new engines for comparison testing, but the 1988 model won't be left behind by many other outboards at the takeoff. A trim switch has been added on the cowl, making it easier to adjust the motor after the boat is on the trailer. The test engine was a bit noisy because of extra breathing passages, but didn't have the ear-piercing whine at top end of Mercurys past.

Mercury's *60*, a three-banger, drew praise from our testers for its exceptionally slow idle. One angler who used the tiller model was able to backtroll into the wind slow enough to fish live baits for walleyes—a tough test for a motor this large. Testers said the 60 was not quite as smooth as the Mercury four-cylinders, but didn't notice

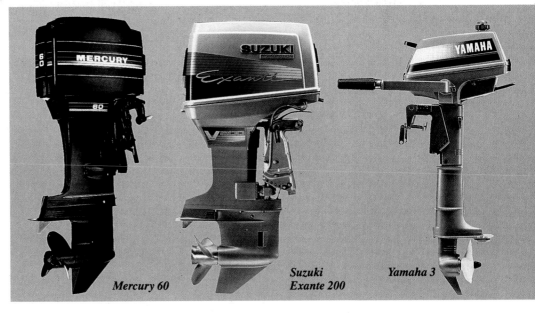

Mercury 60

Suzuki
Exante 200

Yamaha 3

excessive noise or vibration. Some wished the trim unit were mounted on the engine, so the cylinders wouldn't take up boat space. The 60 weighs 188 pounds—the same as the 50-horse. The motor had an impressive top end, and plenty of power to get boats on plane in the lower ranges.

Merc's *45* is available this year with a factory-installed handle, electric start, and power trim—all great for backtrollers. Previously, power trim on this engine was available only as an add-on accessory. It helps get the most from light aluminum boats like the one we used, which really got up and flew as the motor was trimmed. The 45 is very quiet at idle and at speed. The company says a new, filament-wound water pump will resist wear resulting from ice particles, another plus for northern fishermen.

Suzuki has the most unusual gimmick in the outboard field this year with its "talking" engine, the *Exante 200*. Computers keep tabs on the oil level, temperature, and water pressure, and report to you via recording. Back-up gauges also monitor the engine. The 164.3-cubic-inch block features dual spark plugs for each cylinder, and the oil tank is under the cowling, eliminating tubes and tank-storage problems. A stainless-steel prop is part of the package. Aside from the "talking," our test engine was surprisingly quiet. The talking doesn't seem much of an advantage, though, to any boatman used to keeping tabs with gauges.

The new oil-injected Suzuki *30* is a three-cylinder with a weight of 132 pounds, but it offers a lot of big-motor features including a rev-limiter that prevents engine burn-up if the oil level in the cowl-mounted tank gets too low. It's available in both remote and tiller steering. Test users reported exceptionally quiet operation at trolling speeds, and smooth operation in lower ranges after the electronic idle control on the hood was adjusted for extended low-speed operation. Options include oil-flow, water-flow, and oil-level gauges, not common on motors this small.

Yahama's *130* is new this year. It's a smooth-running four-banger with the quietness Yamaha is known for. Extra trim, to minus 4 degrees, makes for easy hole shots, and also helps get the bow down for smooth operation in rough water. Like all larger Yahamas, this motor comes with the new combined LCD tachometer/trim gauge/oil-level indicator. The trim gauge simplifies returning to the right setting for maximum speed—you just count the lighted LCD "windows" to reach the desired level.

A 36-pound *3* has been added to the Yahama line. It's loop-charged and barely sips at the 100:1 gas mix. A 1.5-quart tank is built into the cowling, making a compact package that's easy to get from the trunk to the boat. The motor we used started on the first pull every time. Because it's a single-cylinder, the 3 is not as smooth or quiet as most other Yamahas, but compensates in economy and light weight. One addition we'd like is a reverse gear: presently, the engine must be swiveled 360 degrees to go backward.

The Yamaha jet drives in three-, four-, and six-cylinder models are still in the line, the only factory jet outboards available. We test-drove a *65* and found it would run a 17-foot center console through water less than a foot deep. The boat would also turn and stop on a dime. Reverse can be kicked in at full throttle, since there are no gears, and this really puts on the brakes. The jets are noisier than conventional outboards and burn more fuel, but for shallow water they're great.

Electric Motors & Boat Accessories

Frank Sargeant

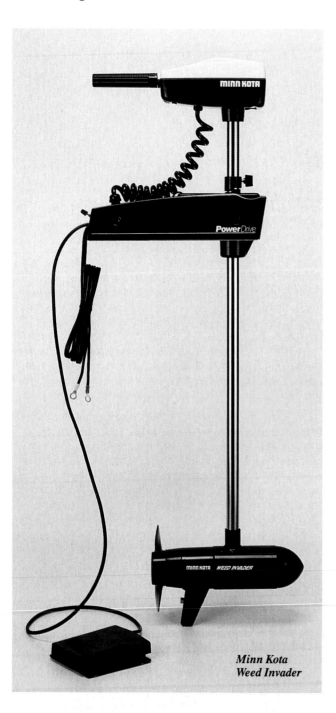

*Minn Kota
Weed Invader*

Electric motors made a quantum leap two years ago with the introduction of pulse modulation, a system of cutting direct current on and off thousands of times a second, greatly extending useful battery life between charges. Last year, radio and electrical remote control made news. There's nothing that earth-shaking this year, but improvements in existing units—more power, better control systems and the use of more durable, corrosion-resistant materials—make the 1988 lineup a great one.

Minn Kota has some of the most advanced units. We particularly like the *795MX*, a more powerful version of the electrical remote-control motor brought out last year. The 795MX puts out 36 pounds of thrust with a single 12-volt battery, and can be operated from up to 18 feet away with the electric footpad, connected to the motor with a flexible cord. The motor is easier to turn than mechanical versions, and the flat footpad makes it more comfortable to use than most. There's also a 24-volt remote-control model, the *799MX*, with 41 pounds of push. Both models feature pulse modulation.

The new 24-volt Minn Kota *Weed Invader* is for prowling the thick stuff. It has a small powerhead— a 3½-inch diameter compared to the 4-inchers common in most 24-volt units—combined with a small, fast-turning prop. The combination works: it's a real lawnmower, judging from our tests in the weedy waters of central Florida. We like the control system, too—it combines electrical foot control and manual hand control, so steering is easy whatever your location. The heavy-duty aluminum prop is a good idea, given the dense cover the motor is designed for. The thrust is only 37 pounds, a bit less than other Minn Kota 24s. One drawback is the noise: the motor is louder than most, because of the higher revs of the small prop.

Minn Kota has expanded its line of horsepower-rated transom-mount models—now included are 2-, 3-, and 4-horse units. The designations by horsepower are primarily a marketing gimmick, but the *4-HP* does stand out as the most powerful electric in the business, generating some 65 pounds of thrust. Byrd has been building a 60-pound-thrust model for some time; but Minn Kota hit on the idea of converting pounds to horsepower, to compete with small gas outboards which electrics excel in ease of starting and steering, and reliability. The 4 draws a whopping 60 amps at full power, but has the Maximizer modulation system and reserves batteries for long operational periods at lower speeds.

MotorGuide has a new tiller model, the *430DA*, which can be switched from stern to bow use by simply turning the head around, provided you have a clamp space on the bow of your boat. It generates 30 pounds of thrust on 12 volts, has DuraAmp 2 pulse modulation, and seems exceptionally quiet. So does the new *Competition Series 665*, a 24-volt foot-control model with 45 pounds of thrust. How well these motors will hold up in the long run is a question, however. Our testers report a number of problems with previous MotorGuide units, including plastic parts that fall off and mysterious power shutdowns while trolling.

Mercury and Mariner finally took the plunge into direct-drive motors with new 24-volt models generating 28 pounds of thrust. The Merc *24/12 Thruster* and Mariner *Stalker R-28 24/12* produce far less noise than the planetary-gear models of the past, and have a smaller, more weedless prop. With lower amp draw, they should give longer battery life than the 12-volters. For those who prefer the large-prop, high-thrust, gear-drive models, several versions are still available under both the Mercury and Mariner logos.

OMC has redesigned the foot control on its Johnson *Power Sneaker 12* and Evinrude *Super Scout 12* remote models, and the Johnson we tested was exceptionally smooth for a mechanical control motor. We also like the retraction system, one of the most effortless in the industry. As always, the OMC entries are among the quietest available. The one thing we might have wished for in the 12-volters is more speeds—the three notches available don't provide adequate selection.

Pflueger has a line of impressive electrics these days, including both electrical and mechanical foot-control units with a completely flat, low-profile footpad that was very easy to stand on in the electrical *BER 50* we used. The pad pivots only 70 degrees, and that's all it takes to turn the motor in any direction, including reverse—a great improvement over the rocker systems that require the foot to be cocked up, and make it tough to stand and fish all day as most bass fishermen prefer to do. The BER 50 has pulse modulation, and a unique systems monitor in the steering head that gives battery power, water temperature, and "stall warning" LCD readings. The motor we used seemed to turn almost magically with the natural pivoting of the foot as we faced in different directions. The 50-pound thrust is more than enough to move the largest bass boat against a strong headwind. A 35-pound-thrust model is also available.

The *DeckHand Electric Anchor* from Minn Kota is a useful device for small-boat anglers who have problems with tangled anchor lines. It features an enclosed reel that controls anchor-line release and take-up at the flick of a switch, which you can mount anywhere in the boat. The unit should be especially useful for live-bait or jig fishermen who like to anchor their boats to

fish a hole thoroughly, but who move fairly often during the day. A locking system secures the 16-pound mushroom anchor in its housing for high-speed runs in rough water.

If you hitch your boat trailer to your car by yourself, you know how difficult it can be to get the ball and the trailer tongue aligned. The *Glide-Rite* hitch solves the problem with a funnel-like receiver that mounts on your car, and a connector that attaches to the tongue. The receiver corrals the tongue, and as soon as the tongue settles into position a spring-loaded pin locks it there. You just back up until you hear a snap, then drive away with the rig securely hitched. It worked great for us the first time we tried it. There are models for both conventional and weight-distributing hitches, and with capacities from 5,000 to 10,000 pounds.

Glide-Rite Hitch

The MotorGuide *DuraAmp 2 Power Pack* converts standard transom-mount trolling motors to pulse modulation—the system that increases the period between battery charges up to four times normal. The pack includes a battery case with carrying handle, the DuraAmp module, and a receptacle for plugging in your motor without taking the lid off the battery box. It operates with motors from any manufacturer. An added advantage is that it gives you infinitely variable speeds even with a motor that otherwise doesn't.

The *Depth Talker,* from Depth Talker Inc., reads depths aloud when connected to your sonar unit. You never take your eyes off the water— a great help while fishing or when navigating a tricky or crowded channel. The unit hooks up to most types of depth finders, and can be set to read depths at various time intervals. It's fairly expensive, but should be worth it to fishermen who dislike spending their day watching the box.

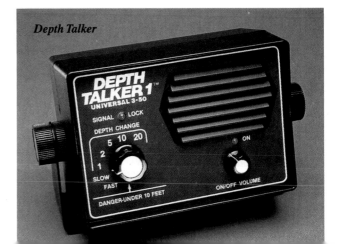
Depth Talker

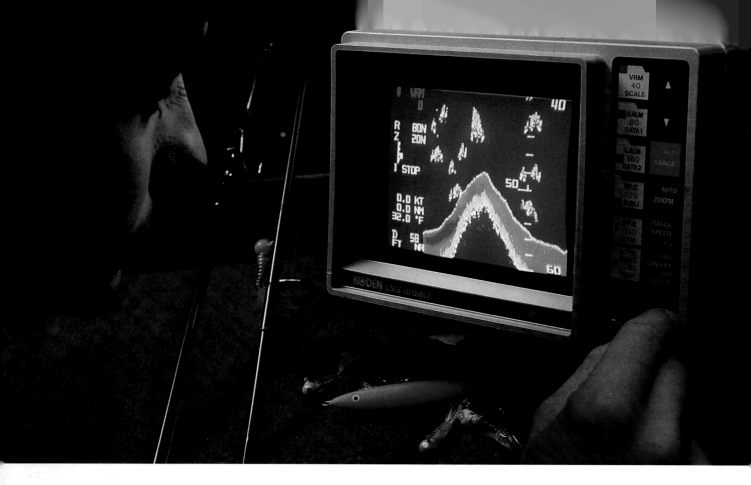

Depth Finders

Frank Sargeant

No other piece of fishing gear has drawn more attention from the technology wizards in recent years than the depth finder. This year's new machines not only chart bottom and find fish, but also indicate boat speed and distance traveled, water temperature, and even (when coupled with Loran) your boat position.

The finders most likely to dominate the field for the next few years are the LCDs, or LCRs. Disliked by many anglers at first because of their poor definition, LCDs have improved so much they're now the choice of nearly all buyers except deep-water anglers who want the last word in detail, no matter what the cost. LCDs have tiny individual pixels, or cells of liquid, that change color when hit by an electric current. They now provide more information than most paper-chart recorders, at half to two-thirds the cost. There's no paper to change, ever—a convenience and cost-saver. And with LCDs, maintenance problems are largely a thing of the past. There are no moving parts to wear out—period.

Videos, or CRTs, once strictly for seagoing commercial fishermen, have gotten smaller, much less expensive, and about as easy to operate as the more complex of the LCDs. But videos display their information in as many as eight colors, with different hues for bottom, vegetation, baitfish, gamefish, and more. They offer all the on-screen readouts supplied by LCDs: speed, log, temperature, and position. Other than initial cost, the only negatives are that videos take up more space on a bass- or pike-boat console than LCDs, and some don't come in waterproof housings—a lethal failing for open boats.

For serious bottom study where the ultimate in detail can make the difference between a big catch and none at all, there's still no match for computerized chart recorders, capable of blowing up a tiny portion of the water column to near-perfect definition on a broad sheet of graph paper. The faithful old flasher is still around, too, but appears headed for obsolescence as the LCDs drop to the same price level while offering volumes more information.

LCDs

The Eagle *Z-7500* is an exceptionally sharp LCD with 192 vertical pixels. The machine largely takes care of itself once you hit the "on" button: everything adjusts automatically to give the depth reading and gain. We liked the zoom key for instant homing on the bottom half of the screen, doubling its size for detail study—handy when you're trying to separate gamefish from bait. The depth range of the zoom window can be changed with arrow keys.

The fish alarm can be set to beep only on fish passing within a particular range, thus avoiding the almost continuous beeping you get from units that read everything in the water column. If you know the salmon are between 90 and 100 feet, you can set the window for that depth and not be bothered with excess beeps from alewife schools at 30 feet. The machine will also read temperature, speed, and distance traveled, but you need to buy the optional sensors.

The Lowrance *X-50* is a deluxe model of the Eagle above. It has more keys, more functions, and 500 watts more peak power: at 3000 watts, it's the most powerful machine in the business. It also offers a 192-pixel vertical definition. To operate it, all you need to do is hook up the cables (which take a bit of wiggling to get into place, but feature waterproof connections) and turn it

on. You really don't have to touch the keyboard the rest of the day.

If you want, however, the X-50 can perform a multitude of functions that would make an IBM PC blush. By hitting the "2nd" key, you can double the functions of all the 32 keys. Any depth range you can think of can be punched in on the numeric pad, and temperature, speed, and distance sensors are available. The unit is totally submersible, the manufacturer says, and we tossed it overboard to find out. It took the licking and kept on ticking. The machine can store two screens of information, even when disconnected, for those who want records of especially productive spots.

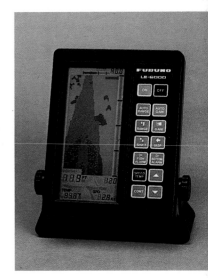

Furuno's *LE6000* has a 6-inch vertical screen, one of the tallest in the industry; with 160 pixels vertically, it defines even small targets very well. The 14-button keypad is simple enough that basic functions can be accessed without looking at the manual: temperature, digital depth, and boat-speed readouts appear in a dedicated area at the bottom of the screen, an advantage over machines that put this information in the active part of the screen, in our estimation.

The Impulse *Microtrac 2800* is a sharp-definition machine despite its small size. With a screen comprising 160 × 128 pixels, the picture is a match for just about anything in the field. A feature we especially liked was the enclosed bracket for flush mounting in the console—a sensible place to put a small unit like this in many bass boats, because mounting on top of the console may interfere with the driver's vision. The basic functions are easy to crank up from the simple keypad. A unique and useful feature is the bottom-coverage readout, which shows the distance the sound cone is covering—helpful in precisely locating fish shown on the screen.

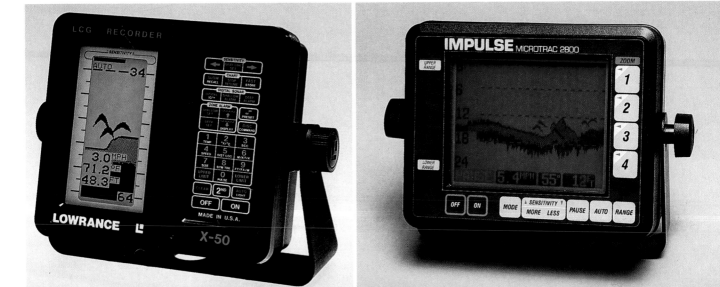

Another good feature of the 2800 is a ten-minute temperature-trends graph that can help you locate spring outflows or hot-water discharges. The optional portable power pack could be useful if you often fish in rental boats: it allows you to take the unit along without worrying about battery hookups. The only possible problems we saw with the machine are the electrical and transducer connections, which are not waterproof and could fail in wet weather in an open boat. Actually, the 2800 may offer too many goodies for the average fisherman. You could spend your entire day running through the seemingly endless functions that can be accessed from the keypad—most of them of questionable use to anglers—and forget to wet a line.

The King *920* offers an exceptionally easy-to-understand screen, with most of the functions always on and always appearing next to their labels on the unit housing. Included are digital depth, temperature, and speed readings, and an extra window to indicate remaining battery voltage—very useful for those who run their trolling motor and depth finder off the same battery. We liked the fact the peripheral information is separated from the chart area itself—it's confusing when all those numbers are scattered across the screen as in some units.

The 920 also has a feature called "fish loupe" which gives a compressed picture, in the left ¼-inch of the chart surface, showing everything below the boat, regardless of where the clutter control is set. The idea is to make sure no fish are missed when the gain is turned down, but the extra line there may make the screen harder to read for some anglers. The machine can recall three screens, even after being disconnected and reinstalled, and it remembers the last range setting before disconnect—a blessing for those who don't like tapping buttons to reprogram a machine every time it's turned on.

In fact, because the 920 has automatic ranging and gain control, you never have to touch it after turning it on unless you want to manually adjust the functions. It's just

2 inches thick and fits easily on the console of a bass boat or inside the electronics box of a pike boat, but the screen is large and exceptionally clear. It has 160 pixels vertically, 128 horizontally, and definition is very good. One possible rap is the water-resistant housing: it doesn't keep water out completely, which could mean trouble if you like to fish in the rain. Otherwise, the 920 is an impressive machine.

The *FD-2* from Si-Tex is a very sharp LCD with a white line feature that sketched the bottom almost as distinctly as a good paper-chart machine. Vertical pixel count is 162, which accounts for the definition. A feature we particularly liked was the ability to reverse directions on the readout. The machine automatically stores the last four screens displayed, so at any time you can hit a reverse button and run them back for another look. And you can program it to hold eight screens in memory, even when turned off—you define exactly what part of the screen you want to reserve with a set of moveable cursors, just as you would on a computer. By displaying this remembered image on only half the screen, reserving the other half for current images, you can perfectly match a particular contour, to relocate a secret hotspot.

The FD-2 has a bar graph at the right side of the screen that helps sort out fish from bottom, but we suspect most users will find little need for it—the manufacturer might have used the space better to expand the readout. The FD-2 has two zoom ranges, 2x and 4x, which you tap in with a single button. If you want to run it on full automatic, with the circuits figuring out depth, gain, and range needed, the Si-Tex will take care of it—you're up and running on auto by pressing only two buttons.

The Micronar *M-810* is a unique concept in small-boat sonar—it's the only side-scan LCD currently available, and it sells for little more than most machines with fixed transducers. The transducer mounts under the boat, and sweeps constantly back and forth to take in any arc you set it for, up to 90 degrees. It allows you to locate schools of fish in open water beside or ahead of the boat. The controls are very simple—you set the arc by pressing arrow keys. The bottom depth is always displayed in numerals at the upper right of the face.

Since we're used to looking at vertical readings, we found the M-810 a bit hard to understand at first, but the concept is intriguing. The definition is not the greatest, owing to the minimal number of pixels, but extreme sharpness is not what the machine is designed for. Anglers who fish open water for schooling stripers, trout, or salmon may find the 810 highly useful. And the company says that with practice you can even pick out schools of bass hiding along a river bank.

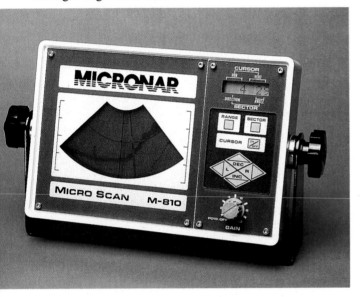

Videos

Television-type depth finders invaded the recreational fishing market only recently, because the prices had been too high for most weekend anglers. But these days, a number of machines are available for under $1000—and some for a lot less than that. The Koden *CVS-101MK-2* color video sells for around $800 at discount houses, but offers full eight-color screens and automatic operation simple enough to have you up and fishing with the basic functions in minutes. We found the resolution was at least as good as that of the best LCDs, and maybe better.

The bright colors make this Koden easy and fun to use: reds indicate the strongest echoes, blue the weakest. After a bit of practice it's not difficult to distinguish a school of bait (generally a cloud of light blue or white with a few red dots) from a school of gamefish (primarily reds and oranges). Hard bottom reads red, mud reads orange, vegetation green or white. The control pad has only eight buttons, but they access a wide variety of functions including on-screen temperature and speed readings.

A nice feature is the "triducer," which combines all the sensors into one unit to hang off the stern and connects to the machine with only one cable—much simpler and neater than the three or even four cables of some other machines. You do need an extra cable if you want to use the built-in Loran positioning function, however. The mounting hardware is notable, two or three times stouter than that on any other machine we tested.

In spring 1988 Koden plans to release the *102* color video, with features very similar to the 101's but with a pair of transducers combined in a single unit. These will allow switching from a 15-degree cone to a 42-degree cone. The option should be helpful to anglers who fish both very shallow and very deep water, with the narrow cone for the depths, the wider cone for the shallows. Rated at 200 watts, the 102 will also have twice the power of the 101.

Furuno's *FMV-602* is a strikingly sharp video in a case measuring only $7\frac{1}{2} \times 9\frac{1}{2} \times 8\frac{1}{2}$ inches. It sells for little more than top-of-the-line LCDs, yet has full Loran interface capabilities; speed, log, and temperature readouts; a temperature graph to show trends; and many other features. One of the more unusual aspects is the dual-frequency transducer. You can select either 50 or 200 khz echoes, and display both at once on a split screen if you like. The screen has three shades of amber, with the brightest marks for the strongest echoes. There's a "shadow-line" feature that reverses the contrast, making fish show up bright and dimming the bottom—useful for finding fish close to cover. The range is adjustable from 0-15 to 0-1000 feet.

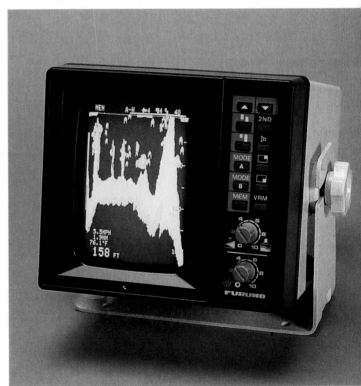

Testers of the FMV-602 were impressed by the accurate picture of action below the boat. One angler fishing in the Great Lakes was watching the trail of his cannonball on the screen when he saw a fish swim into the picture and attack his lure. At that moment, the rod bounced. He picked it up and watched the fish fight its way to the surface, every turn and twist showing on the video. It turned out to be an 8-pound coho salmon. Testers said the basic operation is simple—two buttons are all it takes for automatic operation, and most anglers won't need the instruction manual after the first trip.

The Color-C-Lector:
Godsend or Gimmick?

One of the most controversial fishing products introduced in recent years is the Color-C-Lector, manufactured by Lake Systems Division, Mount Vernon, Missouri.

According to the advertising, you can lower a probe into the water and a meter will show you the color that gamefish are most likely to strike under various combinations of sunlight intensity and water clarity.

To get a better feeling for the merits of the Color-C-Lector, we assembled a panel of experts, including the inventor of the device, Dr. Loren G. Hill of the University of Oklahoma. Dick Sternberg, director of the Hunting and Fishing Library, served as the moderator. The panel members conversed via telephone for more than two hours. Following are the high points of that conversation:

Moderator: Dr. Hill, tell us how the Color-C-Lector was developed.

Loren Hill: I didn't set out to develop the Color-C-Lector, but to investigate whether fish could see color. In the initial experiments, with blues and greens, I found out they actually could.

The next question was whether fish were capable of seeing all the various colors of the electromagnetic spectrum, from violet all the way to red. After more experiments, there was no question. They could differentiate between all the colors, and even between shades of these colors.

Then we conducted tests to determine what colors they could see best under different light intensities and in different water clarities. With the results of these tests, we developed the Color-C-Lector, a light meter with colored bands corresponding to the colors that fish saw best in the experiments.

Moderator: You mentioned that you set out to learn whether fish can really see color. There have been a lot of color-vision studies over the years, but many of the early researchers failed to determine whether fish were actually seeing colors, or were simply reacting to different shades of gray. As a result, most of this early research has little value.

Later color-vision research was done by testing a color against a confusing series of grays. Only in this way could it be determined if fish really see the color. Did you test your colors against comparable shades of gray?

Loren Hill: No, I did not, but I'm convinced that the fish could see all colors including subtle shades.

Rich Zaleski: I find the idea of fishing with the color that fish can see best to be questionable. There are instances when high-visibility colors work, usually with high-speed retrieves, but most of the time you're trying to convince fish that your lure or bait is something they would normally eat. Most types of forage are well-camouflaged, so excessively visible lures usually appear unnatural. In fact, visibility can be a negative trigger. Highly visible lures may actually alarm or intimidate fish at times.

Rudolph Miller: Prey species develop color patterns that match the background in their particular habitat. Predator fish must be able to distinguish between the prey and its background.

I personally believe that most shallow-water fishes have reasonably good color vision, but it's still very possible the factor that makes the big difference is brightness or contrast. Some fish may prefer a lure that contrasts very little with the background, and others may prefer one that contrasts greatly. Movement is also a big factor. Game species probably have good movement-detection systems.

Dr. Hill was attempting to prove that different wavelengths [colors] of light caused different feeding responses in his test fish. But I don't think he proved that. To draw such conclusions, he would need more replications.

One big problem with Dr. Hill's experiments is that they don't demonstrate that the fish are reacting only to the wavelengths of light. They may be reacting to some combination of color and brightness. It's not just a simple matter of one color versus another.

Moderator: You say that was one problem. Do you see some others?

Rudolph Miller: Yes, I do. The major problem with using the study results to calculate color preferences is that all the experiments were done in test tanks only a foot or so deep. The fact that water selectively absorbs the different wavelengths of light was never considered.

If a bright red lure is only a foot deep, it will appear bright red. But the same lure, even in perfectly clear water, would gradually appear more brownish as it goes deeper and would actually appear black in 25 or 30 feet of water. A blue or deep green lure would change least with increasing depth. But most colors would change significantly through the depth ranges in many reservoirs and lakes.

Some of the experiments evaluated the effects of varying light intensity due to shifting position of the sun, and varying degrees of turbidity. But light absorption by water at increasing depth is another matter entirely. You can't make shallow-water experiments and draw valid conclusions about deep-water situations.

We need to know what fish can see under different light conditions. I think that's one of the major pluses of Loren's work. He made an attempt to see what happens at different light intensities, but I don't think his research is anywhere near complete.

Tom Neustrom: I have a question, Dr. Hill. As I understand it, the Color-C-Lector was developed based solely on tests conducted with largemouth bass. So it's fine to say the device works for largemouth and possibly other members of the sunfish family, but how can you say it works for other species of fish?

Loren Hill: Okay. Now all the experiments that I conducted were with largemouth bass. Since that time I've had an opportunity to view the mosaic patterns of the rods and cones in the eyes of other fish. It's almost impossible to see the difference. So it's likely that all fish have pretty much the same color-vision capabilities.

Tom Neustrom: I know it's probably not good marketing, but I think you or somebody at Lake Systems should say, "We don't know everything there is to know on the colors that other species of fish can see, but we feel we know something about largemouth bass."

Loren Hill: I get phone calls from people all over the country who have had good luck using the Color-C-Lector for other species.

Moderator: Dr. Hill, from what I know about color vision in fish, it's misleading to say that all fish have similar color-vision capabilities. Some species of fish are known to have complete color vision. But extensive research on color vision in walleyes has been conducted at the University of Minnesota, and it shows that walleyes are essentially blue-yellow color blind. They see all colors as shades of red or green.

Given this fact, there are certainly going to be times when the Color-C-Lector recommends a color that the walleye doesn't recognize or that it sees as a shade of red or green. Isn't it possible that maybe half the colors the Color-C-Lector tells me to use are colors a walleye can't even recognize?

Loren Hill: I don't know whether I could back up that statement or not. I don't know.

Moderator: Dr. Miller, do you think all fish have similar color vision?

Rudolph Miller: No. Significant studies have shown that different fish species have different types of receptor cells, which respond to different colors. Although there isn't much data on the popular freshwater gamefish, there are enough differences among other fish species to suggest that there are also differences among the freshwater gamefish.

Tony Bean: The majority of my clients want to catch two kinds of fish, big smallmouth and stripers. We find that these two fish are worlds apart in their habits and their selection of baits and colors.

We use a lot of live bait for stripers, and the Color-C-Lector helps tell us what kind of bait to use. We found that on one day we might need a silver shiner; on another, a bright orange pumpkinseed sunfish; and on another, a green sunfish. Some days it made no difference at all.

Seven out of ten times the color indicated by the Color-C-Lector caught the most fish—not the exact color, because naturally we couldn't get the exact color.

When I fish for smallmouth, there are seven colors I use to catch them. I want to give them my best shot first, so I use a Color-C-Lector. I drop the probe down to the depth where I think the fish should be, and it grabs the color. This gives me a starting point, and I feel I'm four jumps ahead. It doesn't work every time—sometimes I have to use another color.

Moderator: What if the Color-C-Lector tells you to use, let's say, fluorescent pink, but this isn't one of your favorite smallmouth colors?

Tony Bean: I probably wouldn't use it.

Moderator: But how is the average guy going to know that he shouldn't be using that color?

Tony Bean: The average guy isn't going to know. That's the problem. Let's say a person gets a Color-C-Lector, then drops the probe down, and the dial says red. He finds a red crankbait or jig, or something else that's red, and he throws it for two hours and it doesn't work. So he automatically says the Color-C-Lector doesn't work.

You've got to put together all the factors, like location and presentation—not just color.

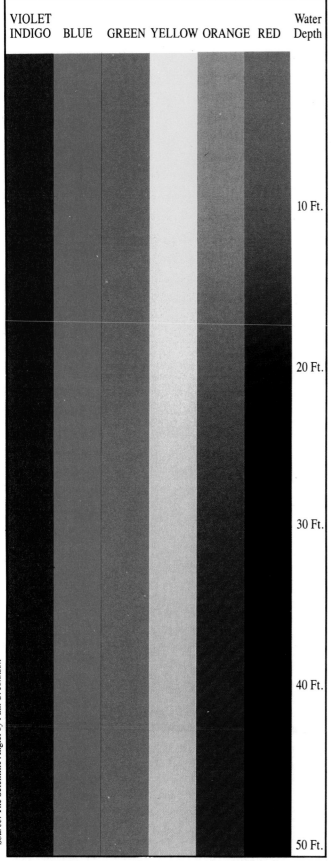

VIOLET INDIGO	BLUE	GREEN	YELLOW	ORANGE	RED	Water Depth
						10 Ft.
						20 Ft.
						30 Ft.
						40 Ft.
						50 Ft.

Source: The Scientific Angler *by Paul C. Johnson*

This chart shows how nonfluorescent colors fade or darken at increasing depths in clear water. A red lure 20 feet down, for example, appears nearly black. Fluorescent colors persist much deeper.

Moderator: Seems to me that unless someone has the knowledge you do, and recognizes there are certain colors that simply won't work, he might try five wrong colors before getting to the right one.

Tony Bean: That could happen, but I don't think it's going to.

Moderator: Tony mentioned that the striper is a completely different fish from the smallmouth, and that the two have different habits and prefer different baits and colors. I've noticed the same thing with the species I fish for.

In one of my favorite lakes, chartreuse generally works best for walleyes, pink-and-white for crappies, and smoke for smallmouth bass. Have most of you found the same thing, or do you think the same colors usually work for all species of fish?

Tony Bean: Stripers and smallmouth above 20 feet tend to relate to the same colors. Below 20 feet, I can't say they do.

Rich Zaleski: Particularly when I'm jig fishing, subtle colors seem to work more consistently than bright colors, at least for bass. But bright colors seem to work better for walleyes. I can go out to a hump on Lake Champlain and selectively catch different species of fish by throwing different-colored lures. If I throw smoke, I catch smallmouth and a few largemouth. If I throw yellow, I catch mostly perch and walleyes.

Tom Neustrom: I change colors for different species. I like to use smoke and shades of brown for smallmouth. For walleyes, I normally use green, yellow-green, orange, or yellow-orange. Northerns like red-and-white. Color doesn't make much difference for muskies—they'd hit an old ashcan if you threw it out there.

Bob Dillow: The tournament I just won was an early-morning situation with heavy fog on the water. I was throwing a white Charger spinnerbait, which the Color-C-Lector told me to throw. I was catching fish by working the bait so shallow I could actually see it coming through the water.

Then about 10 o'clock the sun popped through and the fog cleared. I could've thrown the spinnerbait all day long, but the fish weren't going to hit it. So I moved out to water about 4 feet deep and dropped the Color-C-Lector again. This time it read brown, so I tied on a brown-and-orange jig and more or less vertical-jigged it very slowly, until the fish hit it.

Moderator: Did you try a white jig in the deeper water?

Bob Dillow: No sir, I didn't.

Moderator: Then how do you know a brown jig worked better than a white jig?

Bob Dillow: Well, I tried a black jig with a chartreuse chunk, and a black jig with a red chunk, and neither worked—although they had on the afternoon of practice day.

On tournament day, I knew what I was going to do when the sun came out. I went to a brown-and-orange jig with a slower presentation, because the fish had fed all morning and their bellies were full. I jigged that jig in front of their noses, and they finally got mad enough to take it. But I do believe it had to be a bait they could see.

Tom Neustrom: But the thing is, while you're changing the color you're also using a different type of bait and working it differently.

Bob Dillow: What I'm doing is putting all the factors together.

Moderator: Dr. Hill, I have a question in regard to calibration of the Color-C-Lector. Several fishermen we interviewed tested different Color-C-Lector units alongside each other. In every case, the units gave different readings under the same light conditions.

So we borrowed three new units and conducted our own test. We got three different readings. Evidently there's a problem with calibration of the units when they leave the factory.

How can a fisherman be sure his unit is working properly?

Loren Hill: I warned the manufacturer that calibration would be a problem. But now there's a way to keep the units in calibration. We've designed a calibration device that attaches to the unit. It costs $9.95.

Moderator: That's what we found out from calling the factory. But they couldn't describe what it was or how it works. They said there was no way of calibrating the older units—only the new ones. What about people who have the older units? Is there anything they can do?

Loren Hill: Send them to the plant.

Moderator: Are you advising everyone who owns a Color-C-Lector to make sure it is calibrated properly?

Loren Hill: Yes.

Tom Neustrom: I have a question for Dr. Hill. A lot of well-known people in the fishing industry, like Roland Martin, Bill Dance, and Al Lindner, have stuck their necks out on television ads, to say the Color-C-Lector will put more fish in your boat. A lot of fishermen look upon these guys like they were Moses and believe whatever they say.

That's a good selling thing, but what happens when the Color-C-Lector doesn't do anything for the user? Do you feel the credibility of these people is somewhat down from what it was before?

Loren Hill: No, I don't. People from all over the country are using the Color-C-Lector with great success. I can give you names of people to talk to. When we first contacted Bill Dance about promoting the Color-C-Lector, he was the biggest skeptic I'd ever met. He wouldn't promote any product he didn't truly believe in.

COMMENTARY

by the Editors of
The Hunting & Fishing Library

In preparation for this panel discussion, our researchers interviewed dozens of experienced fishermen across the country, attempting to assemble a panel of experts that was evenly divided on the issue of the Color-C-Lector.

The vast majority of these fishermen were skeptical about the device or did not believe it improved their fishing. Of those who believed in the Color-C-Lector, many were somehow tied into Color-C-Lector advertising or sales, so their opinions could be affected. We had a difficult time finding experienced fishermen who could give a convincing endorsement of the device, yet were not tied in.

From the start of the panel discussion, there was a great deal of disagreement about the merits of the Color-C-Lector. Fishermen from the North were unanimous in the belief that the Color-C-Lector was of little or no

value. But southern bass fishermen expressed the opposite view.

In checking with retailers who sold Color-C-Lectors, we found that none had even heard of the calibration device, so we were unable to get our test units calibrated.

Color obviously makes a difference in fishing success, but we have a major problem with the idea that fish necessarily strike the color they can see best. And even if fish did always strike whatever color they could see best, the Color-C-Lector would still be likely to give misleading color recommendations because of calibration problems.

In sum, we do not believe that Dr. Hill's color-vision research adequately backs the claims made for the Color-C-Lector. The research has never been published, so there has been very little scientific review.

Tony Bean conducts fishing seminars in the Midwest and has written two books, *Tony Bean's Striper Guide* and *Tony Bean's Smallmouth Guide*. He averages 250 fishing days per year, using the Color-C-Lector "in certain situations, but not as much as I used to." He lives in Nashville.

Bob Dillow, who lives in Ohio, is the host of *Fishin' USA*, a television show appearing in 27 states. He's finished in first place in several major bass tournaments, including the 1986 Budweiser Bass Classic on the Ohio River. He attributes that win partly to his use of the Color-C-Lector.

Dr. Loren G. Hill, a professor of zoology at the University of Oklahoma, is the inventor of the Color-C-Lector. He's also done research on the effects of pH on fishes, publishing several technical papers on the subject and developing an electronic pH meter for fishermen. Dr. Hill is an enthusiastic angler.

Dr. Rudolph J. Miller is a professor of zoology at Oklahoma State University, specializing in ichthyology and animal behavior. He's made valuable studies of the sensory capabilities of fishes and other vertebrates. He likes to fish and hunt, and is a professional wildlife artist.

Tom Neustrom says he gets the most enjoyment "out of fishing tough lakes under tough conditions." Considered one of the Midwest's top walleye anglers, he conducts fishing seminars each year in Chicago, Milwaukee, Toronto, and other major cities. He's been guiding anglers in northern Minnesota for fourteen years.

Rich Zaleski is a fishing writer who lives in Connecticut. He's won dozens of pro bass tournaments, including the North American Bass Association Tournament of Champions held in New York. He has a book in progress about simplifying bass fishing—"making it a human-level sport again."

Carl Lowrance with early Fish Lo-K-Tor, circa 1958

The Quick-Fix Syndrome

Dick Sternberg

When Carl Lowrance unveiled his red box in 1958, I doubt he envisioned the effect it would have on the world of fishing. The sport had entered the age of electronics.

The red box was simply a scaled-down version of the sonar device used by the U.S. Navy in World War II. But it gave fishermen a look at the world beneath the water—a world they had never before seen. It enabled them to find reefs and other structure they had never known existed, and even to locate schools of fish. The few anglers fortunate enough to use the device soon realized it was helping them catch more fish … a lot more fish.

Later, Lowrance began to mass-produce his sonar in a green box, and the rest is history. Today you can choose from dozens of flashers, graph recorders, liquid-crystal recorders, and video recorders. All these modern products are simply refinements of the original sonar unit.

Sonar has improved the success of millions of fishermen, but in doing so has created a psychological malady that now affects a good share of the nation's anglers. I call it the "quick-fix syndrome." A typical case is the angler who buys a computer-generated chart to tell him when to go fishing, purchases all the electronic devices that claim to show him where to find fish, and squirts his bait with some magic potion the fish supposedly can't resist.

All of this gadgetry is an attempt to find a quick fix, an easy substitute for the basic ingredients of successful fishing: namely, a knowledge of the fish's habits, and a skillful presentation of the lure or bait.

After Lowrance introduced his green box, it didn't take long for would-be entrepreneurs to note the development of the quick-fix syndrome among the country's fisher-

men. Soon, the angling world was bombarded with ads for other electronic devices such as temperature gauges and oxygen meters.

Water temperature and dissolved-oxygen level are important factors in determining where fish are located, so these devices seemed to hold a good deal of promise. But fishermen who purchased them soon found they did not produce the miraculous results implied in the ads. In fact, the temperature and oxygen data often turned out to be misleading. The fish were not in the temperature zone where the manufacturers claimed they would be, and were often found in low-oxygen zones where the manufacturers claimed they would not be.

Biologists were not surprised by these developments, because they know that fish are affected by dozens of factors, not just temperature and oxygen, and that trying to find them according to one factor alone is hopeless. Of course, the factor that outweighs all others is food. Fish will go wherever they must to find a meal. In doing so, they will swim into water that "the book" says is far too warm or way too low in oxygen.

This is not to say these devices have no use in fishing. A temperature gauge, for instance, can be a valuable tool under the right circumstances. It can help you find fish in springtime by identifying pockets of warmer water where baitfish congregate. It can help you catch northern pike in summertime by locating spring holes. And it can help you in finding coldwater fish like trout, which have more definite temperature preferences than most warmwater species. But it is not a miracle tool and has nowhere near the everyday value of a flasher or graph.

As a professional fisheries biologist, I must admit I'm a real skeptic when it comes to new products that are

47

supposed to help me catch more fish. Many writers have expressed a philosophical concern that these products are taking the sport out of fishing, and that the fish don't have a chance against an angler armed with his arsenal of modern gadgets.

My concern is not philosophical. Because you're playing on the home court of the fish, they have a huge advantage. Even the experts come home shaking their heads a good share of the time, despite what they may lead you to believe on television. So the idea of using electronic devices or any other new products doesn't turn me off. In fact, I'm constantly looking for any new development that can tip the odds in my favor. If you looked in my boat, you'd find two flashers and two electric trolling motors (one of each on the bow and stern), a graph recorder, a temperature gauge, a trolling-speed indicator, a marine radio, and even a Loran-C navigator to help find my fishing spots.

What I'm concerned about is the sales explosion of new products that have little, if any, scientific merit and prey on anglers afflicted with the quick-fix syndrome.

Some of these products measure something or other in the water, then use this measurement to predict where the fish will be or what they're going to strike. Others use some secret set of factors that program a computer to predict the best fishing times. There's even an "everything meter" which measures the pHcline, the oxycline, and the thermocline. And once you've located the fish using all these "clines," it will tell you what lure color to use.

The design of these devices is based on the manufacturers' claim that fish will react in a certain way to a particular factor, like pH, or to a set of such factors. For example, I recently read a magazine article explain-

ing how a pH meter could be used to catch more walleyes. The manufacturer's representative stated that walleyes prefer a pH of 7.4. The anglers proceeded to look for water of that pH and, naturally, they caught a bunch of walleyes.

I was curious where the figure 7.4 came from, so I called some biologists and fish physiologists. None had ever heard of any research to show that walleyes had any specific pH preference. One prominent biologist vehemently disputed the figure, saying his research showed no differences in walleye behavior between pH levels of 6 and 9. Then I called the manufacturer's representative who came up with that figure. Turned out it was nothing more than an opinion based on one fishing trip.

Computer programmers know that the information generated by a computer is no better than the data fed into it. You've probably heard the programmers' phrase "garbage in, garbage out." The same phrase could be applied to fishing gadgets. If you're expecting miraculous results from erroneous data, forget it.

The garbage-in, garbage-out principle also applies to computerized fishing forecasters and fish-activity charts. Until scientists discover all of the factors controlling fish behavior and determine the relative importance of each of them, these forecasters and charts will remain in the realm of wishful thinking. Personally, I don't think scientists can ever learn enough about fish to predict when they'll bite. Even if they can, those discoveries are surely many years away.

Another result of the quick-fix syndrome is the burgeoning popularity of scent products. Here the picture is a little more clouded, because scientists have learned that fish can detect certain scents even at extremely low concentrations. The question is: Do the scent products on the market today make fish bite?

There's little doubt that scent is important in triggering some fish to feed. Catfish and bullheads are primarily scent feeders. To a lesser degree, bluegills and trout use scent to find food. So if a manufacturer could discover which scents trigger these fish to feed, he might have something.

Most authorities believe that scent is much less important in triggering predatory fish like walleyes, northern pike, and bass. These species rely more heavily on eyesight and their lateral-line sense.

I would like to believe that scent products could help me catch more fish. I've seen some evidence that certain types work for catfish and bluegills. But after trying a variety of products intended for walleyes, northern pike, bass, trout, and salmon, I haven't seen one scrap of evidence to indicate they could improve my fishing.

Some claims made by scent manufacturers are so ridiculous I find it difficult to take their products seriously. Recently I heard a fishing talk show on the radio. The guest was a prominent scent manufacturer, who spent a good deal of time making spectacular claims for his product. Then the host invited phone calls on scents or any fishing-related subject. One call went something like this:

Caller: "I do a lot of fishing on a shallow lake. It froze out last winter, but it's connected to a deeper lake. Will fish from the deeper lake repopulate the shallow one, or should I try another lake this year?"

Host: "I think the fish from the deep lake will eventually move in, but it will take quite a while. If I were you, I'd find another lake."

Scent Manufacturer: "Before you hang up—there may be a way to draw fish into the shallow lake. Soak some rocks with my scent product, then drop them in the shallow lake. The scent will filter into the deep lake and attract the fish."

Caller: "Uh, thanks." Click.

I don't know what the caller was thinking after that conversation, but I'll bet he didn't rush out and start soaking rocks. Or, maybe he did.

I'm certainly not the only skeptic when it comes to scents. Many other well-known fishermen feel the same way. Some, however, look at it like this: "I'm not sure if scents help, but they can't hurt. So I'll use them just to be safe."

Unfortunately, this philosophy may cost them some fish, especially if they apply scents to live bait. What could smell better to a fish than the odor of real food? Why attempt to mask this odor with something that may be completely foreign to the fish? On one walleye-fishing trip, I treated my leeches with a new walleye scent; my partner, however, did not treat his. Normally we catch

about the same number of fish, but that day he caught eight nice walleyes while I failed to get a bite. I don't recall having ever been outfished that badly. Maybe I was just unlucky, but I'm inclined to think the scent actually repelled the walleyes.

What has amazed me most about scents is how quickly new manufacturers were able to get products on the shelf once the scent craze hit. Think of the difficulty of testing hundreds of potential ingredients to find the ones the fish like best. Seems it would take years, especially if you wanted to develop different products for different species.

Today, there are well over a hundred scent products available, and there's no end in sight. Is it possible all these products have undergone even minimal testing? I've requested test results from some manufacturers. The usual response is: "Our work is top secret and we're not willing to share it." I'd categorize the results that I've actually seen as "highly suspect."

My advice on scents is this: Wait until reliable test results are available before spending your money.

No doubt the sales explosion of products that prey on anglers afflicted with the quick-fix syndrome will continue. Unfortunately, there is no "consumer's guide" to fishing products, and most outdoor writers have failed to take a critical look at products that are introduced. Practically every article written on a new product gives it a favorable review.

The reasons for this milquetoast journalism are numerous. Many outdoor writers lack the technical background needed to review a high-tech product. And those who venture to write unfavorable reviews soon find that magazines are not willing to publish them for fear of losing advertisers. Still other writers are reluctant to express their feelings in print, because they were given the product and don't want to offend the manufacturer.

Recently, I've seen a new approach to promoting questionable products. Many magazines are running columns that appear to be fishing tips, but when you read them, they're nothing more than product hype. In most cases, you'll see the word "advertising" in small print above the column, but in some instances it isn't there. If you read these columns, recognize them for what they are—advertising.

The bottom line is this: It's up to the buyer to protect himself. If you read about a product that sounds too good to be true, it probably is. Remember, there's no quick fix that will bring you fishing success. You can improve your odds by owning up-to-date, proven equipment and by keeping abreast of current fishing literature. But there's no way to avoid paying your dues, and that means putting in time on the water.

Dick Sternberg is the director of The Hunting & Fishing Library. *He has written several books in the series, including* The Art of Freshwater Fishing, Walleyes, *and* Smallmouth Bass. *For sixteen years he worked as a professional fisheries biologist.*

Muskie at Night

New Techniques

Largemouth Bass

Steve Price

As the best bass fishermen get better and their equipment grows more specialized, they keep coming up with more and more effective techniques.

Sometimes these new ways of doing things are inspired by new lures. Tournament anglers may be the innovators, since they generally get the first crack at new gear and are always searching for new tactics to outfish the competition.

Or sometimes the new ways are simply fresh techniques for old lures: variations on classical themes. Some unsung expert—it might be you—comes up with an original approach to the difficult fishing after cold fronts, for example.

Easy Does It with Dead Worms

One new discovery that's panned out well on many bass lakes is known as dead-worming. A plastic worm is made to appear lifeless rather than full of action—completely contradicting the techniques most anglers have been taught.

Dead-worming works best in three different situations: in dense weeds or brush, on lakes with extremely heavy fishing pressure, and on those bluebird days when the barometer is rising after a strong cold front. In all these situations, bass are reluctant to come out, move around, and feed.

You rig the worm with a cone sinker and embed the hook Texas-style, then cast into any cover where you think bass are hiding. But instead of slowly crawling the worm back out, you let it sink to the bottom and rest motionless there.

Finally, after a minute or longer, hop the worm gently two or three times with your rod tip. Then leave it alone for another 30 seconds. In the situations described above, bass seldom hit very hard and the only indication of a strike may be a slight twitch in the line, or simply a sluggish, weighty feeling when you raise the rod tip.

How long you let the worm lie motionless is generally dictated by the fish. Sometimes they pick it up in the first minute; other times they wait much longer. If you get no strikes after hopping the worm, reel in and cast to a new spot. On lakes hit with really heavy fishing pressure, make long casts to avoid spooking nervous bass.

Wacky Worms for Weeds

Another new worm-fishing technique, worked out by guides at Toledo Bend Reservoir, is for springtime fishing over beds of coontail and milfoil. It's known as the wacky-worm system, and to try it you'll need a 6-inch plastic worm, a 2/0 to 4/0 worm hook, and an ordinary roofing-shingle nail.

Snip or bend off the nail head, leaving a section of nail about ½ inch long. Insert this section completely into the head of the worm. Its purpose is simply to add casting weight so you can use stout baitcasting tackle. In coontail it works much better than a cone sinker, which will catch on the coontail as it slides up and down the line.

Wacky Worm

The worm is hooked in the same way a live nightcrawler might be hooked lightly for maximum action. Simply insert the point into the midsection of the worm and then bring it back out, so the point and barb are completely exposed. Both ends of the worm will dangle free.

Because of the way it's hooked, the wacky worm really does act wacky. It wiggles and squirms just like a real worm dropped in the water. When you retrieve it a few inches below the surface, this lifelike action draws bass up and out of the thick vegetation.

The wacky worm also takes fish in sparse vegetation. Here you allow it to settle all the way to the bottom, then retrieve it with short hops so it acts like a salamander. This way of fishing seems to work best on calm, clear days.

Doodle-Worming in Deep Water

Devised in California, doodle-worming is now catching on wherever bass inhabit deep, clear lakes. In most of these lakes there is very little shallow water and not much cover, and the bass generally stay close to anything they can find—piers and boathouses, for instance. They're reluctant to venture out to strike a traveling lure. But doodle-worming can save the day.

What you need is a thin, 4- to 5-inch worm, a 1/0 worm hook, and a 3/16-ounce cone sinker. Rig the worm Texas-style, using 4- or 6-pound mono. The technique calls for a light spinning rod with a stiff butt and midsection, and a soft tip to absorb shock and reduce line breakage.

Make a short cast or drop the worm vertically to whatever cover is available—pilings, flooded brush, a rocky hump or point. Let it sink to the bottom beside the cover, then lower your rod tip within 8 or 10 inches of the water. Shake the worm—"doodle" it—by bouncing the rod tip rapidly up and down. The worm should dance in one spot, rising and falling only 4 to 6 inches. Wary bass are attracted to the hopping worm, and if you keep it hopping, sooner or later one of them will fall for it.

Doodle-worming takes its name from the old technique of doodle-socking, which is similar but used in very shallow water. An accomplished angler can doodle-worm effectively in water as deep as 60 feet, pulling fish off humps and breaks pinpointed with a depth finder.

Flipping the Pixton Rig

The technique of flipping was introduced several years ago, and by now is familiar to almost every bass angler in the nation. A long rod is used to swing—or "flip"—a plastic worm or jig into holes in heavy, shallow cover like milfoil, submerged trees, and brushpiles. It's close-range fishing, highly efficient and effective.

When the lure is a plastic worm, it's always been rigged Texas-style, often with the cone sinker pegged at the worm head to reduce snagging. But now a brand-new setup called the Pixton rig is coming into use, particularly in Florida where it originated.

The Pixton rig incorporates a patented sinker, which looks like an ordinary bullet-shaped cone sinker but has

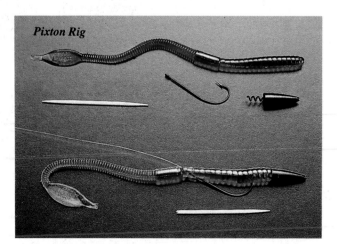

Pixton Rig

a small wire corkscrew at the base. The sinker has no hole, so it's not threaded onto the line. Instead, the corkscrew is twisted into the head of the worm, holding the sinker in place.

This arrangement allows you to place the hook practically anywhere along the worm. Inventor Dennis Pixton recommends inserting the point midway along the worm, then pulling the point, bend, and shank on through the worm so the eye is buried, and finally reinserting the point and barb near the head of the worm. A toothpick through the eye holds the hook in place.

This way, the worm will sink headfirst with the hook point aimed upward, rather than downward as with a Texas rig. The big advantage is that the hook is in a much better position to penetrate the fish's mouth. You can drive it in instantly, and make connections on many more of your strikes. Also, the worm is less likely to hang up in weeds.

Pixton sinkers come in weights from 1/16 to 1/2 ounce, and can be ordered from The Pixton Rig, P.O. Box 222, Coral Springs, FL 33065.

Plunge Deeper with Plugs

One recent technique that's won plenty of fans is extra-deep fishing with crankbaits. Deep cranking is particularly effective in warm weather when bass holed up near deep points or flats want a fast-moving lure. Other kinds of lures can be fished deep—jigs and worms—but to keep them down there you have to reel at a snail's pace.

The key ingredients in deep cranking are the new crankbaits designed to dive 18 or 20 feet, plus 10-pound line and a 7- or 7½-foot rod. The relatively light line has less water resistance, so the lure can dig deeper. The long rod helps, too. After the cast, you point the tip down a foot or more into the water and hold it there throughout the retrieve.

But sometimes you want to fish plugs even deeper than deep cranking will allow, or you want to fish them deep but slow, a trick not really possible with deep cranking. In these tough situations, an even newer technique known as Carolina cranking takes over.

For this, you modify the familiar Carolina worm rig, in which an egg sinker is positioned on the line a few feet above a plastic worm. All you do is replace the worm with a thin minnow plug or a shallow-running crankbait. The rig comes in handy when bass hang out near deep ledges or other deep structure, or when they suspend just a few feet above a deep bottom.

Rigging up is simple. Thread a ¾-ounce to 1-ounce egg sinker onto your line, then tie the line to a swivel. To the other eye of the swivel, knot a length of mono about 4 feet long; tie your plug to the end of the mono. Heavier line, 12- to 17-pound test, can be used with this technique, because the large sinker gives you all the depth you need.

The long rods now popular for ordinary deep cranking are ideal for Carolina cranking, because they make it easier to cast the somewhat unwieldy rig. You lob out a long cast, give the rig time to sink, then reel it in slowly. With this slow retrieve, a thin minnow plug will actually run slightly shallower than the sinker, to minimize snagging. The retrieve can be steady or erratic—whatever works best at the time.

Because the egg sinker slides on the line, it's a bit more awkward to cast than a pinch-on or Rubbercor, but it offers an important advantage with this technique. If the egg sinker does hang up on the bottom and you break your line, the lure will float back to the surface where you can recover it.

New Way to "Spook" Bass

"Spooking" is an old, effective technique used with the Zara Spook, a cigar-shaped lure that zigzags across the surface when the rod tip is worked rapidly from side to side. Now there's a new variation of spooking, used with the Rebel Pop-R. The big difference is that the lure not only skips across the surface but also darts below it.

The Pop-R is much smaller than the Zara Spook. It has a slightly concave face, which makes a dull popping sound when the lure is skipped across the surface. Other chugger-type plugs are usually fished slowly, but not the Pop-R. You work it fast, just like a Zara Spook. It darts, dives slightly, then pops back to the surface.

Rebel actually discontinued the Pop-R in 1979 because it hadn't sold well. But then several tournament pros learned the secret of fishing it successfully, and Rebel brought it back. The pros not only used it to win several big national tournaments, but also kept its potential a secret for many years.

Spooking with the Pop-R works best in calm water, over submerged weeds or in sparsely matted weeds on the surface. In very clear water, the surface commotion can pull bass up from rocks, logs, stumps, or other cover as deep as 20 feet. The pros work the Pop-R with 15- to 17-pound line. The most productive period to use the technique is late spring through late summer.

Willow-Leaf Spinnerbaits in the Weeds

Fishing a spinnerbait in thick weeds isn't new, but by using a big willow-leaf spinnerbait, a recent innovation, you can fish the weeds a new way. The lure can be worked right down in the weeds. Normal spinnerbaits with broader blades must generally be fished above the weeds, to keep from fouling.

A willow-leaf spinnerbait has a blade up to 4 inches long, but no more than 1 inch in width. Because of this shape it cuts through thick greenery without hanging up and clogging on every cast. The narrow blade spins very rapidly, producing lots of vibration and flash, and seems to resemble a large, slender baitfish like a golden shiner.

You can fish this bait almost anywhere in the weeds that bass might be hiding. One good approach is to position your boat just inside or outside a weedbed, and cast obliquely across its edge. On the retrieve, the lure always travels close to the edge of the weeds. This is an exploratory technique: the idea is that the bass may be either in the weeds or in the open water, but either way they're likely to hold near the edge.

Steve Price has written articles on fishing, hunting, and boating for most of the national outdoor magazines. His book World Championship Bass Fishing *covers advanced techniques for largemouths.*

Willow-Leaf Spinnerbait

As long as anglers have fished for smallmouths, they've faced some frustrating problems that seemed unlikely ever to go away. But at last a number of new fishing techniques have come along to help. Some of these are adapted from techniques first developed for largemouths, and even for saltwater fish.

Sliders for Cold Weather

As winter approaches, most smallmouth fishermen just hang up the tackle and dream about fishing until next year. And it's true the smaller bass stop feeding when the water temperature drops below 50°F. But a few anglers are demonstrating that this is actually the best time to hunt trophy fish—and it remains productive down to about 37°!

When the water gets cold, large rivers are more productive than small ones, since the smallmouths tend to

Smallmouth Bass

Lefty Kreh

settle downstream. Locating the best areas can be surprisingly easy. You need a set of favorable conditions, but these occur often in the fall (and in the spring as well).

Smallmouth rivers usually flow at moderate speed, but when they rise 1 to 2½ feet, the current gets so swift the fish move to quiet places along shore. Rocks, logs, and other debris sticking out from the banks obstruct the current and create miniature eddies. These shelter the big bass, and also concentrate the baitfish they feed on.

When a river rises to these levels, and remains moderately clear (if you can see your rod tip a foot under the water you're okay), that's the time to go fishing.

The first-choice lure for this technique is a ⅛- to ¼-ounce slider jig dressed with a 4-inch curly-tail worm. Also effective is a small pig-and-jig, or a small stand-up or bullet-head jig with a brush-type hook guard and the same curly-tail worm.

Motor along the shoreline and look for the eddies. Using an anchor or an electric motor, hold the boat off the bank, then cast your lure into an eddy and allow it to fall to the bottom. Be certain it gets all the way down—this is very important. Then, slow-hop it across the bottom in the same way you'd fish a slider or pig-and-jig for largemouths.

Recently, quite a few 4-pound smallmouths and some 5-pounders have been taken by an elite few anglers using this eddy-fishing technique.

Lead-Eye Flies

Sculpin

Hellgrammite

Crayfish

Shock Leaders for Smallmouths

In smallmouth fishing, light lines generally work best. Many experts, in fact, use 4-pound test almost exclusively. The reasons? Most smallmouth lures don't weigh much, and to cast them as far as possible you need the lightest lines. Also, light lines have less water resistance and permit your lure to dive deeper.

But smallmouths feed a great deal on a boulder or rubble bottom, and if you fish down deep, as you usually must, your line is going to rub across it. This abrasion is most damaging to light lines, since they offer little safety margin to begin with.

There's a helpful trick, however, from saltwater fishing, one that's new to almost every freshwater angler I get in the boat with. Light-tackle experts in the salt use a shock leader to prevent sharp-toothed fish from cutting off the lure or bait. A shock leader is simply a length of heavy monofilament attached to a lighter line.

By adapting shock leaders to smallmouth fishing, you can keep your light lines, yet buy some insurance against break-offs while playing fish. Also, a rod-length shock leader allows you to put more punch in your casting strokes without snapping the fragile line.

Make the leader long enough to give yourself a few turns on the spool when casting. Use 6- or 8-pound mono if fishing with 4-pound line; 8- or 10-pound mono with 6-pound line. Saltwater anglers tie a Bimini twist in the end of the line, forming a length of double strands, then tie this to the leader with an Albright knot. For smallmouth fishing, a much quicker way is to tie your line, undoubled, directly to the leader with a surgeon's knot.

Shock leaders are especially useful with the new extra-deep crankbaits, reputed to go 20 feet deep when trolled. You won't get them down that far when casting, but with light line and long casts they'll still dig to 14 feet. That can mean bottom-bumping right among the rocks, where smallmouths feed.

Extra-deep crankbaits were first made in big sizes for largemouths, but are now available in miniature versions for smallmouths. Look for models measuring 1½ to 2¼ inches long, not counting the lip.

Bottom-Bumping with Lead-Eye Flies

Fly fishermen have also come up with some productive new techniques. Lead eyes, as the name indicates, are made of lead, and they resemble a miniature dumbbell. They're painted and lashed onto the front of the hook, and then the rest of the fly pattern is tied on behind them. This concentrated weight enables smallmouth anglers to bomb flies down to greater depths than ever before. Many fishermen also feel the appearance of the eyes helps draw strikes.

Lead eyes can be obtained from many fly-tying catalogs and shops. They come in six sizes, but the four smallest are most applicable to smallmouth fishing: $\frac{1}{100}$, $\frac{1}{50}$, $\frac{1}{36}$, and $\frac{1}{24}$ ounce.

You can fish lead-eye flies in several ways. Nymphs with $\frac{1}{50}$- to $\frac{1}{100}$-ounce eyes are very effective when worked deep in long pools. If you see a scattering of rises indicating the start of a hatch, don't try to fool those few risers with surface flies. Instead, switch to a dark brown or black nymph, cast across stream, and allow it to dead-drift deep. You'll take many times the bass you would by fishing on the surface.

With lead-eye hellgrammite flies, you can now fish deep in the swift riffles where smallmouths lie in warm weather. Get off to the side of the current and cast your fly upstream and across, and then let it dead-drift back. For the first time, you'll be putting a hellgrammite fly down near the bottom in fast water, where the bass are looking for such offerings.

Sculpins and crayfish live right on the floor of a river or lake, but the realistic deer-hair imitations have always resisted sinking. With lead eyes of $\frac{1}{24}$ or $\frac{1}{36}$ ounce, however, these imitations go right to the bottom, where you can sneak them along in front of smallmouths by slowly stripping line. Use a long leader, and give the fly time to sink before retrieving.

Line Up for Deep Smallmouths

Another way to get a fly deep for smallmouths—any fly, in this case—is to rig your own special fly line. Cut 10 feet from a 550-grain shooting head (the type called Deep Water Express, manufactured by Scientific Anglers), then attach it to the front of any 9- or 10-weight floating line. You can use this to fish deep in big-river currents—for example, right on the bottom in those high-water eddies discussed earlier.

A conventional sink-tip line doesn't work well in such situations, because the tip isn't heavy enough to drop down sharply. You need a head that sinks like an anvil, along with a floating line thick enough to resist being dragged under. The leader should be no longer than 18 inches. When fished, the floating line stays on the surface while the extra-heavy tip hangs almost vertically, the fly dangling below it.

Anchor near an eddy or other likely spot, cast the fly (sculpin and crayfish patterns are my favorites), and let the line tip and fly plummet to the bottom. Then retrieve slowly, crawling the fly along the stream bed. With the tip hanging down, the floating portion of the line acts like a bobber, so any subtle strikes can be spotted immediately.

To connect the head to the floating line, strip 2 inches of the coating from each, then sew the braided cores together with a small needle and size A nylon fly-tying thread. Make a whip finish over the sewn area with the same thread. Finish the job by applying a flexible waterproof glue such as Pliobond to protect the wraps.

Lefty Kreh has written several books, including The L. L. Bean Guide to Outdoor Photography *and* Fly Casting with Lefty Kreh. *He instructs at fishing schools and has made fly-casting videotapes.*

For 95 percent of the daylight hours on a typical trout stream, there is no major insect hatch occurring. Yet most of the flies I carry in my box and most of the techniques I've learned over the years are designed to match hatches. And I'll bet I'm no exception.

As I sat recently on the bank of a favorite stream, hatchless, I turned my mental vest pockets inside out for some tricks I could pull—new tricks, or at least little-known ones, that fishermen can use when the bugs don't cooperate.

Skating a Caddis

This technique is so easy and effective I often feel guilty using it. Twitching a fly on the surface to imitate a caddisfly is nothing new. Old-time wet-fly anglers, fishing three flies on a leader, would often use the bottom fly as an anchor, skittering the top flies across the surface. Leonard Wright, in his classic 1972 book *Fishing the Dry Fly as a Living Insect*, formulated a technique called the "sudden inch" where the fisherman casts an upstream curve, twitches the fly upstream an inch, then lets it drift with the current.

Wright used drag as a subtle tease, but skating a caddis is brash. You cast obliquely downstream, just above where you think a trout is lying. As soon as the fly hits the water, you raise your rod tip to about 10 degrees

Trout on Fly Tackle

Tom Rosenbauer

below vertical and wiggle it from side to side slightly while stripping in line, about 2 feet at a time. When you've moved the fly 5 or 10 feet, drop the tip quickly almost to the water and let the fly drift downstream with the slack that's accumulated.

My friend John Harder uses this technique all over the country; and seldom is the day, no matter how dismal, when he can't hook a dozen fish. But it's most impressive on the Battenkill, one of the world's toughest trout streams. Blind-fishing this river with a Wulff or Adams or weighted nymph will yield you one trout every two or three hours. Yet John can fish downstream through a lifeless pool and make it come alive, as if his rod were a magic wand. Wise old browns that ignore a well-placed, dead-drifted dry fly will chase his caddis 3 or 4 feet, splashing and somersaulting to nail it.

"There are secrets to this technique other than moving the fly properly," he says. "I like a rod about 9 feet long with a matching 4- or 5-weight line, so I have enough reach. The fly has to be a good high-floater, like a well-hackled Elk Hair Caddis or Henryville. I like sizes 14 or 16, but sometimes an 18 or 20 will work. If the fly doesn't skate well enough, trim the hackle tips so it rides on stiff, blunt ends. And here's the real secret: grease your leader all the way to the fly so it slips over the water and doesn't pull the fly under."

The Drift-Boat Shuffle

A rainy day or even dirty water doesn't have to ruin a fishing trip. Streamers and bucktails are flies best used at very specific times—either during a rainstorm or when a river begins to rise and color up from recent storms. A large trout that has been a good neighbor to fry and yearlings will suddenly pounce on them during a rainstorm.

Most anglers retrieve streamers too slowly and concentrate in one spot too long. A trout takes a streamer out of reflex. He doesn't mull it over. Your streamer hits the water and *foodeatnow* goes through his tiny brain and he pounces. He'll see the streamer or sense it through his lateral-line system from 4 or 5 feet away, so there's no need to hit each and every spot. But precision casting is necessary.

I cover a pool with a method I call the drift-boat shuffle, which is based on float fishing in the West. There, the guide holds the boat at what he sees is a comfortable casting distance for the client. The fisherman casts so his streamer lands inches from the bank, makes three strips, picks up the line and casts to the next spot. By then the boat has drifted downstream to a fresh area.

You can use the same technique while wading, in the West or East, as long as the river is wide enough for you to cast across stream without hanging up on your backcast. Standing at the head of a pool, decide which bank looks better—which is deeper, has more cover, or just looks fishier. Find a comfortable casting distance from the bank, probably between 25 and 40 feet.

Start walking slowly through the pool, casting as you go. One cast to each likely spot, then three or four strips away from the bank, pick up, and throw to the next spot 5 or 10 feet downstream. By walking with the current you conserve energy and create fewer disturbing waves. Almost never will repeated casting to a spot produce a strike. If a trout swirls at your fly but doesn't take, don't bother with more than two or three follow-up casts. In any pool, only a small percentage of the trout will take a streamer. Persistence is not a virtue in streamer fishing.

Fly patterns are of secondary importance. If a trout is primed to take a streamer, a "better" pattern will produce only a marginal increase in strikes. Size, though, does make a difference. For smaller trout I use a size 8 or 10. Where I know there are big trout, a size 2 is not too large. If you must have pattern recommendations, I'd use a Black Ghost for rainy weather with clear water, and a Muddler Minnow or Wooly Bugger for the dirtier stuff.

Big Flies for Little Streams

Here's another tough situation: You arrive at a famous river for a three-day fishing trip, only to find the trout feeding in the morning and late evening, with no activity during the day. How about trying a feeder stream?

Feeder-stream trout can be as big as those in the main river, but they're easier to fool because they aren't fished over as often. And you'll catch them on bulky dry flies you thought would only work on the Yellowstone or Snake.

Fishing the Battenkill in June, you often have to go down to a size 18 for the evening hatch. During the day, you might need a size 22 for fish rising on the flats. Yet you can travel 50 feet up a feeder stream and catch brook trout and even browns on a size 10 dry fly like a Humpy or an Irresistible.

On a feeder, you want to use large flies because you're generally fishing bubbly pocket water and it's tough to see your fly. But the interesting part is that a size 16 or 18 is seldom as effective as the larger 10s or 12s. And slim-bodied flies like a Light Cahill or Quill Gordon don't draw as many rises as fat ones like Irresistibles and Humpies. There seems to be a threshold bulk that catches their attention enough to make them rise.

No creek is too small for this business as long as you can get a few feet of backcast room. It's worked for me on tributaries of Pine Creek and Kettle Creek in Pennsylvania, of the Snake in Wyoming and the Madison in Montana, and even of that hatch-matching shrine, the Beaverkill. The lure of fishing these famous rivers keeps people off the tribs.

As in streamer fishing, work fast and cover a lot of water. Many times the best trout will be in the tails of the little pools, so be careful. If there are brown trout around and they boil at the fly and miss or refuse it, you can kiss them goodbye. Twenty casts to the same spot won't be any more effective. Brookies, rainbows, and cutthroats may come to the fly three or four times.

I've even hooked brookies, had them shake off after a second and then go back to the same fly. This happened to me in a tributary of a famous stream that regularly hosts record crowds. But that little guy had probably never seen a dry fly.

Tom Rosenbauer is the editor of Orvis News, *author of* The Orvis Fly-Fishing Guide, *and has written articles on fishing for* Rod & Reel, Fly Fisherman, *and* Audubon. *He helps develop new equipment for the Orvis Co.*

It was a major tournament. Salmon were scarce, so I needed some big lake trout. The problem was time (less than an hour officially remained) and the fact the lakers had their bellies practically cemented to the bottom. As plenty of fishermen have discovered, taking these bottom-huggers with downriggers can be tough.

Wire line would have been just the ticket, and I would have traded a new downrigger for a wire-line rig right

Lake Trout on Downriggers

Terry R. Walsh

then. But sometimes a pressure fishing situation jogs the memory just right. A downrigger trick I'd learned from Frank Arleth, a charter skipper based at Frankfort, Michigan, came suddenly to mind, and it helped me win a mighty nice check. Here's how it works:

Burying the Ball

That name may sound strange, but it's apt.

When lake trout seem to be right on the lake floor, most anglers will lower a cannonball until it hits bottom and then bring it up a foot or two, figuring that's about how far above the bottom it will continue to run. Others will watch the descending ball on their sonars until it appears to touch bottom, and stop it there. But both groups are way off bottom with their lures.

In the first case, though the ball hits bottom when lowered straight down, it swings astern and shallower as soon as the cable is tightened. In the second case, the ball travels even farther off bottom, since the fishermen haven't allowed for the pulse width of their sonars. A 50-kHz unit, the most common and useful type in deep-water fishing, generally has a "dead band" of 3 to 5 feet, so the bottom will be that much deeper than the graph or screen indicates. The sonar simply fails to show those last few feet at the lower end of the signal cone: when the ball appears to touch bottom, it's still well above it.

So instead of those mistaken methods, try burying the ball. Lower the weight until it first touches bottom, and give it a minute or so to adjust to the current and trolling speed. Then lower it again. Keep repeating this process until the downrigger boom bounces steadily, indicating the weight is in regular contact with the bottom.

The downrigger is now accomplishing the same thing a wire-line rig would: the ball has swung astern, but you've gradually released enough cable to compensate. Your lure is running right in front of the bottom-hugging trout. At the same time, the ball is stirring up bottom debris, which triggers strikes from lake trout more often than not.

After I resorted to burying the ball—so named because it drops the weights too deep to be seen with sonar—I took my five biggest lake trout of the tournament, the largest a 15-pound-plus beauty that was the best fish any boat caught.

Walking the Bottom

While the foregoing tactic is highly effective, the rocks and rubble of good lake trout bottoms often rule it out: frequent hang-ups would cost you plenty of downrigger tackle. But there's another trick to achieve the same goal on rocky structure, while virtually eliminating expensive cannonball losses.

Drill a vertical hole through the center of an 8-pound downrigger weight, then slide a 16-inch piece of 3/8-inch threaded rod through the ball so it protrudes roughly an inch out the top. Tighten a nut on the top of the weight and another on the bottom, to hold the rod in place. In the top 1/4 inch of the rod, drill a horizontal hole large

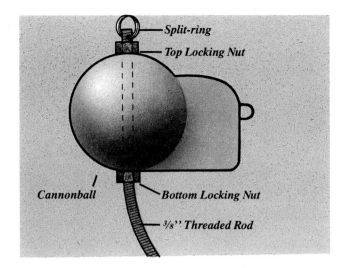

Split-ring

Top Locking Nut

Cannonball

Bottom Locking Nut

⅜" Threaded Rod

enough for a big split-ring to fit through; this ring is for attaching the downrigger cable. Now bend the bottom part of the rod approximately 30 degrees, and you've built an unusual bottom-walking weight.

You can fish this in constant contact with a rocky bottom, because it's virtually snagless. Only the protruding rod actually touches. If all this sounds vaguely familiar, it's because the weight with its rod insert is simply an adaptation of the wire-and-lead walking sinker so many of us have used when trolling for walleyes in snag-infested rivers. And believe me, this big-water version works every bit as well.

Adding a Dropper Rig

The two tactics described so far will work most of the time when fish are tight on the bottom. On days when they don't work, I suspect the reason is that lakers won't always tolerate the disturbance created by an 8- or 10-pound weight dragging along the bottom. Still, when the trout are lying low and won't respond to lures trolled even a few feet above them, your only choice (other than the laborious wire-line techniques) is to put your lures right down where they are.

How can you do that without spooking them with the huge thumping ball? Here's another trick, not quite as convenient as the two already presented, but effective when all else fails.

First, you'll need a weight that has a rudder of some sort, and the rudder must have a release eye molded into it. Big Jon and Cannon both market such weights. Next, cut a 3-foot length of downrigger cable, and use crimping sleeves to secure a heavy-duty snap-swivel on one end of it and a heavy three-way swivel on the other. Knot one end of an 18-inch length of 30-pound monofilament to the bottom eye of the swivel, and the other end to a 1-pound lead ball. Snap this completed dropper rig to the rudder eye.

One final step remains. For this, you need a couple of pad-type releases like the ones marketed by Lee or Offshore Tackle. Clip one release to the middle eye of the three-way swivel; clip the other to the rudder eye where you just secured the dropper rig.

To make the entire apparatus operational, first let out no more than 6 feet of line with your favorite attractor and lure on the end. Next, fasten your fishing line into the pad release on the three-way swivel. Then, with the 1-pound ball hanging straight down, clip the fishing line into the pad release at the rudder eye.

Finally, lower the entire rig into the water until steady bottom contact is indicated by the vibrating or frequent jerking of the downrigger boom. Big Jon's flexible booms are ideal for this tactic, since they're more sensitive to the light bottom contact than stiffer booms.

Only the 1-pound ball touches bottom, while the big weight rides above. The ball doesn't create enough disturbance to spook wary lakers, yet it keeps your lure traveling very close to the bottom. If the ball should hang up, the monofilament dropper will break and only the ball will be lost, not the bigger and far more expensive weight.

The reason for the second release on the big weight is that it lets you put a good tension arch in your trolling rod. If just the release on the three-way swivel were used, the rod would have to stand almost vertically in its holder. The 1-pound ball is too light to produce much tension and would lift right off the bottom, defeating the whole purpose of the rig.

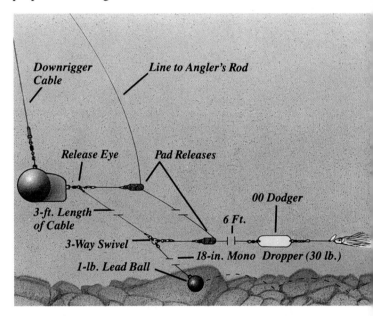

Downrigger Cable

Line to Angler's Rod

Release Eye

Pad Releases

00 Dodger

3-ft. Length of Cable

6 Ft.

3-Way Swivel

18-in. Mono Dropper (30 lb.)

1-lb. Lead Ball

When using any of the foregoing tactics, I've found a 00 dodger or a single attractor blade ahead of the lure works best. Bigger dodgers and multiblade attractors are far more likely to end up as bottom decorations.

And there you have it — three advanced downrigger tactics guaranteed to add to your catch when the lake trout are glued to the bottom and normal downrigger presentations won't work.

Terry R. Walsh is a Lake Huron charter captain operating out of Harrisville, Michigan. He also works as a field editor for Great Lakes Fisherman *magazine, writing frequently about lake trout.*

Trout & Salmon
in Streams *Keith Jackson*

In the past two years, the hottest angling news to hit the Northwest has been the record-breaking runs of chinook salmon in the Columbia River. The second-hottest story is that the best way to catch these fish is by flutter-jigging, a brand-new salmon technique for rivers.

And two other unusual stream techniques have recently appeared: match fishing and glow-balling. Though little known outside the regions where they originated, they're proving effective wherever trout or salmon anglers give them a try.

Flutter-Jigging for Giant Fish

In a sense, flutter jigs aren't new—they're simply big spoons. The most popular type, the Luhr Jensen Krocodile spoon, has been made since the 1940s. For flutter-jigging, Krocs are used in weights from 1½ to 2¼ ounces. Other spoons in this weight range also work, if they measure about 4 inches long and 1 inch wide.

Flutter-jigging was discovered early in the 1986 Columbia run, when the chinooks weren't responding to traditional methods. Two Luhr Jensen employees tried jigging the Kroc and a similar spoon, the Nordic. And they started catching chinooks in six-fish limits.

Flutter-jigging is easy, once you locate the salmon. In the Columbia, they bunch up near the mouths of cool tributaries such as the Klickitat, White Salmon, and Deschutes. You spot the salmon rolling and splashing, or pick them up on a depth finder.

Then, you run upstream, cut your motor, and drift back through the school. Free-spool the spoon to the bottom. Engage the reel and take in just enough line to lift the spoon a little. Next, start the upward jigging stroke; do this slowly, to avoid snagging fish. Then rip the spoon upward. The stroke may be only a few inches long, or several feet. At the top of the stroke, stop your rod tip abruptly; then lower it just slowly enough to keep your line slightly taut while the spoon flutters toward the bottom.

The fluttering is what triggers the fish. Big chinooks—some weighing near 70 pounds—usually hit when the spoon is close to the bottom.

Flutter-jigging works not only for salmon and steelhead in deep pools of rivers, but also for large rainbow, brown, and lake trout in streams and lakes.

Match-Fishing Techniques for Trout

This postgraduate live-bait technique has been around for a while in Europe, but is new in the United States. It surfaced here in trout tournaments in the Southeast. The technique is the same one used in international match-fishing competitions. It's based on a precisely balanced system of rod, line, float, split-shot, and bait.

The heart of the system is the bait: maggots that have been fed dyed turkey meat. They take on the dye tint, which resembles the coloration of insects such as caddis larvae or mayfly nymphs. Sold under the name EuroLarvae, the maggots come in red, yellow, and blue-green, and also in an undyed color. You hook them lightly through the skin at the blunt end.

Usually two or three are fished on the hook at once. The rest of the tackle is just as unusual. A graphite rod 10 to 12 feet long, with a soft tip and stiff butt section, is rigged with a small, precision, underhanging spincast reel. Many anglers use the Daiwa 125M reel because of its exceedingly smooth drag and easy operation.

The drag is important, since the line is very light. Wazp Products, which imports most of the match-fishing gear, recommends 2-pound 6-ounce mono line, and a leader only half that strength. But for the average angler trying the new technique, 4-pound line and 2-pound leader work well enough.

The float has a bulblike body and a long, thin, brightly colored "antenna." Enough split-shot are used to keep the body barely submerged. The antenna stays above the surface, twitching at the lightest bite. Floats come in several sizes, from 3 to 6 inches long. The sizes differ in buoyancy, and are selected for proper presentation of the bait in currents of various speeds and depths.

The idea of match fishing is to drift the bait as naturally as possible. The delicately balanced tackle helps eliminate drag—which is any unnatural movement caused by the current pulling on the line. Drag is just as undesirable for the match fisherman as it is for the fly fisherman.

Ideal water for match fishing is a run less than 10 feet deep, with moderate current. Also good are the breaks between the faster main current of a river and the quieter water near shore. The break line shows up as a "crease" in the surface.

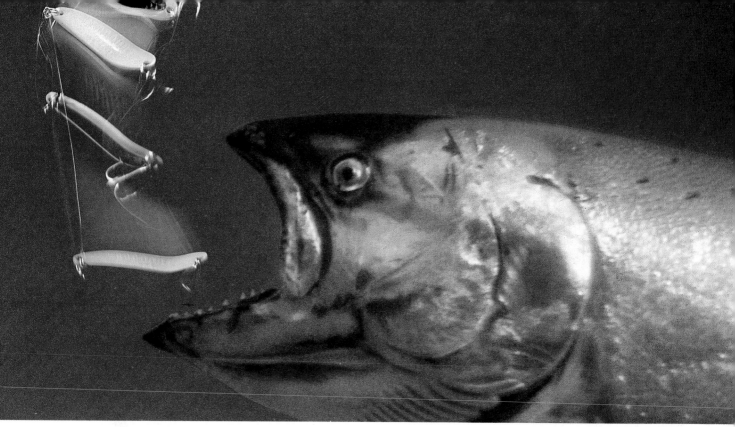

Flutter-Jigging for Chinook Salmon

Rig your float so the bait drifts just above the bottom. Most casts are sidearm or lob casts, especially when the line beneath the float is set long to fish deep. (For fishing deeper than 6 or 8 feet, a slip-float and bobber stop are used.) The long rod makes lob casts easier, and also helps guide the float along the current edges.

You can try the match technique without investing in all the tackle. You definitely need a long rod—the longer, the better. The butt and midsection should be stiff, for controlling hooked fish. The tip should be more flexible, to absorb shocks that would snap the leader. A 10-foot telescoping crappie rod serves fairly well; so does a fast-action 9-foot fly rod. The guides should be ceramic and stand well away from the blank. Standard guides would allow the fine-diameter lines to cling to the blank when wet, interfering with casting.

But there's no substitute for a precision reel with a sensitive drag. The Daiwa mentioned earlier is relatively inexpensive, and will handle the lightest lines a beginner is likely to use.

Bottom Fishing with Glow Balls

Steelhead fishermen in the Northwest have been keeping this technique a secret. It's extremely effective for all trout and also for salmon. Called glow-balling, it's a way of fishing a luminescent drift bobber in low light.

The drift bobber—or glow ball—is about the size of a dime. During fishing, it must be charged occasionally with artificial light. Simply playing a flashlight beam on it will make it glow for a while, but many anglers supercharge it with a camera flash. The result of this intense light is remarkable—the bobber looks to be on fire.

The glowing ball alone, without bait, will often trigger strikes. But for more inducement, many anglers thread salmon-egg clusters, shrimp, or yarn on the hook.

To sink the bobber close to the bottom, pencil lead is rigged on a 4-inch dropper attached to a three-way swivel. The slender shape of the pencil lead reduces snagging. The amount of lead used varies with the current speed and water depth; if the lead gets hung up constantly, it's too heavy.

The bobber floats the hook off bottom so it won't snag. The bobber is strung on a leader and rests on the hook eye, or on a bead above the eye. The leader, tied to the swivel, is usually about 20 inches long. In fast or murky water, where fish hold near the bottom, it may be as short as 1 foot; in clear water, as long as 3 feet. The hook, about size 1/0, has a short shank and turned-up eye.

Cast the rig at an angle upstream. It will drift back along the bottom, the sinker barely tapping the rocks. In low light conditions—at dusk, after dark, at dawn—the ghostly green glow of the bobber really turns the fish on.

Glow balls also take fish during daylight, if the water is murky. Under such conditions they work much better than ordinary drift bobbers that don't glow. For more luminescence in the murk, anglers use larger bobbers—as large as a quarter—or two bobbers together. With the large bobber you need a big hook, up to size 3/0, so the point has enough clearance for sure hooking.

Keith Jackson, who lives in Spokane, has been an avid trout and salmon fisherman all his life. He's the Washington State editor of Outdoor Life *magazine, and he's working on a book about steelhead fishing.*

New Techniques:

Walleyes

Tom Neustrom & Dick Sternberg

I f walleye experts have discovered anything new in recent years, it's that many of the long-accepted "truths" about walleye fishing are false, or at least not true all the time. And several new techniques have evolved to catch those walleyes that are breaking with tradition.

Downrigging for Walleyes

Downriggers are catching on for a lot of fish besides trout and salmon, and walleyes are no exception. Until recently, most fishermen assumed that walleyes spent practically all their time on the bottom. Downrigging was not considered, because running a cannonball close to bottom would be asking for trouble.

Lake Erie fishermen were the first to discover that downriggers worked for walleyes. They found huge walleye schools suspended at depths of 10 to 50 feet in water as deep as 200 feet. By running several lines at different depths, they could quickly locate the walleyes. Once they found the most productive depth, they set their other lines accordingly. Soon, controlled-depth fishing began to produce impressive stringers.

It didn't take long for the word to spread to walleye fishermen in other areas. At Lake of the Woods, on the

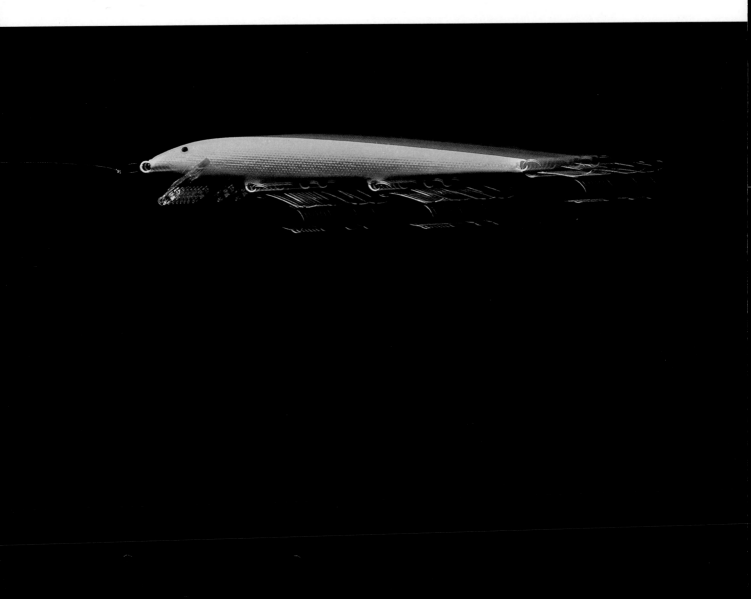

Minnesota-Ontario border, downrigger fishermen discovered untapped concentrations of suspended walleyes, many topping the 10-pound mark. Fishermen flocked to the big lake in the hope of landing a trophy walleye, and literally hundreds were caught during the first summer of downrigger fishing. Local fishermen had always known the big walleyes were there, but before downrigging became popular, there had been no consistent way to catch them.

Downrigging for walleyes is still not a widespread technique, but will undoubtedly catch on in years to come. It works best in large lakes and reservoirs with expanses of water of a consistent depth. And it seems most effective in summer, after a lake has formed its thermocline. This is the time when walleyes are most likely to suspend.

In addition to downriggers and 8- to 12-pound cannonballs, you will need line releases that can be adjusted to trip easily. Otherwise, you may wind up dragging hooked

walleyes across the lake. Another important consideration: the releases should not scuff the line. A simple yet reliable release is a light rubber band.

Most fishermen use electronic gear such as graphs, LCRs, and videos to help them locate the walleyes. But you can get by with a flasher, periodically changing the depths of your lines until you find the fish.

Almost any type of rod and reel will do, but serious downrigger fishermen prefer 6- to 7-foot medium-action baitcasting rods and level-wind reels spooled with 6- to 10-pound mono. Shallow-running minnow plugs are the most popular lure, but spinner-live bait rigs baited with nightcrawlers, leeches, or minnows also work well.

Always set your downriggers so the baits or lures track a few feet above the fish. Walleyes, like most other gamefish, are more likely to strike a bait tracking above than one below.

Snap-Jigging

Here's another new technique that violates the walleye rules. For decades, walleye fishermen have operated on the principle "slow is good, slower is better." But any anglers who spend a day fishing with Dick Grzywinski, ace walleye guide on Minnesota's Lake Winnibigoshish, will probably revise their thinking.

Grzywinski's technique is a form of jig-trolling, which in itself is not unusual. But he adds a few new twists that seem to produce almost magical results. He trolls much faster than other jig-trollers, and he snaps his rod sharply all the time to make the jig dance. If the jig fails to hit bottom, he doesn't really care. The violent up-and-down motion triggers walleyes that ignore slower offerings.

For many anglers, snap-jigging is a difficult technique to master. Grzywinski uses a 7-foot, fast-action spinning rod, usually with 10-pound mono. The long rod makes snapping easier, and the heavy line keeps the jig from sinking too fast and gives walleyes more time to strike. He trolls forward rather than backward because he wants to move at a fast clip. If he were to backtroll that fast, waves would slosh over the transom. His favorite lure is a ¼-ounce feather jig, white or chartreuse, tipped with a 2- to 3-inch fathead minnow hooked through the eyes.

One of the reasons fishermen have trouble catching fish with the snap-jigging technique is that they lower the rod too fast while the jig sinks, allowing the line to go slack. If a walleye hits a jig sinking on a slack line, you'll never know you had a strike. The fish inhales the jig and spits it out in a fraction of a second. This is a common problem in all jig fishing, but snap-jigging exaggerates it because the sharp snap is more likely than a gentler jigging action to create the troublesome slack.

The key to detecting strikes is to drop your rod back slowly as the jig sinks, so the line stays barely taut at all times. Usually the strike will amount to nothing more than a slight twitch or tap. Don't drop your rod back *too* slowly, though, or the line will tighten more than necessary and interfere with the lively jigging action of the lure.

On the drop, be sure to return your rod all the way to its original position. If you start the next snap with the rod only part way back, you will not have enough leverage for a strong hook-set.

Snap-jigging works best from late spring to early fall, when walleyes are most active. The best location is a long, gradually sloping breakline with light vegetation. The most productive depth is 5 to 10 feet, shallower than most fishermen are accustomed to fishing when the water is warm. Even if most of the walleyes are deeper, there are usually some in the shallows. And the fish in shallow water are the ones most likely to bite.

Playing the Wind

Walleye anglers have always known that wind has an important role in their sport. Even novices recognize that walleyes bite best when there is a "walleye chop" on the water. But most walleye fishermen, including many experts, do not understand exactly how to use the wind to their advantage when planning their fishing strategy.

Typically, when a small-boat fisherman is making a decision on where to go walleye fishing, he makes at least one of two possible mistakes. Let's say there's a strong northwest wind. There are two lakes in the area with good walleye populations: one has a northwest-southeast orientation, the other a northeast-southwest orientation. Mistake number one: the angler chooses the latter lake, thinking that it will be easier to fish because the wind is blowing across it rather than along its length.

He launches his boat on the south side of the lake, but the wind is blowing onto that shore. Mistake number two: he heads for the north side to get out of the wind. These two mistakes have just about insured that he will not catch walleyes.

Why not? Because walleyes in calm water are much less likely to bite than those on reefs, points, or other shallow structure exposed to the full force of the wind. The wind blows plankton in, stirs up bottom organisms, and may pile up warm surface water, causing baitfish to move in; it breaks up the surface and may produce a mud line along shore, reducing light penetration; and it creates underwater currents which draw walleyes. Better he had selected the other lake and found some shallow structure exposed to heavy wave action.

Another advantage of fishing in the wind: walleyes often bite all day, as long as there is good wave action. On the lee side of the lake, walleyes may feed for a while in early morning and again around dusk, but midday fishing is probably a waste of time. Also, walleyes along the windward shore are less likely to spook from boat movement or noise.

Any type of shallow structure exposed to the wind can draw walleyes, but the following spots are usually best:

• A rocky point with an extended lip less than 6 feet deep. A point with a shallow lip is better than one that drops off rapidly, because more bottom is exposed to wave action.

• A shallow, gradually tapering rocky reef that tops off at 6 feet or less.

• Small points, inside turns (pockets), and isolated weed clumps along a shallow breakline. These areas offer "something different," and tend to concentrate walleyes.

• A bay or a large pocket on a breakline where warm water is "funneled in" by the wind. Structure like this prevents the warm water from mixing with the surrounding water as it would along a straight shoreline. Sometimes, water in a bay or pocket will be 5 to 10 degrees warmer than water in the main lake.

When these spots are pounded by 2- to 4-foot waves, walleyes often move into the shallowest part of the structure and start feeding. Some die-hard fishermen prefer even larger waves.

When looking for productive structure for fishing in the wind, keep the following rules in mind:

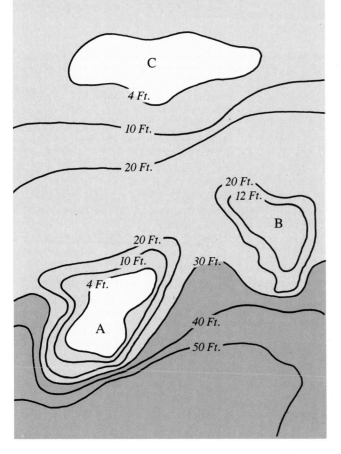

A sea anchor works well for slowing your drift or reducing your trolling speed. When trolling in very heavy seas, throw out your sea anchor, point your bow into the waves, then run your outboard in forward. This technique is much safer than backtrolling and gives you surprisingly good boat control.

Shallow-running crankbaits and minnow plugs work well for casting to shallow structure. Walleyes in rough water are aggressive, not hesitating to chase fast-moving plugs. Small jigs, about ⅛ ounce, are also effective. Most fishermen tip their jig with a minnow. If you don't get a few snags with a jig, you're probably not fishing in the right spot.

You can avoid snags by using a slip-bobber rig baited with a leech. Set the bobber stop so the leech dangles just above the rocks. The waves produce a jigging action that walleyes find irresistible.

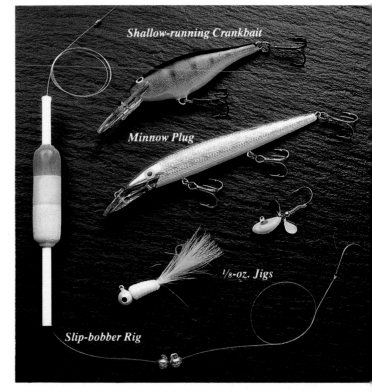

• The deeper the structure, the less it will be affected by wind. A reef that tops off at 4 feet *(A)* is a better bet than one topping off at 12 feet *(B)*.

• On shallow structure, the most productive area is generally where the water is roughest.

• The best structure is near deep water. Walleyes are more likely to move up on a reef that drops quickly into 50 feet of water *(A)* than one in the middle of a large 10-foot flat *(C)*.

• The structure should have good cover, usually large rocks or boulders.

• The longer the wind has been blowing into a piece of structure, the more likely it will attract walleyes. Walleyes may move in within an hour after the wind starts blowing, but your odds are much better if the wind has been blowing from the same direction for several days.

Fishing rough water requires a deep, sturdy boat at least 16 feet long. A Lund Pro-V or an Alumacraft Competitor (see pages 30-31) is built for this type of water. Most rough-water walleye boats are equipped with splash guards to keep waves from sloshing over the transom while backtrolling.

Other useful items include a 20- to 25-pound Navy anchor with at least 100 feet of anchor line, and a sea anchor. The Navy anchor is useful when you want to work a specific spot, and the long line insures that it won't slip. Always drop anchor well upwind of the fish zone, then let out enough line so you can cast to the fringe. After working the fringe, let out more line so you can cast farther into the fish zone. If you let out too much right away, you may spook walleyes in the fringe area.

Anglers who know how to play the wind catch a lot of big walleyes. It seems that wind is necessary to turn the big ones on. Under calm conditions, big walleyes are extremely wary; even the slightest noise or movement will spook them. But in rough water, the sound of a motor or the sight of a moving boat usually doesn't matter.

A few hours of battling the wind can really tire you out. Boat control is difficult, and so is casting and detecting strikes. But once you've boated a trophy walleye, you won't even notice the wind is blowing.

Tom Neustrom, one of the north country's premier walleye anglers, has written many articles on walleyes for national fishing magazines. Dick Sternberg is the author of Walleye, *a complete guide to fishing for the species, published by The Hunting & Fishing Library.*

Traditionally, muskies and pike have been considered territorial, object-oriented critters — loners that hole up by a particular log or weedbed and stay put.

The scenario is familiar: a bearded north-woods guide, wearing a buffalo-plaid shirt in an old wooden boat, casts a rusted bucktail spinner or a red-and-white spoon to an island shoreline, hammering a certain fish he's been after for years. That's the way fishing for muskies and pike is supposed to be.

But just when everything seemed cut and dried, some inquisitive anglers had to go and break all the rules. New discoveries by these anglers — and by scientists, too — suggest a thorough overhaul of old theories. On

Exactly why muskies and pike suspend is uncertain. Some anglers believe that warming surface water forces them to do so, yet sonar readings and actual catches prove they continue to suspend in the fall, when surface temperatures cool. The most logical explanation is simply that they go where the forage fish go. The preferred forage — ciscoes, whitefish, shad, and even perch and walleyes — will often suspend in open water. Another reason may be the predatory nature of muskies and pike. Like wolves, they're at the very top of the food chain, with no fear of other predators in their realm. So they're free to swim wherever they please.

The angler accustomed to casting at specific targets — weedbeds, reefs, steep banks — will no doubt feel lost

Muskellunge & Northern Pike

Joe Bucher

these pages you'll find two of the latest twists in fishing technique for muskies and pike.

Trolling for Suspended Trophies

No matter where you find them, big muskies and pike are tough hombres to catch. But there's one situation that does offer some tremendous untapped opportunities: fish suspended in open water. Unlocking the mystery of these suspended trophies has been one of the biggest breakthroughs in modern angling.

Have muskies and pike always suspended? Do they suspend often? When they do, how can you catch them?

Yes, they *have* always suspended. In fact they suspend frequently — the big ones in particular. But only recently have anglers found all this out. The discovery has been made with the new, highly sophisticated sonar equipment — graphs, LCRs, and videos. These devices clearly display the evidence of large predators suspending in open water.

when first trying for suspended fish. Tradition must be pushed aside, and the mind awakened to a whole new approach to fishing.

Trolling with a motor, where allowed, is one of the most effective ways to present lures to these suspended fish. You can cover lots of water quickly, and get your lures down to depths not normally attainable by casting. With 20- to 25-pound mono, cofilament, or Dacron, you can easily troll a deep-diving plug 12 to 18 feet down, compared to 8 to 12 feet on a cast.

Another option is trolling with wire line. Though its tendency to kink and coil makes it harder to work with, it takes lures much deeper than other lines, and allows you to troll at any given depth with less line out. Also, wire digs more steeply into the water, allowing sharper turns for precise control of your trolling course.

By far the most accurate way to troll at the specific depths where fish are suspending is to use downriggers. Long popular for Great Lakes salmon fishing, downriggers have just begun to catch on with muskie and pike fishermen. Very few are yet aware of their tremendous effectiveness.

Your choice of lures depends to a great extent on your trolling method. In standard trolling or wire-line trolling, plugs with long lips perform best, diving sharply and easily to the productive depths. With downriggers, the best lures are those that track at a constant depth, creating minimal drag. A large spoon would do the trick, or a short-lipped minnow plug like the popular large Rapala. A long lip would pull too hard, tripping the line release on the trolling weight. In most cases the lure should be fished 6 to 8 feet behind the weight.

The trolling speed varies with the type of lure and the water temperature. Speed can make a big difference in lure action. A spoon, for example, will wobble properly only within a narrow range of speeds. Troll too fast, and it will spin and cause line twist; too slow, and it won't wobble at all. With a plug you can vary the speed more than with a spoon, though not as much as with a spinner. A bucktail spinner can be effective at almost any speed, as long as the blade turns. Generally, faster trolling speeds work best in warm water, slower speeds in cool water.

Understand that when muskies and pike suspend, they don't always go deep. When suspending in early summer, they may relate to the warm surface waters or to the shallow thermocline. At this time of year it's not uncommon to find a muskie or pike suspended only 5 to 10 feet deep, over 25 or more feet of water.

By midsummer, most muskies and big pike suspend just above the thermocline, commonly at depths of 18 to 35 feet, or even deeper. Occasionally these giants venture below the thermocline, if sufficient oxygen is present. There is very little evidence, however, that these fish below the thermocline are at all active or catchable. When the thermocline disappears after the fall turnover, muskies and pike may suspend at almost any depth—shallow, or down 35 feet or more.

The easiest way to peg the right depth is to keep an eye on your sonar unit. The mere presence of baitfish, with no bona-fide recording of a "lunge" or "gator," still dictates running your lure at that depth. The lunkers most often situate themselves in easy range of the food source.

There are several likely locations for suspended muskies and pike. The deep main-lake basin usually holds a resident cisco population—and muskies and big pike will generally be found nearby. The outside edge of a large shallow food shelf is another prime target: the mouth of a big weedy bay, for example, or the perimeter of a large mid-lake shoal. A series of rocky humps on a deep flat can be a hotspot, too. The main ingredient is food supply. If lots of food is around, trophy fish won't be far away.

Searching out suspended muskies and pike is one of freshwater angling's last frontiers. To get a crack at these little-understood and largely undisturbed fish, anglers must be willing to step out of line and try something really different.

Muskies Round Midnight

"Everyone knows that muskies don't feed at night," said one writer in a major magazine article appearing in 1986. And in fact most muskie anglers have long held that belief. It's funny, though, that the muskies themselves don't agree.

Although most other species in the pike family don't feed after dark, the muskie definitely does. Day feeding may be normal, but under certain conditions muskies revert almost totally to night feeding behavior.

Heavy boat traffic and fishing pressure during the day will quickly set muskies into a nighttime pattern. Muskies are notoriously wary and retiring, and when there's too much commotion they simply won't buy what anglers are selling.

Under such conditions, muskies feed regularly after dark even if the water is very discolored. In 1986 alone, fishermen I guided caught 67 muskies after dark, with equal success whether the water was clear, stained, or cloudy. Only when the visibility is a foot or less does night feeding cease.

But the water clarity does make a difference in how deep the muskies feed at night. If the water is very clear, they're more likely to go deep. The legendary Len Hartman has taken muskies at night as deep as 35 feet. If the water is very murky, on the other hand, they feed on shallow shelves—and may be taken in only 1 to 3 feet of water.

Heavy boat traffic and fishing pressure during the day will quickly set muskies into a nighttime pattern.

The two greatest nemeses of the daytime muskie angler —ultraclear water and cold fronts—can also promote great action after dark.

Muskies in gin-clear water are especially alert to the presence of anglers, and shy away from the hardware tossed at them. But these spooky fish can be had under the cover of darkness.

In the past, anglers have often thought sustained warm weather was necessary for night feeding. Yet muskies also feed at night under cold-front conditions. When a cold front passes, leaving dry air, chill north breezes, and mile-high bluebird skies, muskies get the classic lockjaw in the daytime. Then, night fishing may be the only productive method—period.

If you're going to fish just after a cold front, time your trip carefully. In stable, warm weather, muskies generally feed for long periods each night. But in the wake of a cold front they may feed only a few minutes—generally within the first hour of darkness. To score, you have to fish the high-percentage spots during this brief period, without letting up.

When gearing up for an outing, be sure to get a good night light. Lights that mount on headgear work best, since they free both hands for knot-tying and fighting and boating muskies. Some muskie stalkers like a miner's hard hat, but most prefer a lightweight headband and a belt with a 6-volt battery pack.

Standard muskie rods and reels will do the job after dark, but stronger lines and leaders are advisable. Because of the reduced visibility at night, extra-heavy lines and leaders will not diminish your chances at all.

Lure choice is more critical for night fishing than for any other muskie angling. Select types of lures that the fish can see easily and detect by sound or vibration. Smaller types that dart and dance erratically are tough for them to locate and connect with. Rather, opt for oversized, 9- to 12-inch lures that move steadily through the water emitting strong vibrations. Large jointed crankbaits and bucktail spinners are superb choices.

Lure color is a simple matter after dark: Use black. Any color may produce some results, but solid black makes the most visible silhouette. A muskie feeding at night will almost always be looking upward. There's always a little light in the sky, even at night, and black lures make the most intense silhouette, showing up much better than brighter ones.

In many cases nighttime muskies respond best to a slow retrieve. If the water is clear and warm, however, they may pounce just as readily on a lure reeled fast. Experiment on every trip to determine what does the best job.

Don't become a "bank beater" after dark. It's tempting to stay close to shore, so you can keep your bearings more easily. While many shoreline spots may be good, areas farther out can be more productive. The same mid-lake weedbeds, rock humps, sand bars, and flats where muskies hang out in the day will be great after-hours spots, as well. One difference is that muskies may venture shallower after dark. Sections of a hotspot that are too shallow for muskies in the daytime will often be prime at night.

But never travel on a body of water after dark unless you're totally familiar with it. Hitting a stump or shallow rock is doubly devastating at night. Thoroughly familiarize yourself—during daylight—with the bottom topography of the area you'll fish and all its potential hazards.

Remember: Safety first. And not only when you're navigating. Be extra-cautious when casting and whenever boating a fish.

With that in mind, get ready for some heart-stopping action. Who knows? You could easily have the fishing experience of a lifetime—tangling with a trophy muskie in the dark.

Joe Bucher works as a muskie guide at Boulder Junction, Wisconsin. He manufactures muskie and pike lures, and has written a book, Bucktail Fishing for Muskies. *Every summer he conducts a three-day school on muskie fishing.*

Striped Bass

Stu Tinney

Publishing *Striper* magazine keeps me off the water more than I care to admit. But it also keeps me in touch with many of the most innovative fishermen in the country. Give a striped-bass angler a difficult set of conditions, and he'll meet the challenge with a new technique.

Crank the High Banks

Stripers like to feed along the high, rocky banks of lakes like Mead, Powell, Norris, and Cumberland. These banks are very steep, sometimes vertical. Plankton wash close to the rock face, and shad swim close to feed on them. The shad, in turn, attract stripers—sometimes in the 30- to 40-pound class.

But big stripers under high banks can be tough to convince. You need to position your lure close to the bank, but sneaking into casting range with your outboard is almost impossible. The motor noise reverberates off the rock. And the lures typically fished on steep drops—jigs and jigging spoons—aren't long enough to match the big shad the stripers usually want. Nor do they displace enough water or have enough action to attract them with sound.

That's where a great new technique comes in. It's the best way I know, bar none, to get those heavy, bank-hugging stripers to come out to play. It scores well all year, except during the coldest winter months. It not only works during the day, but also is dynamite for trophy fish at night.

The requisite lure is a cigar-shaped minnow plug with a long lip. A plug of this type will generally dive 8 to 12 feet. Many different models will do the trick, but Storm's Big and Little Mac are becoming especially popular. The length, including the lip, should be 4 to 7 inches, depending on the size of the shad the stripers are taking. Though stripers may prefer smaller baitfish at times, they're usually after big ones when working the high banks.

Use an electric motor so you can approach the bank slowly and quietly. To avoid running your boat over any stripers that may be holding away from the bank, move no closer than necessary to make your cast. Forget about trying to read fish with your electronics in locations like this.

Cast your lure straight to the bank, dropping it as close in as you can, then crank hard so it dives steeply. Eight to ten turns of the handle will usually get it deep enough. If you use a reel with a high gear ratio—5 to 1—the job will be easier. After cranking the lure down, pause a few seconds so the head can rise and tilt the lure back to horizontal. Then reel again, slowly and steadily. The lure will travel at this same depth for the rest of the retrieve.

When you've made several casts to a short stretch of bank, you can creep in close with your electric motor and cast parallel to it. This way, a larger number of fish along the bank will get a look at your lure. Always test a variety of depths when casting parallel to shore. On one cast, for example, crank eight times before the pause; on the next cast, twelve times; on the next, fifteen.

Any location along a high bank may hold stripers. Many anglers concentrate on the points and neglect the long stretches between. It's true that the inside curve of a high, steep point is especially productive, but shad aren't glued to the points exclusively. Smart anglers often start at a point, but then work their way along the entire length of the high bank.

In this technique—and in most others for stripers—it's essential to fish a lure or live bait of the same size as the prevalent forage in the water. The correct length may vary from 1½ to 7 inches, according to the time of year. Determining what's right is simple.

Just plan to arrive at your fishing destination before daylight. Once there, look for a lighted area on the water. Virtually every bridge, launching ramp, and parking lot has some kind of overhead light that switches on at dark. Baitfish congregate in the illumination and remain all night. If you ease down to the lighted water, you'll discover exactly what size forage the stripers will see that day.

Ballooning with Live Bait

Fishing with live bait is the simplest way for beginners and experts alike to catch a really large striper. But even this back-to-basics fishing can be complicated by difficult conditions—and that's where new techniques come in.

In many impoundments, for example, springtime flooding is a way of life. Flooding also occurs at other times of year, when occasional storms drop tons of water. Big stripers take advantage of the situation, swimming into shallows and feeding on the baitfish the flooded land vegetation has attracted. For fishermen, it's always been tough to work this shallow water without spooking the big stripers. But recently a special technique has been devised to get the job done.

With an electric motor, ease quietly into the shallows. Then, select a large baitfish—a gizzard or threadfin shad, blueback herring, or yellow perch—and hook it through the nostrils or lips so it will swim along naturally when trolled. Use a short-shank, short-barb, bronzed hook like the Eagle Claw 84RP, in sizes 2 to 2/0. Bronzed hooks, unlike stainless types, will disintegrate in any fish that break your line.

Next, attach a balloon to your line several feet above the bait. A balloon 4 to 8 inches in diameter works best, and the line length below it should be a foot or two greater than the water depth. Usually the flooded areas are 4 or 5 feet deep, occasionally 10 or 12 feet. Let the bait out behind the boat 50 to 75 feet, either holding the rod in your hand or setting it in a rod holder. The bait will trail behind the balloon, swimming above the bottom.

Troll at medium speed. With the electric motor you can slip along almost anywhere, and the stripers won't be the wiser. The balloon creates enough drag to keep the baitfish directly astern, so you can position it wherever you want. Without the drag, a large baitfish could swim off wherever *it* wanted, instead. And another plus: in breezy weather, you can anchor upwind of a good spot and simply allow the balloon to float your bait over.

Enlightened Downrigging

Because stripers carry so much fat, they can go for long periods without food, simply waiting for the most favorable feeding conditions. During these rest periods, they form sizeable schools in zones where the water temperature is 65° to 70°F. With your electronics you can find them suspended, usually in deep water. Downriggers are ideal for this situation. Even though the stripers aren't feeding, you can generally catch them if you drag your lures right in front of them with downriggers.

But what do you try when the water is discolored? Stripers are mainly visual feeders, and muddy water cuts down their ability to spot their quarry. Still, if the visibility is at least 3 feet, you can rig brightly colored baits behind your downriggers and draw plenty of strikes. Especially good colors are chartreuse and yellow. Cigar-shaped minnow plugs work well, and vibrating plugs such as Spots and Rat-L-Traps. In this cloudy-water fishing, the downrigger weight helps draw attention, pushing water aside and thereby producing sound.

When the water gets so turbid that these bright lures won't do the trick, most fishermen give up and go home. But even with 1-foot visibility, you can still take stripers with a special technique. Borrowing from the long-line swordfisherman's book, you simply troll Cyalume light sticks behind your downrigger cables, illuminating a small field near your lures. The sticks are attached to the cables just above the weights, with mono droppers 6 inches long.

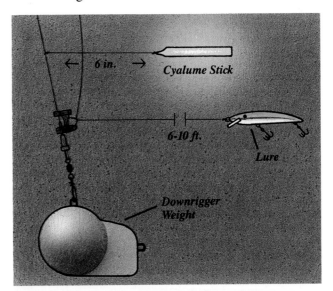

When using light sticks, shorten the lines between your downrigger weights and lures. Instead of 15 to 20 feet as in very clear water, allow only 6 to 10 feet. The fishing may not be frantic, but this technique is still the best way to light up what otherwise could be a dark trip indeed.

Stu Tinney is the editor and publisher of Striper *magazine, in Nashville, Tennessee. He's a leading advocate of striped-bass fishing, appearing frequently on national outdoor television programs.*

Ice Fishing

Joe Bucher

In today's fishing world we're seeing a blitz of new information, new technology, and new techniques. Old theories have been altered or thrown out entirely. Even a sport as traditional as ice fishing has gone through a firestorm of new ideas.

Following are a few of the latest—and hottest—innovations on the ice. Some of these, surely, will become standards in the years ahead.

Meat Strips

Steve Herbeck, a well-known guide from the region around Madison, Wisconsin, has developed what may be the most unusual and effective new system for trophy walleyes and pike. Instead of buying fresh live bait from a dealer, Herbeck cuts side strips off whatever species of forage fish is most common in the lake he's fishing.

It all began on a Wisconsin lake that was highly regarded for its trophy walleyes, though conventional methods and baits would produce very few of them. Herbeck found that the stomachs of most big walleyes from this lake contained remnants of crappies. Normally, crappies are not considered a prime walleye food. So his discovery set off a brainstorm: he hung a tantalizing strip of crappie meat on a treble hook, along with a lively shiner minnow.

Ice Fishing with Meat Strips

Suddenly, those hard-to-catch local trophies became very catchable. Lots of 8- to 13-pound lunkers began falling to Herbeck's new meat-strip method.

Eventually he tried the meat strips by themselves, without assistance from live bait. The results were nothing short of phenomenal. Two or three narrow strips, 3 to 5 inches long, hung on a size 8 treble hook and fished on a tip-up, produced just as well alone as they had with live bait.

What's the trigger? Herbeck says it's the scent and taste of the natural forage strips. Store-bought baitfish, by contrast, usually are raised in hatcheries and don't produce the kind of scent and taste that convince those finicky, survival-keen walleyes. Herbeck claims that even when lunker walleyes do take a non-native baitfish, they'll often drop it quickly. But they'll munch, swallow, and enjoy the meat strips.

One key to success with big walleyes is the freshness of the meat strips. Frozen or old strips are much less effective than freshly caught ones. That's why an accepted part of any fishing date with Herbeck is to spend some time at the outset catching the bait.

Meat strips have great potential for panfish, too. A small strip cut from the flank of a shiner and attached to a jig or jigging spoon will catch plenty of crappies. Take time to examine the stomach contents of the first few crappies you "ice": often you'll find a freshly eaten baitfish of some kind. Don't hesitate to slide off a meat strip and put it to work.

Double-Deep Walleyes

In recent years the books have been rewritten on walleyes. Once regarded only as deep-water fish, they're now taken commonly around shallow brushpiles, logs, stumps, and cribs, and even in weeds. Yet today there remains still another frontier, virtually unexplored: walleyes living in extra-deep water, 35 feet or more.

Until recently, little has been said about these denizens of the super depths—even though they exist in great numbers in those deep, clear lakes that are better known for lake trout. But ice anglers are now going after these untapped walleyes. They're using modern sonar devices to discover the deep haunts, then reaching them with specialized lake-trout gear such as tip-ups with extra-large spools.

These double-deep walleyes usually school around a midlake hump of rock, gravel, or sand, which may have some weeds on top. Another hotspot is a deep finger protruding from a large, shallow midlake reef. These places also are prime habitat in the fall; and going fishing then, just before ice-over, is the best way to get them located for winter. With the water still open, it's easy to pinpoint the fish and pick out landmarks for later reference.

If fall excursions are out of the picture, you can still locate these double-deep spots by using a portable LCR or other sonar unit. Simply brush any snow off the ice, then splash on a small amount of water. Immediately place the sonar transducer on this wet spot, switch on the unit, and you should get a reading.

One of the best aids for locating deep walleyes is a hydrographic chart of the lake you're fishing. A good one will clearly show the large midlake humps. Recent charts, usually more detailed than older ones, may even reveal the deep fingers. Small humps, however, are generally neglected.

Once you've located a likely hump or reef, thoroughly map its configuration in the snow. Move around and take depth readings with your sonar unit, marking spots where the readings are identical, then connect these spots by dragging your feet in the snow. The resulting contour lines will give you a picture of what lies underneath.

Walleyes in extra-deep water often school very tightly. You can group your tip-ups closer than normal: six to nine in an area 30 feet in diameter is not too tight. Set your rigs 6 to 12 inches above the bottom. Walleyes may hold on top of the hump or finger, down along its sides, or on the hard lake floor close to its base. Use ample weight—at least ⅛ ounce—to get the bait down and keep it there.

One drawback to catching deep walleyes is the fact their air bladders may invert when they're pulled up from the depths. Often the bladder will actually protrude from the mouth. It's not wise to release such fish, since they'll almost certainly die anyway. The best policy is to keep every fish until you've taken a fair share or (at most) your legal limit. Then pull your rigs and head for home.

Walleyes in these deep spots may bite all winter long. First ice—as soon as it's safe—is an especially productive time to fish. The middle of winter can also be good. In fact, ardent ice anglers may find that double-deep walleyes are the only ones consistently catchable then. And late-winter fishing, where legal, often provides superb action: the change of season puts fish on the feed.

Quick-Strike Pike

In ice fishing for pike, the biggest recent advance is the quick-strike hook rig from Europe. Traditionally, North American pike anglers have used either a single large treble hook with live bait, or the famous Swedish pike hook with dead bait. Either way, the hook is attached to a heavy wire leader. Rigs like these are obvious overkill—much too cumbersome for the size of the bait, and heavier than necessary for the fish to be caught.

A quick-strike rig, by contrast, consists of a pair of small, strong, ultrasharp hooks attached to microthin wire. This rig coordinates much better with the bait and makes it far more appealing. But the biggest advantage is what its name implies: when a pike grabs a bait on this rig, there's always a hook in position to penetrate. You can set it immediately, confident you'll connect and hold on.

My own experience with the quick-strike rig has been satisfying and somewhat amazing. Previously, my catch-to-strike ratio had been about 70 percent. Then my first outing with the new rig resulted in an unbelievable 28 catches for 28 strikes. There's no doubt in my mind that the quick-strike will produce nearly twice as many pike in a winter as a traditional rig.

You can make your own quick-strike rigs using thin braided wire, small black swivels, and tiny bronze treble hooks. In place of the trebles, however, most European anglers prefer special double hooks that penetrate and hold extremely well. The V.B. hook, as it's called, has two back-to-back bends unequal in size. The point of the smaller bend is anchored in the baitfish, while the point of the larger remains exposed and ready for pike. The sharpness of the V.B. is second to none, and its remarkable strength enables you to land fish of 40 pounds and more.

Quick-strike Rig

To rig a minnow, first insert the lower hook into the nose area, then snug the wire by pulling it toward the tail. Notice where the upper hook meets the back of the minnow—generally near the dorsal fin—and insert it shallow at that point.

Lower the rig through the ice, and prepare yourself to strike a big pike. Quick.

Joe Bucher is a fishing guide in Wisconsin. He writes and publishes a monthly fishing newsletter, In the Same Boat, *and teaches at fishing seminars throughout the northern states.*

Salmon Fishing on Wood River, Alaska

1988 Regional Hotspots

MAINE

Lake Champlain

VT.

Sebago Lake

Portland

N.H.

Oneida Lake

Syracuse

NEW YORK

MASS.

Connecticut River

Hartford

R.I.

CONN.

PENNSYLVANIA

Pittsburgh

Raystown Lake

Philadelphia

N.J.

MARYLAND

DEL.

WEST VIRGINIA

Charleston

New River

1988 Hotspots:

The East

"I fancy I am amphibious," wrote Thoreau, a famed eastern angler, "and swim in all the brooks and pools in the neighborhood, with the perch and bream, or doze under the pads of our river amid the winding aisles and corridors formed by their stems, with the stately pickerel."

A century and a half later, it's not so easy to entertain Thoreau's subaqueous vision. At Walden Pond he had space for inspiration. To wet a line today in many eastern waters, fishermen wade shoulder to shoulder, troll gunnel to gunnel. Yet there's still an abundance of productive water in the East, and countless great angling opportunities are largely passed up. Who, for instance, cares much today about the lowly bream? Or is likely to appreciate the stateliness of the pickerel? Doubtless there are many who do, but to most the pickerel is nothing more than a nuisance that shortstops plugs and flies intended for bass or trout.

Foremost among the missed opportunities are the thousands of minuscule ponds and creeks too tepid for hatchery trout, the lost and not-yet-found waters where the only launching ramps are mud slides reserved for the local otters. Part of the fun of angling these unremarked spots is to discover exactly which species of fish make their homes there. The other part, just as enjoyable, is to find such a spot in the first place. On your own.

The following pages describe a number of larger eastern waters where the most popular gamefish remain plentiful and where fishermen still have ample room to roam. All these waters—lakes and rivers alike—can absorb more angling pressure than they're presently getting. One of them, Lake Champlain, has a vastness and variety no angler could explore in a lifetime of leisure. All but the Connecticut River lie some distance from the big urban centers, but still within a few hours' drive. West Virginia's New River can be reached more easily by train than by car if you're traveling from Washington, Baltimore, or other cities on the coast. Amtrak winds through the damp, spectacular river gorge, otherwise roadless, and deposits you at the weatherworn Thurmond station where guides will pick you up by prior arrangement. It's a scarce kind of angling trip these days: high adventure the whole way.

Thoreau passed his hours afloat "communicating" with the fish "by a long flaxen line." The tackle has changed, but not the essence of the communion itself. All in all, there's more good angling in the East than most easterners imagine, and far more than most others would dream possible.

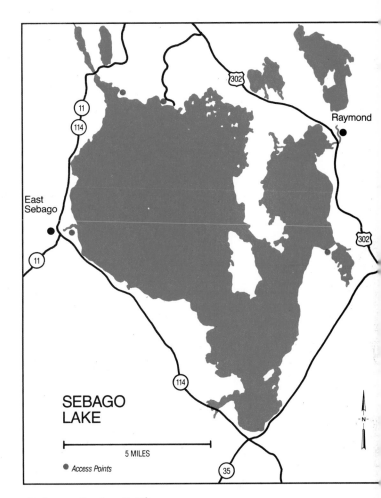

Sebago Lake, ME

This is the lake that produced the world-record landlocked salmon of 22½ pounds way back in 1907, and fisheries workers were reported to have netted a 36-pounder here that same year. The angling for landlocks is still excellent today. The species reproduces naturally in Sebago, but the population is now supplemented with approximately 20,000 stocked landlocks each year. Anglers take fish averaging 2 to 4 pounds by casting or trolling with spoons and minnow plugs. April, May, and June are most productive. In addition, lake trout were introduced in the early 1970s and have caught on so well that stocking has been discontinued. Lakers average 4 pounds, and reach a maximum of about 20 pounds. In summer, downriggers are effective with spoons, plugs, and dodger-and-fly rigs; in winter, good catches are made by jigging through the ice. Sebago also holds lots of smallmouth bass, which most anglers overlook. Jigs, crankbaits, and live bait pay off around rocky points and reefs.

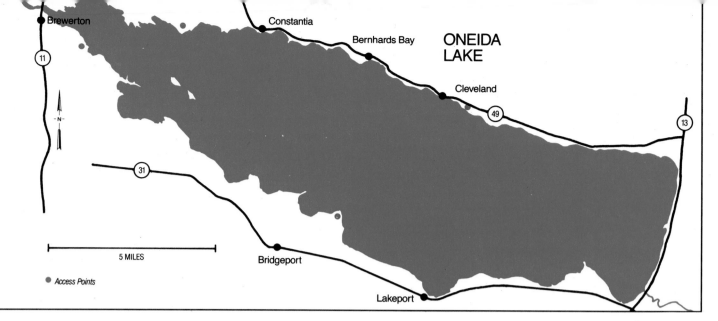

Oneida Lake, NY

One of a growing number of places, in several states, where local boosters claim the title of "Walleye Capital of the World." Whether or not Oneida is really number one, it does offer top-notch fishing for walleyes, about 300 million of which are stocked each year. The average catch is a 1½- to 1¾-pounder, with a few reaching 8 pounds. Walleye angling peaks in late spring and early summer. Old hands here generally prefer live bait— nightcrawlers, leeches, and minnows—either fished alone or trailed from spinners, jigs, or floating jigheads.

Both drifting and trolling are popular. The most intriguing form of the sport at Oneida is lantern fishing on sultry midsummer nights. With Colemans humming on their gunnels, anglers bounce crawlers for walleyes 20 to 25 feet off the bottom in water as deep as 50 feet. Smallmouth bass are plentiful in Oneida too, schooling on dropoffs of points and reefs, but few anglers make an effort to catch them. Ice fishing is productive for walleyes and especially for the lake's dense population of yellow perch.

Raystown Lake, PA

This fertile reservoir lies half-hidden in a fold of the western Alleghenies, just outside hollering range of the hamlet of Shy Beaver. For several years running, the Pennsylvania striped-bass record has been broken here; it now stands at 38 pounds plus. Survival of stocked fingerlings is high, and the stripers grow fast because of a large shad population, reaching the legal minimum length of 15 inches in only two years. Striper anglers do best in March, April, November, and early December. Muskies and tiger muskies are also stocked regularly, and the managers consider them "underfished." These predators go after shad that have grown too big to interest the stripers. Muskie fishermen drag spinners and big diving plugs in 15 to 20 feet of water in the bays of the lake. Bass strike plastic worms, crankbaits, and pig-and-jigs in these same areas. Largemouths outnumber smallmouths, but both grow fat and fast on the shad. Out in 80 to 120 feet of water, downrigger anglers catch planted lake trout. A 6-pounder is a big one, but the lakers are abundant.

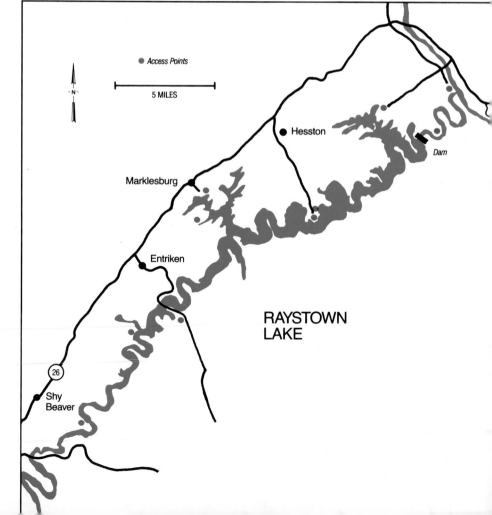

80

Lake Champlain, VT/NY

Big water, big expectations. Champlain has rocky islands and reefs, weed-filled bays, and frigid blue depths. These highly varied habitats support good populations of practically every gamefish species found in the East. The current favorite among anglers is probably the land-locked salmon, which both New York and Vermont stock annually in large numbers. During the warm months anglers troll spoons and dodger-and-fly rigs in open water, often using downriggers. In September and October the landlocks run up rivers like the Bouquet and Saranac, where fly anglers queue up to cast stream-ers. Lake trout do well in Champlain, too. The species is stocked by both states, and is believed to reproduce naturally in addition. There's excellent ice fishing for lakers with jigs and bait; also downrigger trolling and deep jigging in summer. Possibly the most productive fishing on Champlain— and surely the most over-looked—is for smallmouth bass on reefs and other structure. Also abundant are largemouths, pike, wall-eyes, and yellow perch.

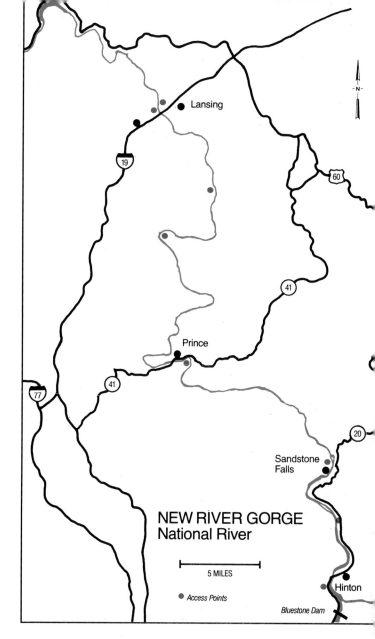

NEW RIVER GORGE National River

5 MILES

● Access Points

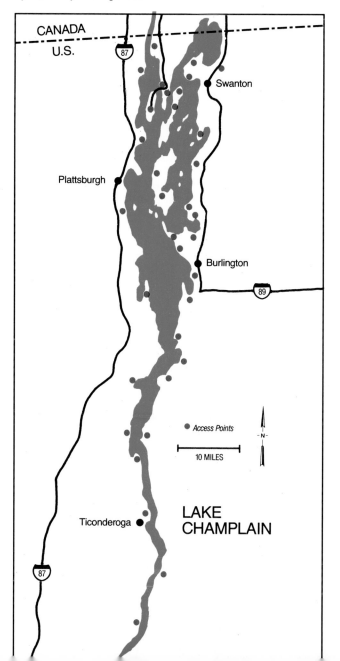

Access Points

10 MILES

LAKE CHAMPLAIN

New River, WV

Imagine one of the celebrated whitewater rivers of the Rockies picked up and set down in the Appalachian hardwood forest. That's exactly what the New River is like: rumbling chutes and falls, many of them rated Class V, for experts only. On a guided trip you can safely float for miles through rocky, roadless gorges, casting for trophy smallmouths wherever you're able to catch your breath. The smallmouths are plentiful, many in the 3- to 5-pound range. Make arrangements with Whitewater Information in Glen Jean, or Rivers Inc. in Lansing. Both use rubber rafts, and Whitewater also has large, comfortable fishing dories imported from the Pacific Northwest. One-day runs are possible, but an overnight trip allows you to fish the prime evening and early morning hours. Most guides encourage catch-and-release fishing; the best ones insist on it. Experienced whitewater canoeists can make a two-day float on their own from Sandstone Falls down to Prince. The small-mouth fishing is good from April through October. Top lures include jigs with grub tails, crawfish-pattern crankbaits, and propbaits.

Connecticut River

Rich Zaleski

In angling circles, the Connecticut River is famed for its spectacular spring run of American shad. Many anglers, in fact, rank this run the best in the country.

But the 350 miles of the Connecticut, pouring from its source in northern New Hampshire to its confluence with Long Island Sound, provide many great fishing opportunities other than shad. Largemouth and smallmouth bass are abundant throughout the river. Walleyes flourish along much of its length, and so do white and channel catfish. Several stretches produce outstanding black-crappie fishing, and a tiger-muskie fishery exists in some of the Vermont-New Hampshire pools.

Perhaps the least recognized of its resources, though, is its northern pike population. Pike occur in much of the river, but the fishing is most consistent in the southernmost stretch: the 45-mile tidal section downstream of the Enfield Dam, in the state of Connecticut. Pike are not usually thought of as brackish-water fish. But Long Island Sound is less salty than the ocean, so salt intrusion into the river is not nearly as great as you might expect. As a result, the Connecticut supports freshwater species everywhere except the last few miles above the mouth.

The pike population in the tidal section has always been good, and since the early 1980s it's been increasing. In five of the last six years, the water levels in early spring have been higher than normal. Thousands of additional acres of marsh have flooded, at precisely the time of year when the pike are seeking out such areas for spawning. Spawning success and fry survival have been tremendous, and the pike population has fairly exploded. In the next few years it should border on fantastic.

The growth rates of the pike have been increasing, too. In four of the past seven years, the freshwater flow has been greater than normal in the summer, so pike have been able to forage in stretches of the tidal section that otherwise would have been too salty for them at that time of year. Traditionally, the tidal section hasn't been known for producing big pike, but the quantity in the 8- to 15-pound range has been good. With the faster growth rates, however, we're looking forward to really big pike—some 20-pounders—starting in 1988.

As any tidewater bass fisherman can confirm, there's something about the brackish environment that builds superb fighting ability into the fish. Certainly that's true of pike. Hook a 10-pound tidewater pike and you'll swear it's a 15-pounder, until you get it in the boat—if you ever do get it in!

Among the most productive pike areas on the tidal section are Wethersfield and Keeney Coves, not far south of Hartford; the islands in and just north of Middletown, and the tributary creeks nearby; the waters around Haddam Meadows State Park, including the Salmon River; and Hamburg Cove, which pretty much marks the downstream limit of the pike's stomping grounds. The warm discharge from the nuclear generator across the river from Haddam Meadows Park is a late-season pike hotspot.

As to tackle and techniques for tidewater pike—if it catches pike anywhere, it'll probably work fine in the Connecticut. Any decent medium- to heavy-action rod and a reel filled with 12- to 17-pound-test line will handle most of the usual pike lures. Spinnerbaits, crankbaits, and live bait are all productive. Most of the regulars on the river rely heavily on lures in bright green or chartreuse.

Live-bait anglers usually opt for large shiners suspended beneath floats. The pike in the Connecticut haven't had

a chance to get familiar with the advanced, European-style methods using natural bait, such as the quick-strike system (see page 73), which some progressive midwestern anglers have adopted in recent years. Sooner or later, someone's going to introduce these methods here, and really clean up.

Like most other fish in rivers, pike position themselves so the current washes food close to them. From their protected lair in a weedbed or behind a log, piling, or other obstruction, they dart into the current to grab a passing meal. Recognize, however, that the tidal effect reverses the current every six hours or so, and the pike reposition themselves accordingly. Bear in mind also that the water level fluctuates 2 to 4 feet with the change of tide. As food-rich marshes are flooded on the high tide, aggressive pike roam far back in the vegetation to feed. Later, as the water recedes, they take up positions in funnel areas, where prey washing out of the marshes is plentiful.

Late in the year, the pike congregate in slack-water coves, and in marinas, boat basins, and other protected areas. Of course a lot of them will lie in and around that warm-water discharge mentioned earlier. I've enjoyed my own best results with late-season pike while fishing light jig heads dressed with small plastic grubs, on 6-pound line. With these lures you'll catch mostly crappies, yellow perch, and bass, but you can also expect to nail a few big pike in the course of a day.

Though the pike have benefitted most from the early-spring flooding, lots of other fish in the tidal environment also offer excellent fishing. Regardless of the time of year, you can enjoy catching one or more of the resident species, or one of the saltwater species that annually invade the river.

For pike, the season is open all year on the tidal section, but early summer and late fall are the most productive times. For largemouths, the fishing is good all summer; for smallmouths, it's usually fastest in early autumn, when the scenery is truly spectacular. Black crappies are most easily found in early spring and mid fall, when they move from the main river into areas with little or no current. White catfish provide good fishing late in the spring and all through the summer, especially during brief high-water periods following storms.

From late April to the end of May, you can sample the shad fishing that brings so many anglers to the Nutmeg State. The shad, which often are aerial battlers, average 5 to 8 pounds, but fish in the 10-pound class aren't uncommon. At any time of year, it's not unusual to hook into a striped bass in the Connecticut; and in late summer, bluefish chase schools of menhaden several miles upriver from the sound. Hanging one or two of these bruisers on freshwater tackle is an experience few anglers ever object to!

Rich Zaleski is the outdoor columnist of the News-Times *in Danbury, Connecticut. His articles have appeared in many national outdoor magazines, and he's working on a book about bass fishing.*

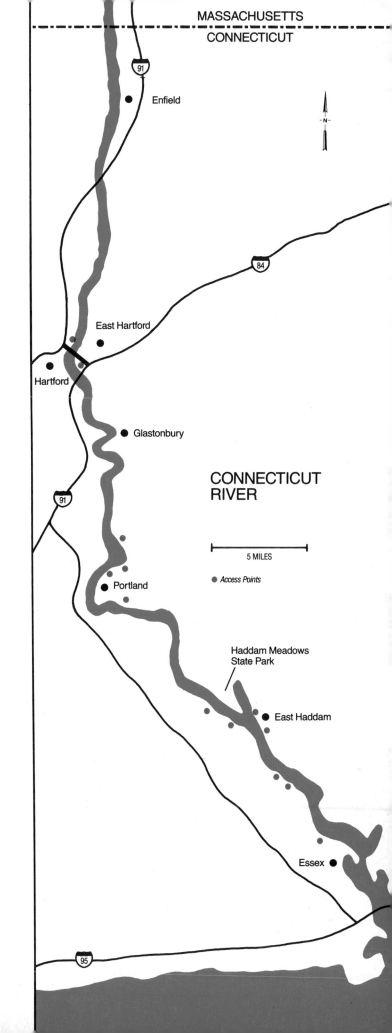

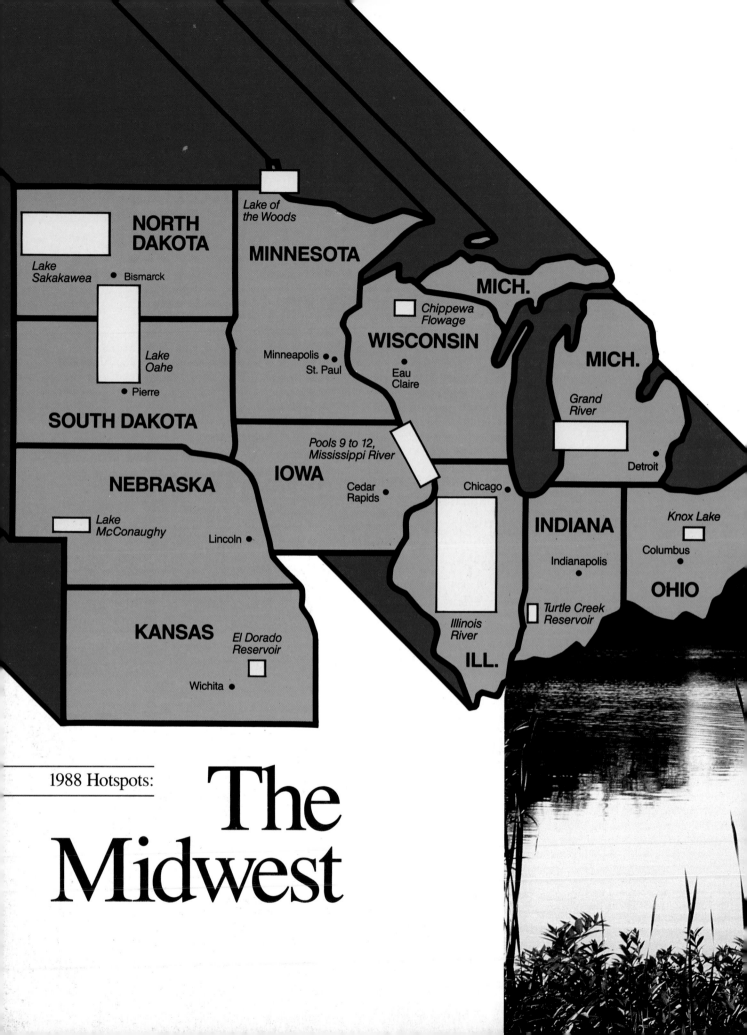

NORTH
DAKOTA

Lake of
the Woods

MINNESOTA

_Lake
Sakakawea_   • Bismarck

MICH.

Chippewa
Flowage

WISCONSIN

_Lake
Oahe_

Minneapolis •
St. Paul

Eau
Claire

MICH.

• Pierre

SOUTH DAKOTA

_Grand
River_

_Pools 9 to 12,
Mississippi River_

IOWA

Detroit

NEBRASKA

Cedar
Rapids

Chicago •

_Lake
McConaughy_

Lincoln •

Knox Lake

INDIANA

Columbus
•

Indianapolis •

OHIO

KANSAS

_El Dorado
Reservoir_

_Illinois
River_

_Turtle Creek
Reservoir_

Wichita •

ILL.

1988 Hotspots:

The
Midwest

The common image of the Midwest as wall-to-wall sweet corn could stand some revision. Of all the regions defined in this book, the Midwest, surprisingly, may offer the most varied opportunities for angling.

It's one thing to drift a hellgrammite for smallmouths in a hill-country creek in Ohio; it's another to slash a 12-inch jerkbait for muskies in a tamarack bog in Wisconsin. And neither of these bears much resemblance to backtrolling a shiner for walleyes in some immeasurable reservoir in the Dakotas; nor to snaking brook trout from a quicksand creek deep in an alder maze in Michigan.

Midwestern angling in all its variety was revealed to the rest of the world as early as 1892, with the publication of Mary Orvis Marbury's *Favorite Flies and Their Histories*. A correspondent from Mechanicsburg, Ohio, reported to Mrs. Marbury that on a "small inland lake … surrounded by spatterdock" his flies had taken 25 pounds of "sunfish, roach, pike, rock bass, and bigmouth black bass," plus "a common *bat,* all in fifty-five minutes, from sundown to dark." Another, from Cleveland, made it clear that catching fish in those days did not depend inordinately on how, or with what, you went about it: "As to theories on the many things connected with fishing implements, I am almost destitute,

as my fishing has been in waters where we could always keep the larder supplied without being compelled to revert to extraordinarily fine work."

In the droll era of Marbury's book, most of the fishing took place in the rivers and creeks. Those flowing waters of the Midwest were still largely unpolluted; and the outboard motor, which later would make fishing in lakes a simple matter, was not yet invented. In our own time, however, reservoirs get much of the attention from midwestern anglers. Though these synthetic lakes too often have been boondoggles that needlessly wiped out irreplaceable rivers, it's true that many of them have created first-rate sport fisheries in locations where angling would otherwise be out of the question. Vast reservoirs like Oahe and Sakakawea are prime cases. In the midst of arid terrain better suited to prairie rattlesnakes than to fish, these waters amount to miniature Great Lakes.

But stream fishing in the Midwest still pays off, too. The midwestern river that hasn't been damaged by some form of pollution—sewage, pesticides, siltation—probably doesn't exist. In the last decade or two, however, many streams once written off for fishing have been rehabilitated. The Illinois River and Michigan's Grand River, both described in the following pages, are examples of the progress seen all across the region.

Illinois River, IL

Pollution cleanup pays off. Not so many years ago, sewage spewed into the Illinois dropped oxygen levels so low in the summers few gamefish could survive. Today, with improved treatment plants, saugers and white bass have come back strong. The saugers are whoppers; fish between 2 and 3 pounds are common, and quite a few over 4 pounds are caught. The Starved Rock State Park, near Utica, is the prime location. On the stretch below the Starved Rock Dam, anglers troll fathead minnows with Lindy rigs, crankbaits, minnow plugs, and Beetle Spins. Shore fishermen take their share by jigging Sonars along the edge of the retaining wall below the dam. The best period for saugers extends from late January into April, with a lesser flurry in the fall. Spring and fall also are best for white bass; there's good action at Starved Rock, but also at many other spots along the 273-mile river. White bass-striper hybrids are abundant, too, with fish over 12 pounds taken. The Illinois also offers largemouths, crappies, bluegills, catfish, and muskies.

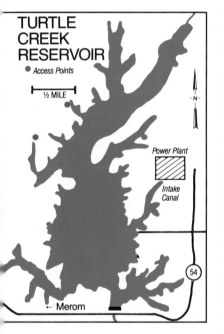

Turtle Creek Reservoir, IN

Eight years old, and a vigorous producer of bass and panfish. This compact reservoir serves a power plant whose warm discharge keeps water open and fishermen in action year round. Crappies win the popularity contest. March through May is the fastest period, then September and October. Work the flooded timber along the old creek channels with minnows and bobbers, or with 1/16- to 1/8-ounce yellow or white marabou jigs tipped with minnows. Jig-and-minnow combinations will take crappies in winter, too, near the discharge canal. Largemouth fishing is also excellent in the lake, owing in part to a two-fish limit and an 18-inch minimum-size restriction. The bass average 2 to 3 pounds; many above 4 pounds are pulled out, and a few over 7. The growth rate is excellent because forage is abundant in the form of threadfin shad. The bass hang out near flooded timber, old roadbeds, and well-established weed growths. Motors are limited to 10 hp, and boat fishing is banned during a few days in summer and throughout the waterfowl hunting season.

Pools 9 to 12, Mississippi River, IA

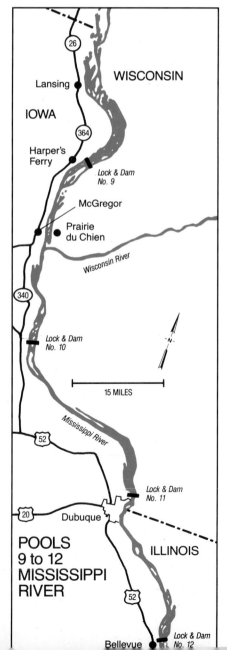

Something for everyone: at least a half dozen different species of gamefish flourish in this long stretch of flatland effluent, some of them above the dams, some below. The premier fishery is for saugers, greatly increasing in numbers the past few years. In size they range from 3/4 to 4 pounds. Anglers flick them from the deep, swirling holes just below the dams, and also from the currents below the smaller wing dams and sandbars farther downstream; the productive depths are 8 to 20 feet. Popular baits include fathead minnows with Lindy rigs, and 1/8- to 1/4-ounce marabou jigs. The action gets under way in late September and lasts through April. Many walleyes are caught, too: same places, baits, and times as for saugers. The largemouth bass angling has also improved greatly, with lots of fish from 12 to 17 inches and quite a few 4-pounders. Bass are found in the stump-studded backwaters of the reservoir pools; so are pike, bluegills, and crappies, all favorites of ice fishermen.

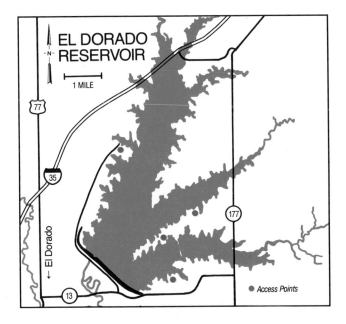

El Dorado Reservoir, KS

This lake is fed by water filtering through native prairie grasslands, rather than the farm-country runoff that loads so many other midwestern reservoirs with fertilizers and silt. It was formed in 1981, and the state has managed it primarily for largemouth bass. Despite heavy fishing pressure, a great deal of it from tournaments, the bass population has held up well by natural reproduction. Last year there were lots of fish just under the 15-inch minimum-size limit. Some 7-pounders have been taken. Much of the good fishing is in the timber left standing along the old creek channels. Timber is also the place for crappies in April and May; angling for this species is extremely productive. Biologists say the big opportunity that anglers neglect at El Dorado is the excellent smallmouth population. Smallmouths are found along the dam, on riprap shorelines near the dam, and around rocky points. Jigs, crankbaits, and live bait will catch them. Despite its newness, El Dorado last year produced the Kansas state record smallmouth of 4 pounds 1 ounce.

Grand River, MI

Whatever fish you want, the Grand can probably supply it in gratifying numbers. A wide variety of warm- and cold-water species have benefitted greatly from a pollution cleanup undertaken a decade ago. A few—such as walleyes and chinook salmon—are now being stocked by the millions each year. Walleyes are abundant throughout the river, but the biggest, up to 10 pounds, are caught on the stretch between Lake Michigan and the first dam in Grand Rapids. Some of these big fish spend the summer in the lake and migrate back into the river in the fall. The most productive angling comes in late April and May, then again in September and October. Bass are numerous, too: largemouths in the frequent backwaters and smallmouths in the deeper upstream eddies, both species hitting well on crankbaits and jigs. The biggest event on the Grand is the fall run of cohos and chinooks, beginning in late August and lasting into October. Some of the salmon migrate as far up as Lansing, leaping several dams and fish ladders along the way. Steelhead run up in spring and fall.

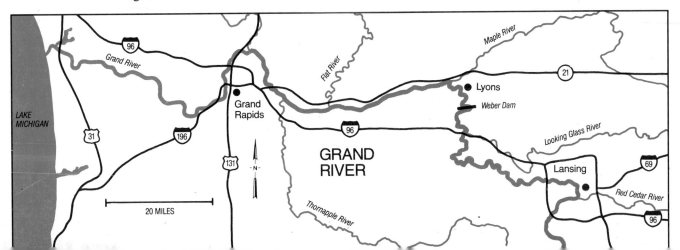

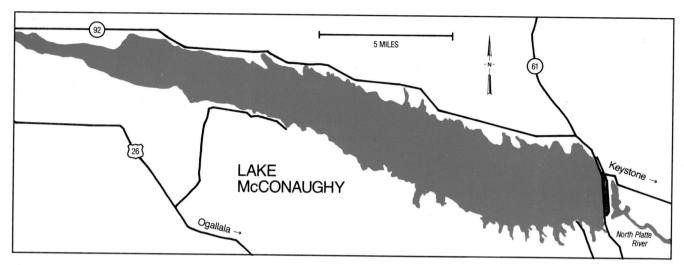

Lake McConaughy, NE

The excellent walleye fishing this lake is known for should continue in 1988. Natural reproduction is good; for many years, no walleyes have been stocked. Fish from the strong year-class of 1983 should make up most of the catch this season; they're expected to run from 1½ to 2 pounds. The best fishing is in May and June. Trolling with minnows on Lindy rigs has proven highly effective. The state has been stocking several different species of forage fish—rainbow smelt, spottail shiners, gizzard shad, and alewives—much to the benefit of the walleyes. Anglers make good catches of suspended fish grazing on the schools of forage, often more than 50 feet deep. Striped bass, like the walleyes, have not been stocked here for many years. McConaughy is one of the few inland waters where any significant natural reproduction of stripers is known to occur. The population isn't large, but the usual size caught is 10 to 20 pounds. The lake does hold a dense population of white bass: fish from the strong 1983 year-class now predominate, ranging from ¾ to 1 pound.

Lake Sakakawea, ND

The big news here is the sauger population, which appears to be peaking. Saugers have been increasing not only in numbers but also in size: 1½- to 3-pound fish are average, and a few over 4 pounds are taken. Anglers do well from ice-out to freeze-up, with the fastest action in April and May, and September through November. Walleyes, though not quite as numerous as in the past, are still doing well in the lake. Some 3 million are stocked in the lower end each year. One especially good spot to catch walleyes is the Van Hook Arm. Chinook salmon are heavily planted in Sakakawea, and good fishing is predicted for 1988; the fish are smaller than in the past, but still average 5 pounds. Two other abundant species are neglected by anglers. Northern pike offer great action in shallow bays on the first warm days of spring; many 25- to 30-pounders showed up last year in state test nets. Smallmouth bass were stocked several years ago, and a sizeable population has been established by natural reproduction. A good spot to find them is right along the dam.

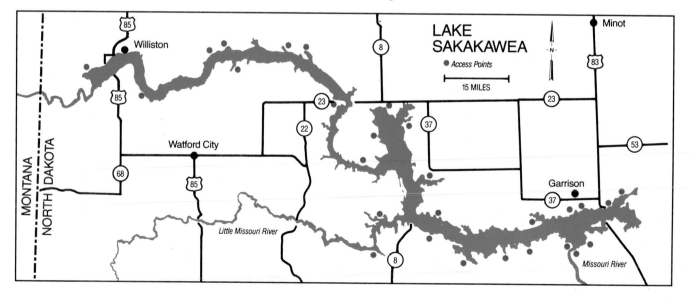

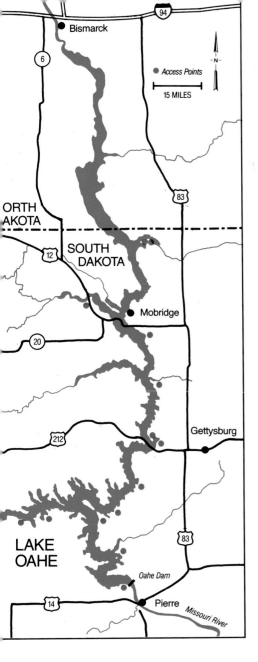

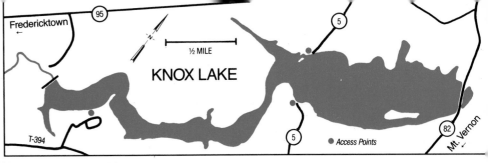

Knox Lake, OH

For the past few years this aging body of water has been given a good rest, thanks to a 16-inch minimum-length limit on its bass. Fishermen had over-harvested the population, leaving only small bass in the lake and not many of those. The new deal began in 1983, and Knox is now turning out more and bigger largemouths than it did for decades. The majority are still below the legal minimum, but there's plenty of action; fish ranging from 2 to 3 pounds are now common, and occasional old residents up to 6 pounds are taken. A good supply of gizzard shad is fueling the growth. Creel censuses indicate that bass fishing at Knox is just as fast in summer as in spring. Summertime bass gravitate to the deep weedbeds and to the remnants of standing timber in the upper end of the lake; crankbaits, spinnerbaits, and plastic worms are effective. Fishing for bluegills is very good, too. With more big bass to control their numbers, bluegills have been growing larger, some going over a pound. Outboard motors on Knox are limited to 10 hp.

Lake Oahe, SD/ND

What makes this lake work is the splintery little smelt. Walleyes, pike, and chinooks all gorge on this abundant forage, packing on the pounds. Limits of walleyes in the 2- to 7-pound range are not unusual. The walleye action warms up in late May, gets really hot in July and August, and continues, a little cooler, after Labor Day. Points and sandbars near shore produce excellent catches. The proven lure is a red, chartreuse, or blue spinner rigged with a night-crawler. Pike fishing is on the upswing, with lots of fish over 10 pounds in the population. For trophies the best time by far is right after the ice goes out in March or April. Effective methods include still-fishing with smelt on quick-strike rigs and casting with Magnum Rapalas. Chinooks will be very plentiful in 1988—a foregone conclusion since South Dakota plants approximately a million in the lake each year. In summer chinooks track the smelt through the deep, cool water near the dam, 60 to 120 feet down, where anglers dredge them out with downriggers. In fall they move into shallower bays.

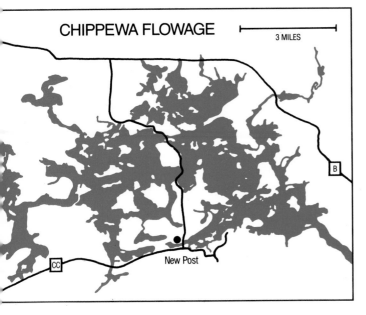

Chippewa Flowage, WI

Biologists who have netted in this impoundment believe no other waters anywhere have a denser population of walleyes. They estimate fifteen to twenty adult walleyes per acre—an enormous number of fish, considering there are 15,000 acres in all. And the nets have turned up some 12- to 14-pounders, measuring as much as 34 inches. Angling is best in spring and fall, around river mouths and along gravelly and rocky shores; the favorite lure is a jig tipped with a minnow. In summer, the walleyes sulk under floating bogs or in weeds and stumps, where leeches or nightcrawlers on slip-bobbers will tempt them. Muskie fishing is top-notch, too. Fingerlings are stocked every year, and many anglers are aiding the fishery by releasing their catches. Early in the summer, bucktails and jerkbaits worked above fresh weed growths are most effective; in midsummer, switch to surface plugs and fish around weeds and stumps from sunset till an hour after dark; in autumn, work jerkbaits slowly along rocky shorelines.

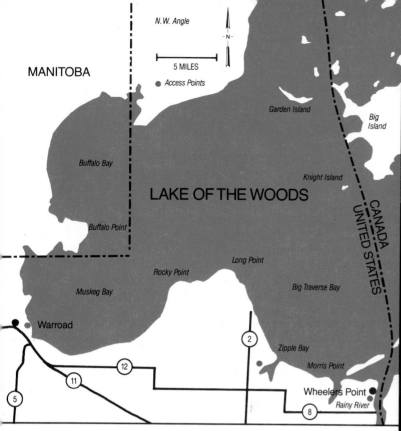

LAKE OF THE WOODS

1988 Hotspots:

Lake of the Woods

Denny Geurink

Big: that's one way to describe Lake of the Woods in northwestern Minnesota. Ninety miles long and 55 miles wide, it's the largest body of fresh water in the U.S. outside the Great Lakes. And with countless pine-covered islands and hundreds of scenic bays, it's a wilderness lake of exceptional beauty. But size and good looks aren't what makes it one of the year's top angling prospects.

Lake of the Woods actually is an international lake shared by Minnesota with Manitoba and Ontario. It boasts excellent populations of big walleyes, muskies, northern pike, and smallmouth bass. But officials estimate that over 95 percent of the fishing pressure is concentrated on the walleyes. The walleye fishing has always been good, and it's been getting even better since Minnesota put the gill-netters out of business in 1985. (Gill-netting is still allowed in Ontario waters, but efforts are under way to curtail it.)

"We have some of the best fishing and biggest fish you ever saw, since they took the gill nets out," says Gary Roach, an avid Minnesota angler and prominent walleye authority. "We always did have good walleye fishing here, but when the state bought out the gill-netters the size and quantity of fish really improved. This year should be great for big walleyes."

Roach considers the mouth of the Rainy River one of the best spots on the lake to catch a big walleye. "Especially in April, just before the season goes out, you can catch some big pre-spawn fish in the river. A lot of 4- to 7-pounders are taken at this time of year, along with a number of fish 10 pounds and over."

The Rainy is also an excellent spot right after the season opens in May. Other good spring bets include the shallows near Zippel Bay, Morris Point, Warroad, and Willow Creek. Roach recommends jigs, crankbaits, spinnerbaits, and live-bait rigs at this time of year.

In June, the walleyes move farther out into the lake. Anglers begin scoring near Rocky Point, Long Point, Knight Island, and Garden Island. By the time July rolls around, the fish have migrated into deeper water off the sunken reefs in Big Traverse Bay. On these midsummer hotspots, anglers have been scoring heavily with downriggers the past few years. In fact, most consider July and August the top two walleye months on Lake of the Woods.

In the fall, the walleyes head back into shallower water. By October they're close to shore again, feeding near the rocky ledges and sandy beaches, prime targets for the jig-and-live-bait crowd. A fine winter fishery is also available to anglers willing to brave the elements.

The art of downrigging for walleyes is rapidly gaining popularity on Lake of the Woods. One of the area's most successful downrigger enthusiasts is Tony Beckel from the Sportsman's Lodge in Baudette. "We've been using downriggers for quite a while now," he says. "They work out well on our charters. We can fish more lines—on the Minnesota side each person is allowed two lines while trolling under power—and we have better control of our baits. We can troll them right over the reefs at the proper depths."

Beckel feels that July and August are the best months to tap into big walleyes. "One day last summer we had a stringer of twelve fish that weighed 109 pounds. We take a lot of fish from 6 to 10 pounds in the summer, and have taken several 14-pounders. I think a state-record walleye will come out of here in the next summer or two, especially since gill-netting has stopped."

Beckel likes to troll in 30 to 40 feet of water, from 15 to 30 feet down. He catches most of his fish over reefs in Big Traverse Bay, trolling 25 feet down. Top walleye baits on Lake of the Woods include Shad Raps, Rapalas, Rebels, and Bass-N-Shads.

While walleyes are the bread-and-butter fish, this sprawling, 2,000-square-mile body of water also boasts fine sauger, northern pike, muskie, and smallmouth bass angling.

"Northern pike, especially, are in good supply," says Mike Larson, a Minnesota Department of Natural Resources fisheries supervisor, stationed in Baudette. "We have good trophy potential for pike, but most of them are caught incidentally to walleye fishing. Not many people go strictly for pike. The fishery is very underutilized."

The same goes for muskie and smallmouth bass, says Larson. "While we don't have as many muskies as they do in Canadian waters, we do have enough to provide a trophy fishery. In fact, we raised the minimum size limit to 40 inches last year, because we have so many fish in the 30-inch class. But they're hardly fished at all. In the case of smallmouth bass, we don't have a lot of them, but we do have an expanding population. Very few people go after them."

Anglers interested in catching these species will find northerns all along the lake's shoreline (the best bets in Minnesota waters are the weedy coves in Muskeg Bay south of Buffalo Point, and Zippel Bay), muskies along the Northwest Angle, and smallmouths in the southeastern corner of Minnesota waters.

Saugers are caught in the same places as walleyes and are generally incidental to walleye catches. But a good fishery for saugers does exist in Big Traverse Bay during the winter, when they become a target species. Good fishing for jumbo perch up to 14 inches and for sturgeon is also available.

Minnesota's regulations for Lake of the Woods are liberal. The walleye season closes for only a month— approximately April 15 till May 15. The pike and bass seasons don't close at all, and the muskie season was recently extended to run from June 20 to November 30. Possession limits are equally liberal. An aggregate limit of twenty fish has been set for walleyes and saugers, but no more than ten may be walleyes. Northern pike and bass limits are six each, and the muskie limit is one.

Anglers interested in fishing the lake on their own will find several public launch sites, including one right at the mouth of the Rainy River. Many lodges also allow unguided anglers to launch for a small fee. For maps and more information on fishing, launch sites, and licenses, contact the Minnesota Department of Natural Resources, Baudette Area Office, Route 1, Box 1001, Baudette, MN 56623; telephone (218) 634-2522.

Anglers who would rather hook up with a guide, stay at a lodge, or fish with a charter captain will find numerous options available. Combination lodging and fishing packages can be arranged. A typical package, offered by Beckel and the Sportsman's Lodge—phone (800) 328-0318 out of state, (800) 862-8602 in state—includes three nights' lodging, two days of fishing, and meals, for $210 per person. For more information on lodging, charters, guide services, and camping, contact the Baudette/Lake of the Woods Chamber of Commerce, Box 659, Baudette, MN 56623; telephone (218) 634-1351.

Anglers fishing Lake of the Woods from Minnesota should be aware of the international boundary, advises Larson. "Use your maps and charts to make sure you stay in Minnesota waters. Unless you have an Ontario or Manitoba license, you'll get into trouble."

Anglers can, of course, purchase Manitoba and Ontario licenses, and when fishing Canadian waters they must abide by local possession limits. For walleyes, the limit is six fish in Ontario and eight in Manitoba. Also, anglers fishing in Ontario but not staying there must purchase an angler validation tag for $3 daily. Both provinces offer excellent fishing opportunities, especially Ontario.

For more information on fishing the Canadian waters of Lake of the Woods, call Ontario Travel at (800) 268-3735 or Travel Manitoba at (800) 665-0040.

Baudette pamphlets proclaim Lake of the Woods the "walleye capital of the world." Anglers have always wondered whether this is true or just a lot of hyperbole. Looks as if 1988 will be a good year to find out.

Denny Geurink is the Midwest regional editor of Field & Stream *magazine. His weekly columns on fishing, hunting, and camping are syndicated in seventeen newspapers.*

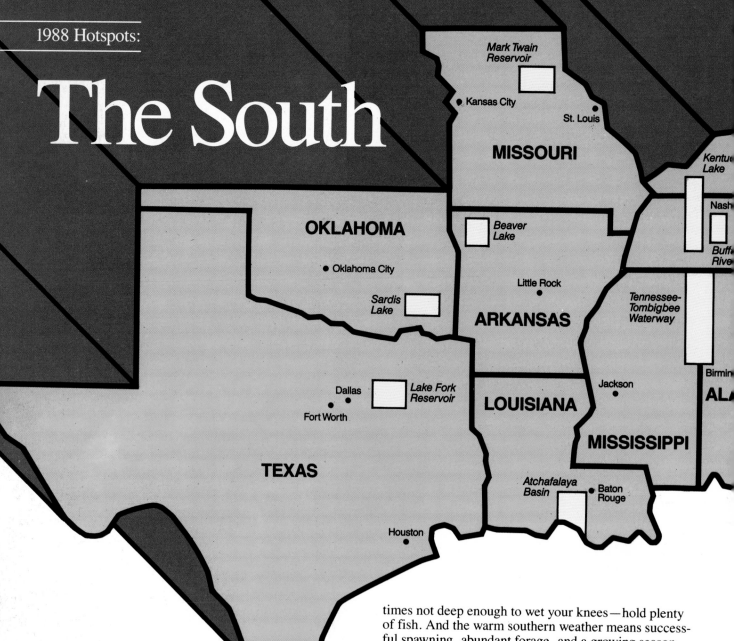

The South

times not deep enough to wet your knees—hold plenty of fish. And the warm southern weather means successful spawning, abundant forage, and a growing season that almost never ends.

Not that the fish are always easy to catch. In most of the South they're active year round, but so are the fishermen—among them the refugee flocks of winter, who seem to many resident anglers less like snowbirds than circling buzzards. Fish that see lures flying overhead all year are not so gullible as those that get a long annual respite. Southern largemouths, for example, may be ravenous and plentiful, but nonetheless pose a real challenge.

Many northerners imagine the South has nothing but warm-water angling. But it also offers a good amount of trout fishing. Along the Appalachian spine all the way down into Georgia, stocked rainbows and browns inhabit the creeks and smaller rivers, while native brook trout hang on in numerous headwater trickles. Acid rain, not to mention acid drainage from coal mines, has severely hurt many of these fisheries. For the most part,

Someday the South will run out of rivers to dam. When it does, all the gentry subsisting on tournaments, boats, and tackle will taste a strange new reality. Perhaps some later-day promoter with a ten-gallon topper can peddle the idea that gizzard shad are gamefish. Suppose Dr. Juice were to come up with a plankton scent....

In the meantime, there are probably more fish to be caught in the South than anywhere else in the nation. Besides all the reservoirs, there are countless waters that actually came with the country: natural lakes, swamps, sloughs, bayous, sinks, rivers, rivulets. In Florida, even the "prairies"—vast, open wetlands, at

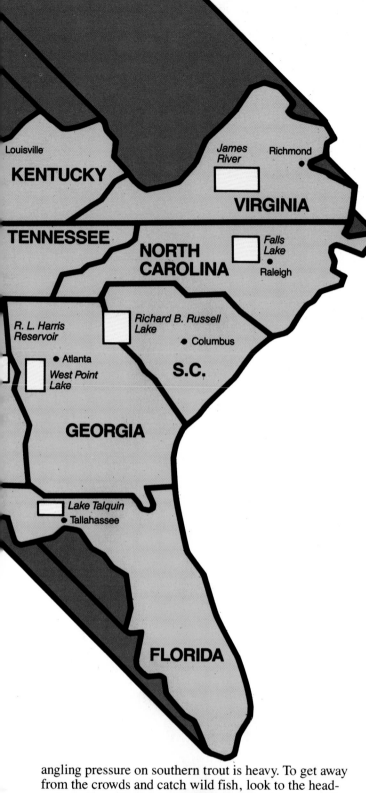

Louisville
KENTUCKY
James River
Richmond
VIRGINIA
TENNESSEE
NORTH CAROLINA
Falls Lake
Raleigh
R. L. Harris Reservoir
Richard B. Russell Lake
Columbus
Atlanta
West Point Lake
S.C.
GEORGIA
Lake Talquin
Tallahassee
FLORIDA

angling pressure on southern trout is heavy. To get away from the crowds and catch wild fish, look to the headwaters. Even there you won't be lonely; but you will find good sport and ample scenic reward if you're willing to do some bushwhacking.

Fishing of all kinds will be better in the South when more anglers start releasing their catches. At present neither the locals nor the visitors seem much inclined to worry about tomorrow. In this, the South is definitely lagging behind other regions. But increasing fishing pressure on many waters is going to make catch-and-release a necessity. Don't wait till regulations are imposed: turn some of your fish loose now, voluntarily.

R. L. Harris Reservoir, AL

Only six years old, this reservoir on the Tallapoosa River has its glory days still ahead of it. Largemouths have been abundant here—overabundant, in fact—but the size has been small and the growth rate sluggish. Now the story is changing for the better. The 14-inch minimum-length limit was lifted in 1986, to pare the population, and threadfin shad were stocked for forage. The shad are taking hold, and now the bass are bulking up. Last year, a number of 8- to 10-pounders came out of the creek arms and from the points and deep standing timber of the main lake. Biologists expect the shad to increase the size of crappies, too. But maybe the best thing about Harris is the elbow room; so far, the fishing pressure has been surprisingly light. The excellent fishing at nearby West Point Lake pulls a lot of anglers away, and the limited launch and overnight facilities at Harris have discouraged some of the tournament crowd.

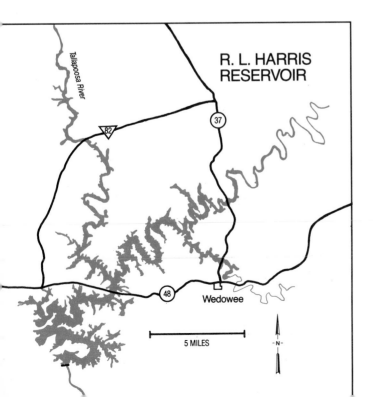

Beaver Lake, AR

Anglers who roam the country in search of striped bass rank this lake among the top three or four. Last spring was the most productive ever on Beaver. And the word from the biologist who knows it best is that stripers should be even bigger and more abundant in 1988. From mid-April to mid-June, they smack 9-inch Red Fins fished on the surface, sometimes homing in from

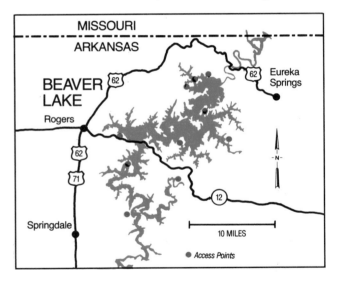

20 feet deep. Live shad hung from bobbers also do the job. In summer, white jigs trolled deep with downriggers are standard fare. By August the stripers collect in the deep pocket of cool water behind the dam; on a graph or LCR you can spot them heaped up like wood shavings. Around the first of October, they fan out once again. According to angling data, they can dash 50 miles up the lake in just two days. Beaver is also one of the best lakes in Arkansas for black bass. Largemouths are plentiful, but spotteds outnumber them two to one. Small Rapalas twitched on the surface work well in spring and fall. During the summer, the spotteds will take smoke-colored twister-tail jigs fished deep in the morning and evening.

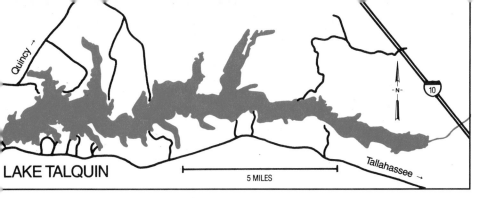

LAKE TALQUIN

5 MILES

Lake Talquin, FL

Here's a reservoir that passed its prime before most of today's anglers were born. By the early 1960s more than half the fish population, by weight, consisted of shad. If a symbol was needed, there was the power plant at the dam—so antiquated it was shut down for keeps in 1970. But in recent years Talquin has turned completely around. The lake has been lowered several times, stimulating plant growth, and the bass and panfish populations have boomed. The most recent management drawdown, late in 1983, was followed by a massive spawn in the spring of 1984. Bass from that year-class have been protected by a slot limit, and this year the females should reach 15 to 18 inches, weighing 3 to 4 pounds. Also, bass older than the drawdown have been growing much faster than before. Still another benefit: bumper crops of panfish, with crappies now weighing between 1 and 2 pounds.

Kentucky Lake KY/TN

One of the largest and most reliable southern reservoirs, and getting even better. Though a few anglers ply the lake all year, most open the season on those damp, warming days when the dogwoods and redbuds ease into flower. In 1988 they should find the largemouths bigger and more plentiful, fish produced a few years ago when the TVA began keeping the lake level up until July. Before then, the water had always been lowered in June, forcing newly hatched bass out of shoreline cover and leaving them vulnerable to predators. Smallmouths are now doing better, too. In recent years the water has gotten clearer, and much of the mud has been washed off the shoreline boulders and gravel, improving habitat for the crayfish that smallmouths feed on. Even the famous Kentucky Lake crappie fishing is looking up. To replace woody cover which has rotted away, heaps of cedar trees and old tires have been submerged. A map showing these attractors is available from the Tennessee Wildlife Resources Agency, in Jackson.

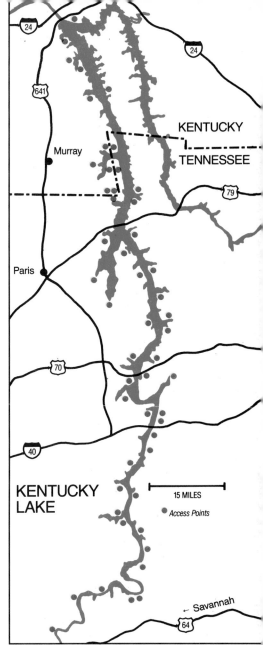

KENTUCKY
TENNESSEE

Murray

Paris

KENTUCKY
LAKE

15 MILES
• Access Points

← Savannah

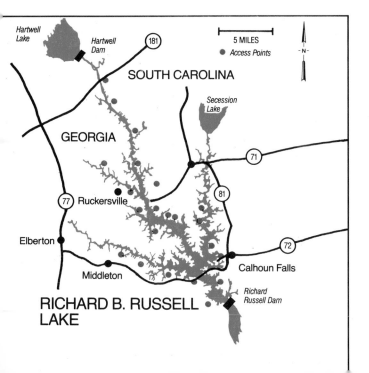

Hartwell
Lake

Hartwell
Dam

181

5 MILES
• Access Points
-N-

SOUTH CAROLINA

Secession
Lake

GEORGIA

71

77 Ruckersville

81

Elberton

72

Calhoun Falls

Middleton

Richard
Russell Dam

RICHARD B. RUSSELL
LAKE

Richard B. Russell Lake, GA/SC

Testimony to the bureaucratic zeal to leave no major water undammed, Russell is a new reservoir sandwiched between two older ones on the Savannah River. It filled in 1984, and the fishing has been everything the managers could have hoped for. Largemouths are flourishing, many in the 3- to 4-pound range and a few up to 8 pounds. Censuses show the catch rate has been four times greater than the average for Georgia reservoirs. Lots of timber was left standing, much of it along the old creek channels, and there's plenty of submerged brush in the shallow water along the shores. In spring, try surface plugs and spinnerbaits near shore in the arms; in summer, jigging spoons and Carolina-rigged worms on points and humps in the main lake; in fall, shallow-running baits along the banks. The tailrace at Russell produces large stripers and striper-white bass hybrids, on cut or live blueback herring. Trout live in the upper end of the lake, some of them stocked there, others settled in from the tailwaters of the Hartwell Dam.

95

Tennessee-Tombigbee Waterway, MS/AL

Aim to get your money's worth: constructed by the Army Corps of Engineers at a cost of nearly $2 billion, the Tenn-Tom has to be the most expensive fishing water in the history of the world. It's 234 miles long, but the bass and crappies are concentrated in a few impounded pools along the way. Columbus Lake, probably the best, has had a slot limit for several years that deflects many anglers to other lakes with looser restrictions. Biologists report that Aberdeen and Aliceville lakes also hold high populations. Nearly all the lakes in the system contain lots of standing timber or stump fields; some, including Columbus and Aliceville, are developing welcome growths of vegetation. Riprap shorelines also produce fish, as do sunken attractors—cedars and brush—marked by buoys. Largemouths run from ¾ to 1½ pounds, with many up to 5 pounds. Among the public benefits of the Tenn-Tom, according to Corps promotional literature, is its proximity to the Elvis Presley birthplace in Tupelo, Mississippi.

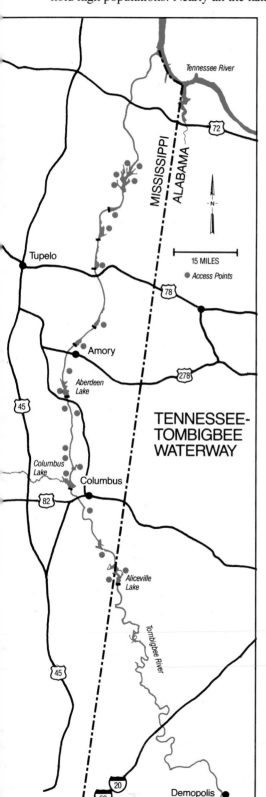

Atchafalaya Basin, LA

The crawfish capital of America—and what's good for the craws is good for the gamefish, too. The Atchafalaya is a vast perplexity of cypress stands, bayous, and pipeline canals. Water diverted from the Mississippi River seeps through the basin, loading it with nutrients and gradually filling it with silt. Year after year the largemouths more than hold their own. Fishing is productive when the water is low; even better when it's slowly dropping. The lower end of the basin has the advantage of clearer water, since much of the silt settles out farther up. Two excellent spots are Duck Lake in the lower end, and Henderson Lake in the upper. But there are plenty of fish—not only largemouths but also spotted bass, crappies, bluegills, and catfish—in countless errant bayous and canals. The largemouths run from 1½ to 2½ pounds, a few up to 5 pounds. Stay alert: the Atchafalaya is a great place to get lost. Newcomers should get a detailed map from the Louisiana Department of Wildlife and Fisheries, and would be wise to hire a guide.

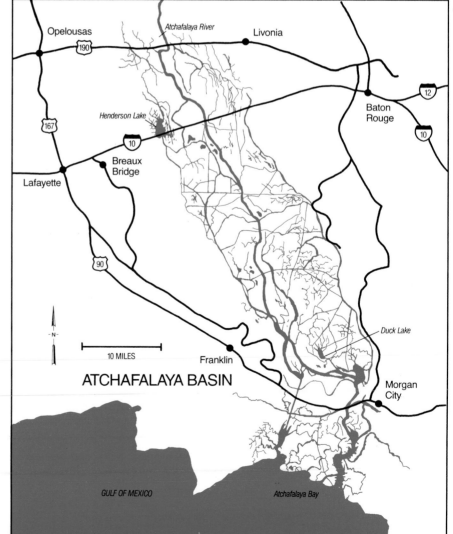

Mark Twain Lake, MO

This year the majority of the walleyes in this new reservoir will be reaching legal size. In 1987 most ran 16 to 17 inches; the minimum for keepers is 18 inches. For three years managers stocked walleye fry by the millions, and have now called a halt to see whether the population will sustain itself. The lake has all the right stuff: limestone outcrops along shore, and plenty of points, submerged ledges and old roadbeds, even standing timber. The most productive period should be late April through June, though spring rains can make the water too roily at times. A spawning run takes place in the tributaries in April and early May. Local walleye aces report that practically anything works: Rapalas, crankbaits, jigs with fathead minnows, Lindy rigs with crawlers or leeches. There's also good angling for largemouths. For now, the bass hang around sunken brush, rock piles, and roadbeds; but weed lines are becoming established. Mark Twain is loaded with crappies, too; lots of them this year should top a pound.

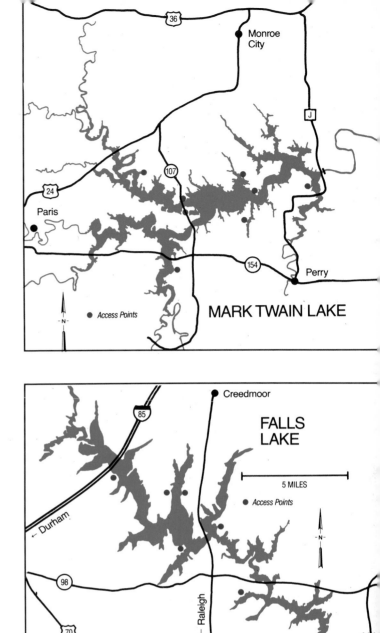

Falls Lake, NC

A young reservoir on the Piedmont, with implants of artificial weeds, discarded Christmas trees, and rubber reefs. Bass fishing at Falls should continue hot in 1988. The Corps of Engineers leased the lake floor to North Carolina, whose fisheries managers had plenty of ideas on how to furnish it. Scout troups and other volunteers have done most of the heaving and hauling. The added cover is marked with buoys, and some of it can be fished from shore. Fishing pressure has been heavy at Falls, but success remains high. The shallow water above the Route 50 bridge gets hit harder than the deeper water below. In the upper section the water spreads out wide, and because of its higher fertility it holds more bass. The lower section is narrow and twisting, with shoals and steep outcrops, and the fish generally are larger. Angling is best from March through May and again in October and November. Favorite lures are plastic worms in red shad, moccasin, and crawdad colors.

Sardis Lake, OK

First, a bit of local history, in the poker-faced prose of an Army Corps of Engineers leaflet: "Sardis Lake is named for a rural community which it inundated." Anglers are faring much better than the former townsfolk. Here, while contemplating the Winding Stair Mountains and the gentle Potato Hills, they cull out limit catches of largemouths, most weighing 1½ to 2½ pounds but many in the 3- to 7-pound class. Sardis was stocked with both native and Florida strains of largemouths, and also with spotted bass. It was flooded in three stages over a three-year period, filling completely in 1985. The idea was to stretch out the period of maximum bass reproduction, and it seems to have paid off superbly. Anglers take bass all year but do best in April, May, September and October. There's also a good crappie population, plus legions of channel cats whiskering their way along the scrubby bottom.

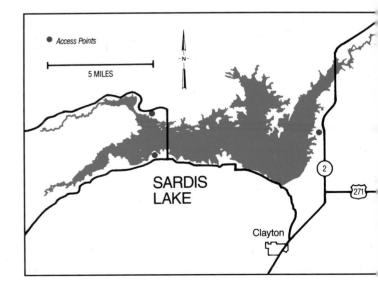

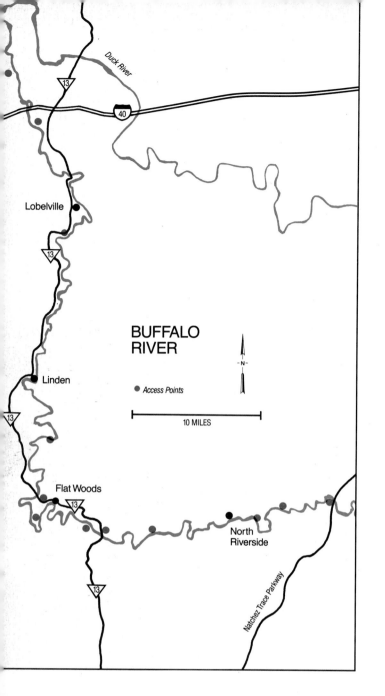

Buffalo River, TN

This waterway may look crowded, but really it's not. All those people thudding past in canoes are mere canoeists: you'll spot plenty of six-packs, but seldom a rod. The pools and eddies hold good numbers of small-mouths, not much alarmed by the spectral Grummans. Naturally, a float trip by canoe or light johnboat is the best way to fish the lower Buffalo. The stretch from Flat Woods down to Linden is scenic as well as productive, and so is the much longer stretch from Linden on down to the confluence with the Duck River. Canoes are available from the Buffalo River Canoe Rental, in Flat Woods. You can wade to the smallmouths, too. Try the headwaters stretch above the Natchez Trace Parkway; the posted signs are mainly for deer hunters, and most landowners will let you fish if you ask. The best time for Buffalo smallmouths is mid-May to mid-June. Use 4- or 6-pound mono, with small Rapalas, A.C. Shiners, or spinners.

Lake Fork Reservoir, TX

This eight-year-old lake has it all: tire reefs, flooded timber, and the Texas state-record largemouth. Texas is tops for bass waters right now, and Lake Fork may top them all. From the start, the Sabine River Authority and the Texas Parks and Wildlife Department plotted to make this the perfect bass hole. Large tracts of timber were left uncut, Florida-strain fingerlings and brood stock were planted, and the lake was filled in stages over five years to enhance spawning. Also, a five-fish limit was imposed, first with a 14-inch minimum and later a 14-to 18-inch slot restriction. Today, Lake Fork turns out tons of bass. Four-pounders are common, and plenty of trophies are boated. The state record, a 17-pound 10-ounce fish taken in 1986, is probably one of the breeders planted early on. Most catches are made on plastic worms and lizards, and on jigs with plastic tails. Crappies, bluegills, and redears also abound; an estimated quarter-million crappies have been caught here in a single spring.

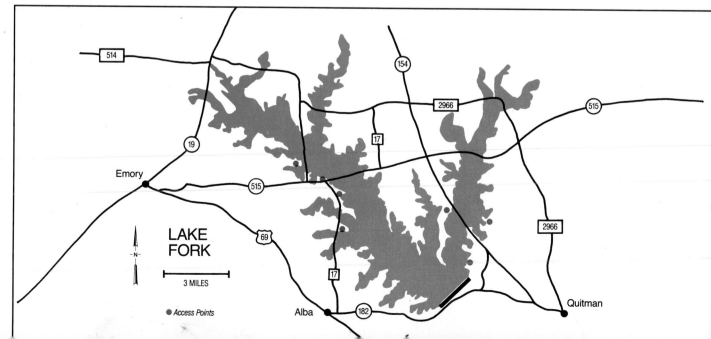

James River, VA

Classic smallmouth water, set amid soft-focus forests and farmlands recollecting the early days of the republic. Smallmouth fishing on the James has always been good, and lately has been picking up. Water quality has improved following the environmental movement of the early 1970s, and an 11- to 14-inch slot limit has been established. Trophies are plentiful: more than 300 smallmouths over 4 pounds have been reported to the state's awards program in a single season. Canoes and johnboats are generally used, but wading anglers can find access, too. A number of the regulars on the river use float tubes to work through the deeper pools with live bait.

The entire 212-mile stretch from Eagle Rock to Richmond is the kind of water that can make you cry if you live somewhere else. The upper part, as far down as Snowden, tumbles through mountainous terrain. At places like Balcony Falls the drops can be treacherous. For those making overnight trips, the U.S. Forest Service has established several no-frills campsites, float-in only. Farther down, the river grows broader and milder with occasional islands braiding the flow. Several recommended runs are Howardsville to Scottsville, Scottsville to Hardware River, Hardware to Bremo Bluff, Bremo to Columbia, and Beaumont Landing to Watkins Landing.

Access sites are numerous from top to bottom, and there are several canoe liveries: one that's close to lots of good water is James River Runners in Scottsville. Some outfitters rent camping equipment, too. Smallmouth guide service is available; check with Van Doren's Orvis Shop in Richmond. Favorite lures for smallmouths include 3/8-ounce spinnerbaits, 1/8-ounce grub-tail jigs, and Tiny Torpedos. The most effective live baits, bar none, are madtoms; also good are hellgrammites and minnows. Fly fishing with streamers is productive; good patterns are Zonkers and Marabou Muddlers in size 2 or 4.

Below Richmond, the James metamorphoses into a slow-pouring tidal river, with excellent fishing for largemouths and sometimes for stripers.

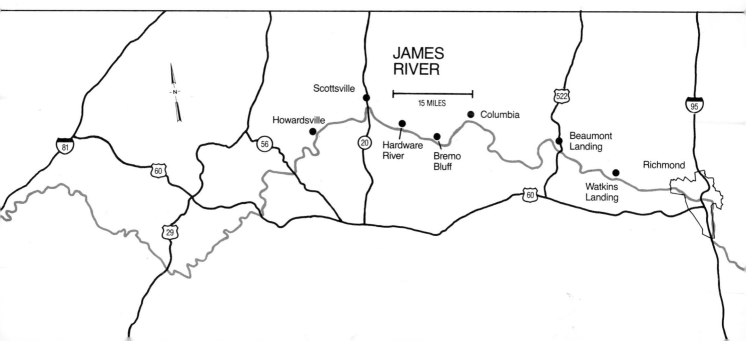

JAMES RIVER

15 MILES

Scottsville

Howardsville

Columbia

Beaumont Landing

Hardware River

Bremo Bluff

Richmond

Watkins Landing

West Point Lake

Steve Price

Few bodies of water have ever surprised bass fishermen as much as West Point Lake, a 26,000-acre reservoir on the Chattahoochee River of Alabama and Georgia. Today, thirteen years after impoundment, rather than slowing down as reservoirs generally do, West Point is producing more and larger bass than ever before.

West Point's claim to fame is not the maximum size of its largemouths (the lake record is a 13½-pounder taken in early 1987), but the numbers caught between 5 and 8 pounds. The best ten-bass stringer local guide Gordon Elkins has ever brought in, for example, weighed 85 pounds, but that was just one of eleven times his ten-fish limit has topped 70 pounds.

For visiting anglers as well, such heavy stringers aren't just dreams, because West Point is a relatively easy lake to fish. With a little consideration of seasonal patterns and a few minutes studying a lake map, a newcomer should be able to locate bass fairly quickly.

The lake not only provides excellent fishing, but also offers beautiful scenery. Cradled by gentle pine-clad hills, it has virtually no commercial or residential development along the shorelines. Instead, anglers frequently see whitetail deer swimming across the shallow coves, and occasionally wild turkeys slipping along the secluded beaches. Ospreys are seen, too, and sometimes even bald eagles.

Located near the cities of West Point, Georgia, and Lanett, Alabama, West Point was impounded late in 1974. On the same river with famous Lake Eufaula, a lake renowned for its trophy bass, West Point was expected to produce similar outstanding action. It did, too, but only for a short time.

Severe fishing pressure, combined with an extremely poor spawn, turned West Point off by 1977. Anglers continued trying to harvest the original 1975 year-class of bass. Meanwhile, gizzard shad, the primary forage species, outgrew the few younger bass and forced them out of living space.

Hybrid striped bass were introduced into the lake in 1978 to help control the shad, and a 16-inch minimum size limit was later imposed on largemouths. The results were spectacular, and during the past several years West Point has rebounded better than most dared hope. The hybrids have fed on the larger shad, while the size limit has allowed the largemouths to spawn at least once before being harvested.

Since there's little cover along the shorelines, the most successful largemouth anglers have learned to fish the edges of the old creek channels in the arms of the lake. These channels are lined with submerged timber.

During impoundment, the Army Corps of Engineers allowed the lake to rise to an elevation of 619 feet, at which time all the timber in it was cut off at the water line. Then the lake was allowed to rise 16 additional feet, to full pool. This not only provided for safer boating, but also left plenty of habitat for the fish below.

Anglers often begin fishing the underwater trees at the entrance of an arm, then gradually work their way up the arm along the old creek channel. Depth finders are extremely useful, making it possible to pinpoint the timber edges and channel drops where the bass are most likely to be. Fishing depths vary, depending on seasonal water levels. The treetops may be as deep as 16 feet at full pool, or may be practically on the surface when the lake is drawn down in winter.

The most popular lure for creek timber fishing on West Point is the plastic worm. Anglers rig it Texas-style with a ⅛- to ⅜-ounce slip sinker, and fish it with a slow crawl through the underwater branches. Jigging spoons are also used, for vertical fishing through the branches. And deep-diving crankbaits will take bass when worked in the openings close to the edges of the timber. The creek timber is productive through most of the year, though the lures change slightly, pig-and-jigs taking the place of worms during the colder months.

Other excellent spots are the flats or gently sloping terraces extending from the shorelines out to the creek timber. These flats have been bulldozed of all cover and may be broad or narrow, depending on the width of the creek arm. In warm weather they produce good catches, as long as water is being pulled through the West Point Dam for power generation. The current draws baitfish onto the flats and the bass follow, moving out of the creek timber and into 7 to 10 feet of water, even during the hottest part of the day.

Here, the best lure is a deep-diving crankbait, cast across the flats and retrieved in the direction of the current. Anglers usually hold their boats out in deeper water, casting up into the shallows.

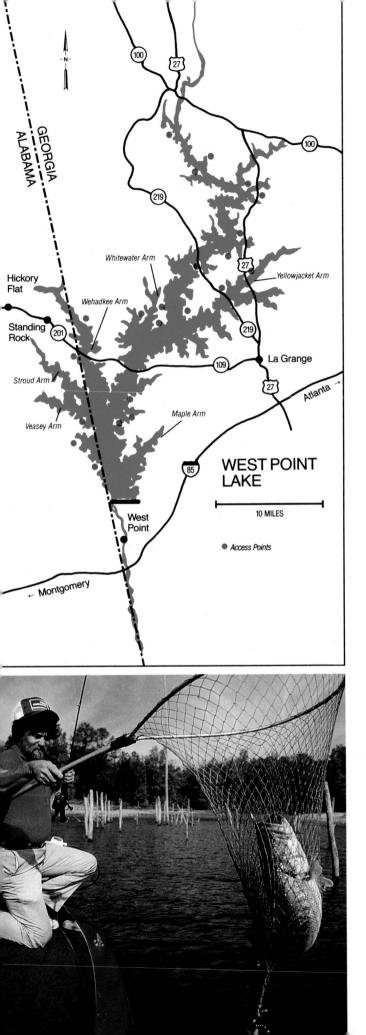

Year after year, the most productive creek arms are Maple, Veasey, Stroud, and Wehadkee, all located on the lower part of the lake. The Whitewater and Yellowjacket arms offer excellent fishing in the upper part. The Georgia Route 109 bridge crosses the lake near its middle, and is usually the reference point for directions.

When West Point was impounded, several roads were flooded, and their submerged embankments frequently offer excellent largemouth fishing in the spring and summer. They're easily located by studying the shorelines, a map, and a depth finder. Old State Line Road across the entrance of the Veasey Creek arm is a favorite spot, as are old Route 109 near the Yellowjacket arm, and Potts Road in the Maple Creek arm.

The hybrid stripers also support a productive fishery. These fish, a cross between striped bass and white bass, are plentiful now and attain weights around 15 pounds. They move gradually up and down the lake with the seasons. In the spring, they're found far up the Chattahoochee River, trying to spawn in the running water. By midsummer, they're often schooling at the mouths of the Yellowjacket and Whitewater arms. And by fall, they're farther down the lake in the Maple Creek region.

Throughout the year, the favorite lures for hybrids are shad-imitation sinking plugs, bucktail jigs, and tailspins. All these are fished in much the same way—first allowed to sink, then worked in quick hops and jumps off the bottom. This isn't the usual way to fish a sinking plug like a Rat-L-Trap, but it works well on West Point.

A pleasant aspect of visiting West Point is that fishing can easily be combined with camping or other outdoor recreation. The Corps of Engineers has constructed launching ramps and recreation areas along both the Georgia and Alabama shores. Several of these areas have campgrounds, swimming beaches, and even fishing piers for those without boats.

There are only two marinas on the lake, Highland Marina (P.O. Box 1644, La Grange, GA 30241) and Burnt Village Park (Rt. 4, Box 385, Lanett, AL 36863). Both offer camping, picnicking, boat launching, and convenience stores. Guide service costs about $200 per day, and can usually be arranged through either marina.

Lake maps, as well as information on additional accommodations and attractions in the area, are available from the Greater Valley Area Chamber of Commerce, P.O. Box 205, in Lanett.

A brochure describing West Point Lake is available from the Resource Manager, U. S. Army Corps of Engineers, P. O. Box 574, West Point, GA 31833-0574.

Alabama fishing licenses are valid only below the Georgia Route 109 bridge; Georgia licenses are valid on the entire lake, including the Alabama waters.

Steve Price is a freelance outdoor writer and photographer who lives in Alabama. His two books are World Championship Bass Fishing *and* Wild Places of the South.

The West

Exactly fifty years ago, when Dan Bailey said good-bye to the sidewalks of New York and opened his fly shop in the sooty railroad and sawmill town of Livingston, Montana, no one could have known such an unassuming venture would become not only an internationally famous institution, but also an inspiration.

The country had not yet recovered from the Depression, and trout fishing was scarcely considered a gold mine. Back in the city, Bailey had been teaching at the Brooklyn Polytechnic Institute and working toward a doctorate in physics; but after a honeymoon angling jaunt to Montana, he decided to abandon all that. One hesitates to feed contemporary bootstrap fantasies, yet the fact is that against very long odds Bailey made his fly-tying business a success. Local trade was modest at best, so he printed a catalog and established a profitable flies-by-mail operation. And in time, since his shop was lyrically situated amid some of the finest trout waters on the continent, it became a kind of boondocks Canterbury for fly fishermen everywhere.

Beyond that, other anglers trout-lorn like Bailey and encouraged by his example have packed up and moved west themselves, determined that fishing would somehow foot the bill. These were square pegs who schemed they could write about the sport in books and magazines (some of whom actually could, and did); others who learned enough about the streams to work at least part-time as guides; and not a few who opened fly shops of their own in fetid cowtowns and subalpine tourist traps.

There's no denying the West comes closer than other regions of the country to realizing the ideal of untouched fishing, the way it was before the notion of Manifest Destiny started messing things up. Alaska has lakes and streams where the ideal remains a fact: no one has yet flown, slogged, or floated in to them and wet a line. In Montana, Wyoming, and other mountain states, certain wilderness waters may go unfished from one year to the next. And even where angling pressure is great, productivity very close to that of virgin waters is often maintained by special regulations.

Also, trout and other salmonids aren't the only game available. The heaviest largemouth bass in recent years have come not from Florida but from California; striper angling is first-rate in numerous desert impoundments; and some of the fastest walleye fishing anywhere awaits in those vast, lonesome reservoirs of the high northern plains.

Other parts of the nation all have their particular allure for anglers; still, have you heard of any westerners who moved eastward to find better fishing? Perhaps that tells the tale.

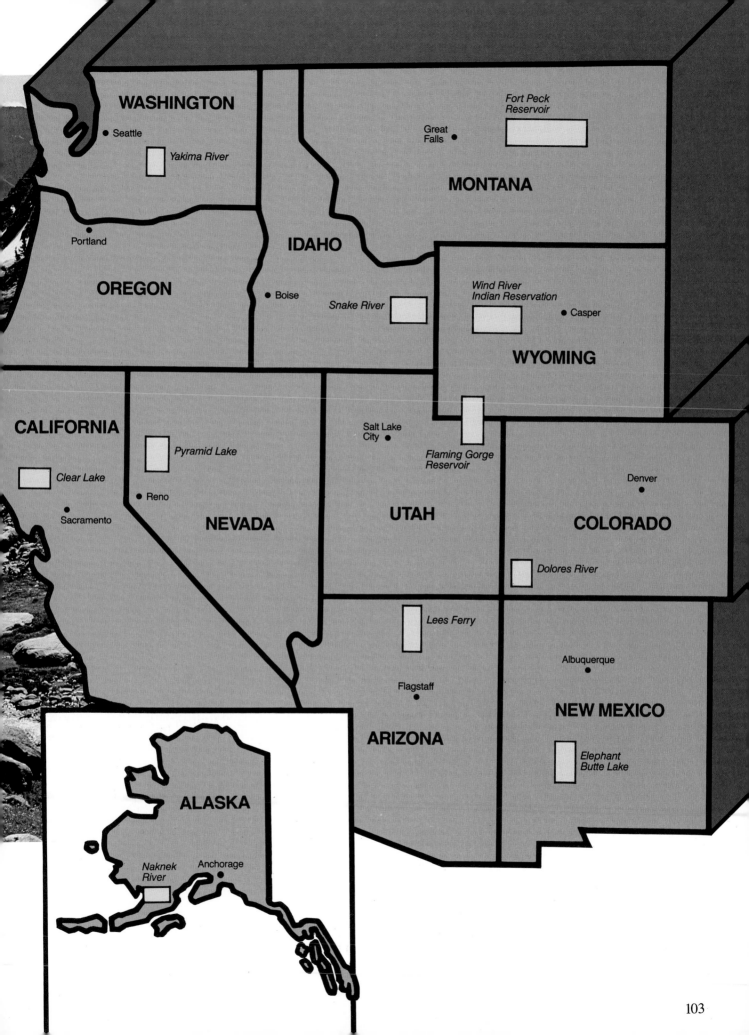

WASHINGTON

● Seattle

Yakima River

Portland ●

OREGON

IDAHO

Boise ●

Snake River

MONTANA

Great
Falls ●

Fort Peck
Reservoir

Wind River
Indian Reservation

Casper ●

WYOMING

CALIFORNIA

Clear Lake

Pyramid Lake

● Reno

Sacramento ●

NEVADA

Salt Lake
City ●

UTAH

Flaming Gorge
Reservoir

Denver
●

COLORADO

Dolores River

Lees Ferry

Flagstaff ●

ARIZONA

Albuquerque
●

NEW MEXICO

Elephant
Butte Lake

ALASKA

Naknek
River

Anchorage ●

103

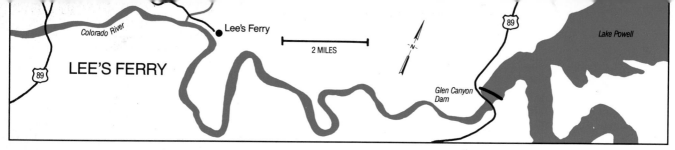

Lee's Ferry, AZ

The lower Colorado River, where canyon temperatures soar above 100° in the summer, may seem the last place on earth to look for trout. But rainbows flourish in several miles of clear, supercooled water flowing from the basement of Lake Powell, and anglers can enter the canyon via the launch site at Lee's Ferry. The angling here peaked several years ago, then dropped off when pressure became too great. Now it's on the rebound, thanks to new regulations. Only artificial lures are permitted, and the limit is four fish per day. Last year saw a myriad of smaller trout — 10 to 12 inches — which by 1988 will be hefty enough to snap plenty of tippets. The trout feed heavily on scuds, and the favorite fly is a scud imitation with one or two 3/0 split-shot on the leader. Many anglers use boats, but those on foot can wade the gravel bars along a 2-mile stretch. Fishing is best when the water is low — generally in early morning and at evening, when power generation at the dam is reduced. Spring and fall are the most productive seasons, and also the most comfortable.

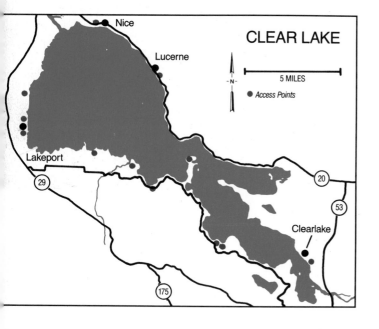

Clear Lake, CA

California's biggest natural lake, producing many of its biggest bass. Ten-pound largemouths are not uncommon, and five-fish limits over 30 pounds are frequently weighed in at tournaments. A Clear Lake bass just under 14 pounds was the heaviest ever caught in a sanctioned tournament anywhere. Because of its size, the lake has been less affected by fishing pressure than the famed but comparatively small reservoirs near San Diego. In the spring, bass move into the shallower waters which warm up first, especially the channels carved into lakefront residential areas. Piers and pilings attract lots of fish, as do flooded willows and beds of tules. In the summer, bass settle below the 10-foot contour, and fishermen use depth finders to work deep points and rock piles. In the fall, the action returns to the shallows. Top lures on the lake are white and chartreuse spinnerbaits, and a variety of darker-colored lures: brown jigs, sometimes with pork strips; brown, black, and purple plastic worms; and crawfish-pattern crankbaits.

Dolores River, CO

Until the McPhee Reservoir was formed a few years ago, the stretch of the Dolores that now lies downstream of it sometimes ran dry. Today the reservoir ensures a steady flow, and the river has transformed into a highly reliable trout stream. The U.S. Forest Service and the Colorado Division of Wildlife have trucked in boulders to create more cover for the fish, and planted willows and cottonwoods to stabilize the banks. Fishing on the 11-mile stretch where this work was done is restricted to catch-and-release, artificials only. The trout — cutthroats, rainbows, and browns — ran from 10 to 16 inches last year, and occasional prodigies up to 4 pounds were caught. Slow and slick, the water demands a catlike approach. Small dry flies and nymphs, size 16 and 18, are usually most effective, copying the tiny mayflies and caddisflies now abundant here. Grasshopper and ant patterns also produce when the naturals appear in summertime. Frost-hardy anglers can match the hatches of midges and *baetis* mayflies on bright winter afternoons.

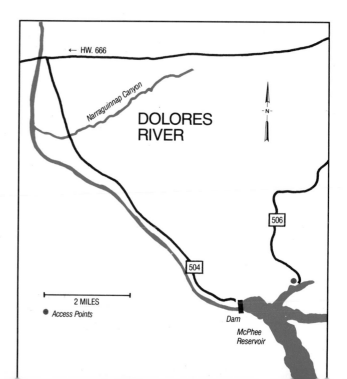

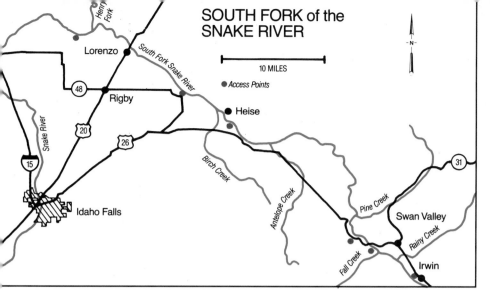

SOUTH FORK of the SNAKE RIVER

10 MILES
• Access Points

South Fork of the Snake River, ID

Not as glamorous as the nearby Henry's Fork, where you feel like a vagrant if you haven't spent half a year's pay on rough-rider haberdashery and excess tackle. The South Fork is bigger water, less celebrated and far less peopled, with spectacular angling for wild cutthroats and browns. It produced the Idaho record brown, a 3-foot, 26-pound hulk taken on a live sculpin in 1981. Fifteen-pounders are caught every year, usually in the fall. The good fishing gets under way in late June, as soon as the spring runoff ends. Anglers have visions all year of the hatch of salmon flies in early July; dry and wet imitations of these bulky, lumbering insects take lots of trout averaging 14 inches, plus quite a few trophies. Later in the summer, drift small dries such as the Adams and Elk Hair Caddis under the banks; in the fall, work Woolly Muddlers deep for big migrant browns. Because of its size, the South Fork is best fished from a drift boat handled by a good local guide. But wading is possible in some areas, especially during low water in the fall.

Fort Peck Reservoir, MT

As reservoirs go, this one is really intriguing: rugged, godforsaken shorelines, and vast, fishy, but lightly fished waters. The northern Montana weather is less than benign and can suddenly get you in trouble, another irresistible draw. The entire lake, 245,000 acres, lies within the Charles M. Russell National Wildlife Refuge. In 1988 the major news is the improving walleye fishing. Biologists say the population has been increasing and spreading out, possibly into some areas which have never been fished for walleyes at all.

Also, the planting of new forage species—ciscoes and spottail shiners—has spurred the walleye growth rate. In the spring, anglers can take walleyes from shore; productive spots with dirt-road access are at Rock, Bug, McGuire, and Nelson creeks, all on the Dry Arm. In June, gravel points 10 to 20 feet deep pay off. Later in the summer, the fish pull away to ledges and points 15 to 25 feet down. In spring and especially in fall, there's good trolling for lake trout along the dam and in the Bear Creek area nearby.

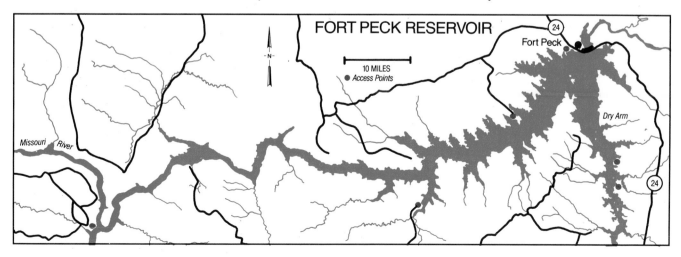

FORT PECK RESERVOIR

10 MILES
• Access Points

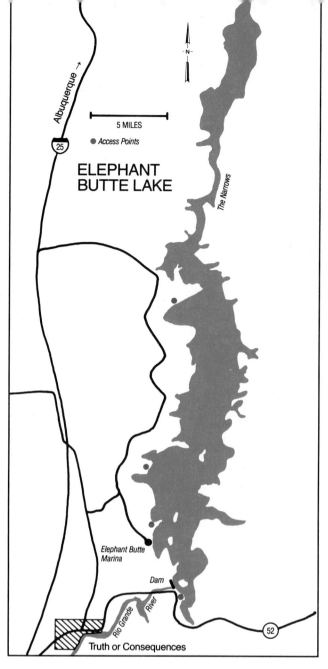

Pyramid Lake, NV

At this haunting, unlikely lake in the high desert, fly-rodders perch on half-submerged stepladders to cast for a rare breed of trout. The Lahontan cutthroat is a beautiful, sunburnt-looking creature, its flanks as ocher as the desert dust. Anglers commonly take Lahontans weighing 5 to 10 pounds, and a few over 15 pounds have been wrestled out in recent years. Native to the lake, the fish are able to withstand its high alkalinity and salinity. An irrigation scheme decades ago wiped all the Lahontans out of Pyramid, but an effort by state and federal agencies and by the Paiute Indians has brought them back. (See "Saving the Old West's Wild Trout," page 132.) By far the best fishing is in the cooler months, October through mid-April, when the fish abandon the depths for the shallows. Fly fishermen working close to the shorelines prefer Woolly Worm patterns; boat anglers troll diving plugs and spoons. Natural bait of any kind is prohibited to all but Indian fishermen. There is a 19-inch minimum-size limit, but release of all fish is encouraged.

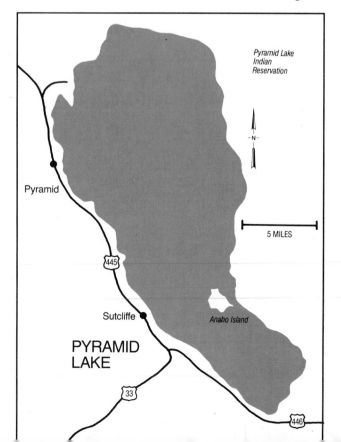

Elephant Butte Lake, NM

When formed in 1916 this was the world's biggest impoundment, but now it's not even close. Despite its age, Elephant Butte has recently been turning out more largemouths and bigger stripers than in the past. At least part of the reason is that the water has been high the last few years. The largemouths are flourishing throughout the lake and are doing especially well in the shallow upper reaches, above the bottleneck known as the Narrows. Until recently this upper part was dry land, so it's loaded with brush. It's high in fertility, too: large doses of inflowing nutrient are trapped here by the Narrows. Numerous largemouths over 10 pounds came out of Elephant Butte last year. The average size is a solidly respectable 3 pounds. Anglers who go for stripers kept outdoing one another in 1987, setting several new state records. The best time for big ones is March and April, when they rendezvous near the dam and along the west shore north to Elephant Butte Marina. Summer finds stripers from the midsection of the lake north to the Narrows.

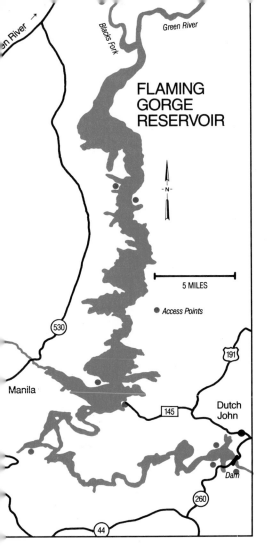

Flaming Gorge Reservoir, UT/WY

A winding, rock-walled body of water, immensely scenic, though scarcely a substitute for the primeval canyon it flooded. No longer the rainbow and brown trout factory it was at first, Flaming Gorge is now turning out blimplike lake trout and plenty of them. Virtually all of the tortuous shoreline—hundreds of miles—is prime spawning habitat for lakers. They grow so fast and so continuously in these waters that no annuli (growth rings) are discernible on the scales or bones, robbing biologists of a ready way of determining their age. Quantities of 25-pounders are dredged out every year. Laker fishing is a twelve-month sport at Flaming Gorge, with excellent ice fishing, but May and June are most productive. Dependable spots much of the time are reefs and bars 60 to 100 feet deep on top. Downriggers, wire line, and deep jigging all have their advocates here. Anglers are encouraged to release all lakers over 25 inches long. There's also some first-rate fishing for Kokanee salmon, and good angling for smallmouth bass; both these species reproduce naturally in the reservoir.

Yakima River, WA

How much can a little restraint help everyone's fishing? The Yakima, only a mediocre fishery a few years back, is now regarded by many as the best trout river in Washington state. In the early 1980s a 15-inch minimum-size limit and a ban on live bait were put into effect from Cle Elum down to Ellensburg; these paid off so well they were extended in 1986 to nearly all the trout water on the river—from Easton up in the high Cascades, down through the foothills all the way to the Roza dam 10 miles above the city of Yakima. Last year most of the trout were in the 11- to 13-inch class, but anglers took plenty ranging from 15 to 20 inches, too. Rainbows are the mainstay, with fair numbers of cutthroats above Ellensburg. In most places the water is too deep to wade, so drift boats and rafts are popular. Anglers float large caddis and hopper imitations close to the banks throughout the summer. Wading becomes more practical in September and October, when the water drops; size 18 and 20 dries are fished in the riffles to match the tiny mayflies then emerging. Guide services operate in Ellensburg and Yakima.

Wind River Indian Reservation, WY

Snow-capped mountains, six kinds of trout, little competition for space to fish. The reservation lies only a few miles from Yellowstone and Grand Teton national parks, and offers similar Fugichrome scenery and numbers of fish. What it lacks, pleasantly, is the crowds of summertime fishermen. Much of the best fishing here is in backcountry lakes and streams accessible only by trail. The reservation boundary winds right along the Continental Divide; up there in gemlike basins where the water is ice-free only a few weeks each year thrive recluse populations of the wild and improbably colorful golden trout. Pack in on horses with Indian outfitters who know the country, or backpack on your own. There's also excellent fishing in waters at lower elevations with access by road. For big fish, the best of several pocket-size reservoirs is Bull Lake, with lake trout over 25 pounds. Other good waters easy to get to are Bull Lake Creek, Dinwoody Creek, Popo Agie River, Wind River, and Little Wind River. Tribal fishing licenses are required on all reservation waters.

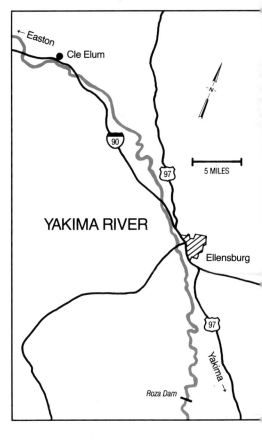

Naknek River

Dick Sternberg

When you're in King Salmon, Alaska, you can't help thinking salmon. The name of the village isn't the only reminder: you'll also see the King Ko Inn (suggestive of king and coho salmon), and the Quinnat Motel (Quinnat is another name for king salmon). And just out of town is King Salmon Creek.

There's good reason for all of these names because the village is on the banks of the Naknek River, one of Alaska's premier salmon streams. From its origin in Naknek Lake, the river meanders about 25 miles before emptying into Bristol Bay, the site of one of the world's most productive commercial salmon fisheries. So it's not surprising that the river draws phenomenal salmon runs.

I learned of the Naknek while doing research for *Freshwater Gamefish of North America*, the latest volume in The Hunting and Fishing Library®. I was looking for an area where we could catch and photograph most of Alaska's popular gamefish, and the Naknek seemed to fill the bill.

Mark Emery, the chief guide at the King Ko Inn, assured me that we would have no trouble catching king, coho, sockeye, and chum salmon, as well as rainbow trout, grayling, Dolly Vardens, and arctic char. Claims like that are tough to take seriously, but when I arrived in King Salmon with the HFL photo team, it didn't take Mark long to convince us that he knew what he was talking about.

It was 7 p.m. by the time we got our bags unpacked, but Mark told us that the kings were in and we still had plenty of time to fish because the sun wouldn't set until midnight. So we grabbed our heavy baitcasting rods and some fresh salmon eggs, then headed for the river.

We pulled into a long, deep run where Mark had been catching some kings. After rigging up with big Spin-N-Glos, we lowered the rigs to bottom, then began slow-trolling downstream.

Within minutes, Bill Lindner yelled, "Fish on." He could do nothing but hold on as the fish sizzled off over 100 yards of his 17-pound-test line. The fish stopped running, and Bill seemed to be gaining line, but soon it was obvious that the fish was not going to come in. Several times,

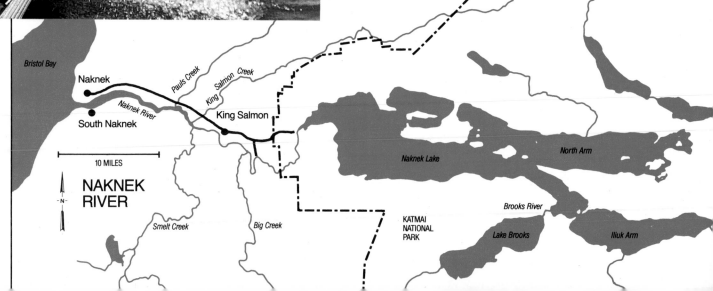

NAKNEK RIVER

Bill worked the fish almost close enough for a look, but each time it ran out another 20 to 30 yards of line.

After about twenty minutes, we caught a glimpse of a huge fish. Bill kept the pressure on, and finally Mark netted a beautiful 45-pound hook-jawed male king. Only then did we realize what was happening. The 45-pounder was only lassoed around the tail, and the line was still connected to another fish. After we untangled the line, Bill finished the job by reeling in a nice 25-pound female. Evidently, the male had followed the hooked female and somehow got tangled in the line.

Mark shook his head in disbelief. "I've seen a lot of strange things in Alaska, but never anything like that."

For the rest of the evening, we hooked kings almost as fast as we could get our lines in the water. Mark was right—the kings were definitely in.

One afternoon, I decided to make a quick king run with Jay Parker, another guide at the King Ko. We already had some great photos, but we wanted to improve on them. This time, the action was even faster than before. In twelve drifts through the hole, we landed twelve kings from 25 to 45 pounds! Only one drift failed to produce a fish, but we made up for it on the next with a doubleheader.

By now, it probably sounds as if catching kings on the Naknek is a sure thing. That's not exactly true, but your odds are pretty good if you follow Mark Emery's guidelines:

• Time your trip to correspond with the run. The first kings move in about June 20. The run peaks about July 10, then starts to dwindle in early August. You can catch a few stragglers until about August 20.

• Watch the tide tables. The best time to fish is usually the hours around high tide. Salmon will move into the river with the incoming tide, and even the ones already there will bite much better than they do when the tide is low.

• On first coming into the river, kings are silvery and are called "bright fish." At this stage, they fight hardest and are best for eating. After several days in the river, the fish start to turn pink. Later, as spawning time approaches, they turn a deep red color. By then, they have weakened considerably and the meat has started to deteriorate. But you can still catch bright fish late in the run if you fish by the tide tables. At this time, the highest tides are most likely to bring in fresh kings.

• Use a proven bait, such as a large Spin-N-Glo baited with a good-sized gob of salmon eggs and rigged with a pencil-lead snagless sinker. We used Spin-N-Glos almost exclusively, but you can also catch kings on large lures like plugs, spoons, and spinners. And Mark has discovered that kings love plastic worms.

• When using a Spin-N-Glo, troll downstream slightly faster than the current. Your bait moves more naturally than it would if dragged upstream, but your line still stays tight so you can easily hook the fish.

• Fish along the edges of deep holes in the channel. Kings follow the edges of the grassy underwater banks. There are always some kings in mid-channel, but you will hook two or three times as many by working the edges.

• Keep your bait ticking bottom as you drift downstream. The pencil sinker keeps snags to a minimum. If your bait is not on bottom, you will seldom catch a king.

During the king salmon run, the Naknek also gets excellent runs of sockeye and chum salmon, although these fish are ignored by most anglers. Then, about the time king fishing hits the skids, the cohos move in. And in even-numbered years, the river gets a banner run of pink salmon. You can catch cohos until about September 5, pinks until August 25.

The Naknek River also boasts some of southwest Alaska's finest fishing for grayling and rainbow trout. These are resident fish, so they can be caught throughout the open-water season.

The upper reaches of the Naknek teem with rainbows from 3 to 5 pounds. We had no trouble catching them whenever we tried. The trophy-sized rainbows, 8- to 15-pounders, bite best in late May, early June, and September, although we caught several in late July. The most productive technique was trolling with shallow-running minnow plugs.

We found grayling wherever there was fast water. Once we'd located the best runs, an egg fly rigged with a split-shot produced a 14- to 18-inch grayling on practically every drift, along with some "bonus" rainbows and Dolly Vardens.

Besides the Naknek River, there's plenty of other blue-ribbon fishing around King Salmon. You can take a boat to Naknek Lake, 32 miles of icy glacial meltwater nestled among snow-capped peaks. The lake is worth a trip just to witness its breathtaking postcard scenery, and its waters are home to giant rainbows, lake trout, and arctic char. Some of its tributaries, like the Brooks River, draw tremendous runs of sockeye salmon.

Although you can catch arctic char in Naknek Lake, your odds are much better if you fly out. From King Salmon, you can charter a float plane and within an hour be catching char on Ugashik Lake or on dozens of other prime waters.

There are no roads into King Salmon, but it is easily accessible by air from Anchorage. Peninsula Airlines and Mark Air have several flights each day. Accommodations for fishermen range from plush resorts to basic motel units. The King Ko Inn (Box 346, King Salmon, AK 99613; phone 907-246-3377) is basic but comfortable. The rooms are about $90 per night for a double. A complete dinner runs $12 to $16. Guide service is $150 per day per person.

Dick Sternberg is the director of The Hunting & Fishing Library. He has sampled fishing spots—some hot and some not so hot—across most of North America.

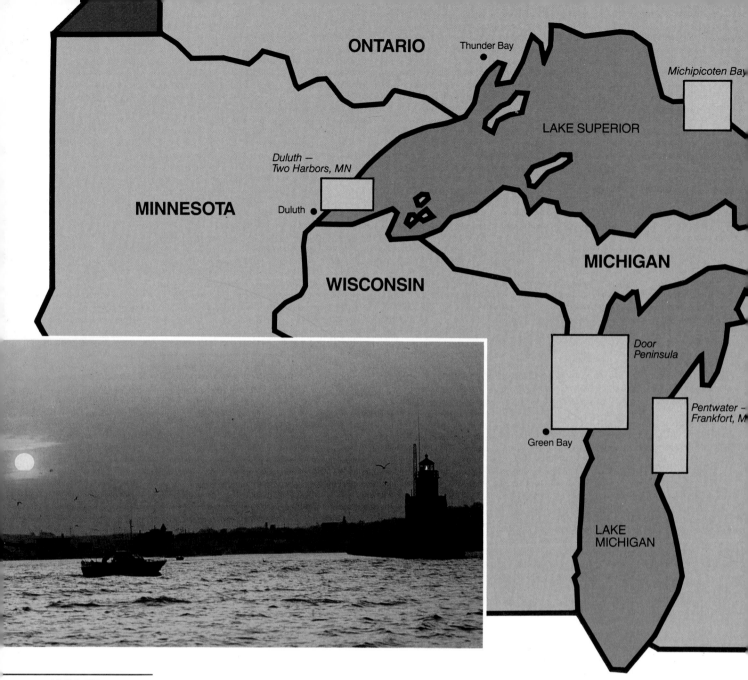

ONTARIO
Thunder Bay
Michipicoten Bay
LAKE SUPERIOR
Duluth —
Two Harbors, MN
MINNESOTA
Duluth
MICHIGAN
WISCONSIN
Door
Peninsula
Pentwater –
Frankfort, M
Green Bay
LAKE
MICHIGAN

1988 Hotspots:

The Great Lakes

Fisheries managers frequently refer to the annual "harvest" made by rod and reel, and nowhere does the term seem more appropriate than on the Great Lakes today. The fish caught most commonly in these waters are salmon and trout, nearly all of which are hatchery-raised and stocked—"planted"—rather than naturally spawned. A fully outfitted Great Lakes charter boat, cutting a broad swath with downriggers, outriggers, and planing boards, bears less resemblance to the rowboats of yore than to a diesel combine rumbling through a grainfield.

In recent years the chinook salmon has replaced the coho as the principal game species in the lakes. Last season was the best ever for chinooks on Lake Ontario, with fish over 40 pounds boated. In 1986, the salmon had been plentiful but looked a little gaunt; the same went for alewives, the primary forage, which apparently had overpopulated. Then the alewives grew scarcer, and both species recovered a healthy girth. Biologists expect 1988 will be a bumper year for chinooks on the lake.

In Lake Huron, salmonids and forage alike appear to be doing well. A specter is looming, however, particularly

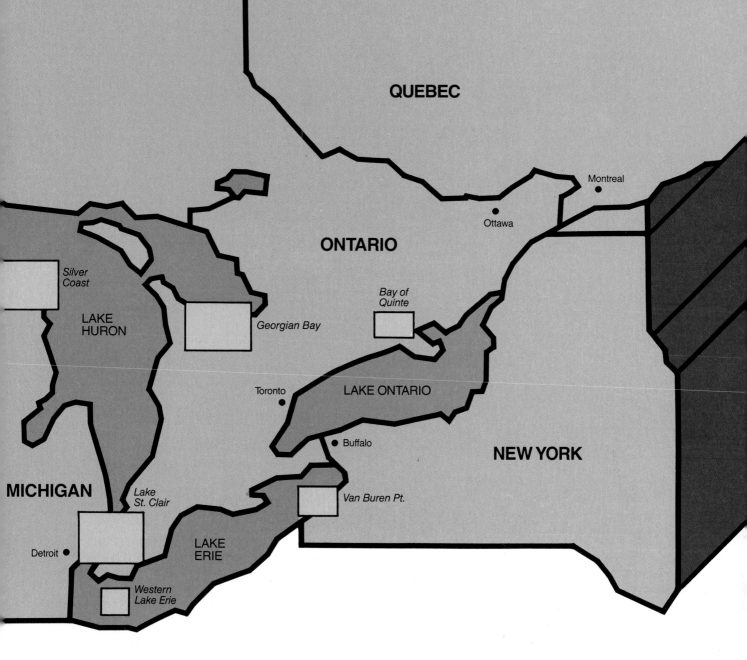

toward the north end of the lake. An increase in the number of sea lampreys, parasitic on all salmonids and especially on lake trout, has recently been noted. Ironically, the increase may stem at least in part from the pollution cleanup in certain streams where lampreys reproduce.

The same problem has hit Lake Michigan, and here there's another as well. Alewives, the main course in chinook meals, have declined to a fraction of their former numbers. What's caused this is a matter of heated speculation. Many anglers say commercial fishermen have netted too many for cat food; the commercial men point out they net only in limited areas of the lake, and imply not very subtly that the anglers are in league with hostile foreign powers. Biologists suggest other possible causes: predatory zooplankton that eat the plankton which alewives subsist on, and predation on alewives by overabundant salmon. The chinooks are averaging smaller, owing possibly to the alewife decline or to an increase in fishing pressure, notably in the early season.

There's good news and bad news from Lake Superior. For several years, the forage base has been changing: smelt have been decreasing while lake herring, a better food source for trout and salmon, have become more abundant. Lake trout also have proliferated, perhaps because fewer of their larvae are being eaten by smelt. Unfortunately, lampreys seem to be on the upswing too. The St. Louis River, where pollution has lessened, could be part of the reason: its wider stretches cannot be economically treated with lampricide.

In Lake Erie, salmonids are far less important than walleyes and other cool-water species. The walleye fishing has boomed since the early 1970s, and anglers credit the halt in commercial netting of the species in Ohio waters. But some biologists suspect an additional factor: the productive walleye years have also been a continuous period of abnormally high water, which creates ideal spawning conditions on the reefs. Regardless, 1988 will be another great year.

Pentwater to Frankfort, MI

Here's where it all got started: The first big returns of Great Lakes salmon took place along this stream-punctuated stretch of shoreline exactly twenty years ago. Today, chinooks have virtually replaced the cohos, but the area is still tops in the state of Michigan for sheer, inconceivable tonnage of salmonids caught. Natural reproduction now supplies a fourth to a third of the chinook population. State biologists have predicted another great year of fishing in 1988, though the average size of the fish is no longer as great as it once was, perhaps because more are being taken in the spring before reaching full growth. Lake trout, uncommon in these waters two decades ago, have become abundant since the lampreys were controlled and the gill-netting ended. Fast laker fishing begins in July and continues until the season on the species closes in mid-August. Steelhead help keep trollers happy in summer, then run up the feeder streams in spring and fall, glomming onto spawn bags drifted through the deeper holes. Brown trout are fairly common, both offshore in summer and upstream in fall.

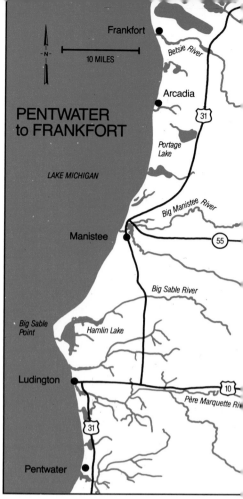

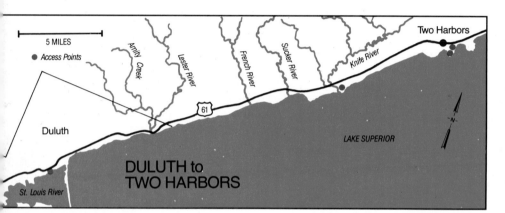

Duluth to Two Harbors, MN

The abandoned ore-loading piers still loom at Two Harbors, rusted and paradoxically romantic: the local economy has now switched over to trailer parks and trolling. Lake trout constitute most of the fishery, and the Minnesota Department of Natural Resources, though stocking them heavily, has set the goal of a completely self-sustaining population. Twenty percent of the lakers now caught here are naturally produced, versus 5 percent back in 1976. Trollers launch into action in May, plowing the surface waters with flat lines and planer boards; shore anglers also do well at this time. By midsummer the lakers go deeper, sometimes to 200 feet, and downriggers are standard. Some of the best laker fishing comes just before the season closing at the end of September, around the offshore reefs. Salmon are caught through the summer also, both cohos and chinooks; but the major fishing is in September and October when the chinooks move into the tributaries. Trollers take a few steelhead, but the spring and fall runs in such rivers as the Knife, French, and Big Sucker provide most of the fishing.

Van Buren Point to Cattaraugus Creek, NY

Despite the deadly subzero weather of eastern Lake Erie, the water stays open all winter in the harbor at Dunkirk. Steelhead and browns hole up in the warm effluent from a power plant, and fishermen catch them from mid-October through April. Toward the end of winter, schools of cohos crowd in as well. Around May first, smallmouth bass begin to hit, though anglers must release them until the season opens in June. Outside the harbor, especially along the lakeshore between Dunkirk and Van Buren Point, good fishing for smallmouths and walleyes gets under way in June and continues through the summer. The smallmouths, running 2½ to 3½ pounds, are caught around structure in water 15 feet deep or more. Walleyes suspend in the open water pursuing smelt, where salmon trollers pick them up on plugs along the thermocline. July and August produce lots of salmonids offshore; in the fall they move in closer. Cattaraugus Creek has a good run of steelhead. New York has begun stocking the big Skamania steelhead, and anglers should catch the first of these fish in 1988.

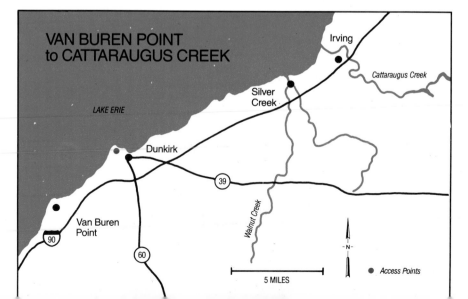

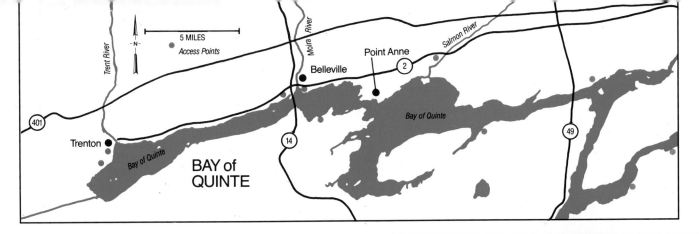

Bay of Quinte, Ont.

One of those stranger-than-fiction places where pollution has been substantially reduced, rather than just studied forever and ever. The big plugging-up here began in 1978, and the fishery has shown remarkable improvement every year since. Now the Bay of Quinte has the best fishing for walleyes on the Canadian side of Lake Ontario, and probably the best on the entire lake. The fastest action starts with the season opener in May, then tapers off sometime in June. During this period anglers work the shallower reefs, sandbars near the shoreline, and the mouths of the Trent and Moira rivers. The favorite lure—here as in other good walleye spots all over the Great Lakes—is the weight-forward spinner with a hefty nightcrawler looped onto the hook. Also good are marabou jigs, and floating jigheads with crawlers or minnows. In late summer and fall, the reefs are the productive spots. Walleyes run from 2 to 4½ pounds, depending on the time of year. The ice fishing is fast, too. The bay also produces lots of perch, and offers some overlooked angling for smallmouths, pike, and muskies.

Islands of Western Lake Erie, OH/Ont.

Those who thrive on challenge may find the walleye fishing here *too* easy at times. In early summer, when the fish suspend in clouds off West Sister Island, it would actually be difficult to avoid catching them. The walleye population boom began in the early 1970s and shows no signs of subsiding—certainly not in 1988. Several outstanding year-classes of mature fish are present. The long-time favorite walleye lure here, a Lake Erie specialty, is the weight-forward spinner, usually tipped with a nightcrawler. But deep-running crankbaits are becoming more and more popular, along with vibrating plugs like the Rat-L-Trap. Though trolling is the traditional walleye method on the lake, most anglers today prefer casting. As the summer progresses, the fishing slows in the western part of the island region and gradually picks up further east. Spots productive early on—Niagara and Crib reefs, for example—give way to late-season locations like Chickenolee Reef southeast of Pelee Island, and the deep water east of Kelleys Island.

There's also some first-rate fishing for other species, especially yellow perch and smallmouth bass. Perch are caught year round: in the spring, summer, and particularly in the fall, the reefs and rocky shorelines produce them by the ton; in winter the Bass Islands offer good ice fishing. Smallmouths are abundant and grow fat, with

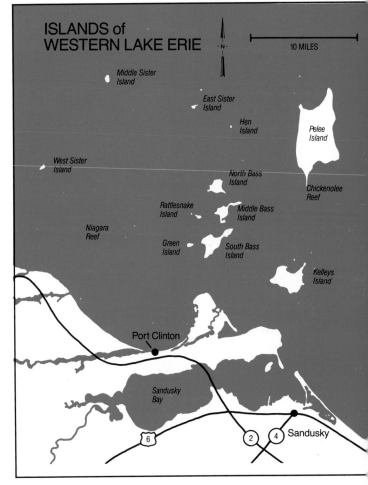

many over 4 pounds. They're not so widely and haphazardly distributed as the walleyes often are, so more knowledge of the reefs and humps around the islands is required. Crawfish and emerald shiners are the favorite baits, but crankbaits, vibrating plugs, and spinners also produce. Smallmouths strike well in late April and May, lie low during the post-spawn period in June, then return to feeding from mid-July through October. White bass fishing, if not quite as spectacular as in the past, is still very good. Vast schools of 10- to 12-inch fish may feed for hours over shallow points and reefs. A weight-forward spinner is the only lure needed; heave it across a surfacing school and retrieve as fast as you can.

Western Lake Erie is dangerous water for small boats and inexpert boatmen, but hundreds of licensed guides operate out of ports along the Ohio shore—notably Port Clinton and several on the Marblehead Peninsula.

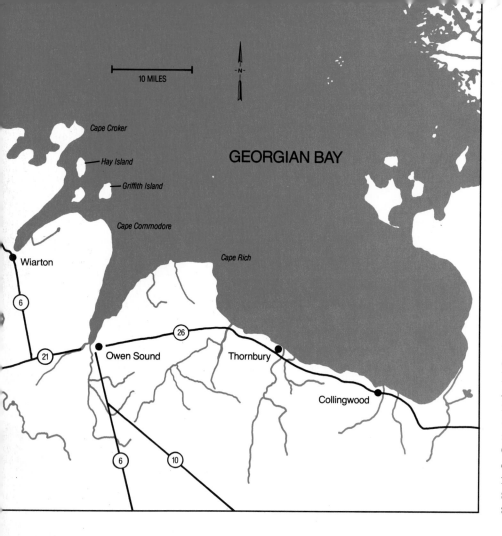

Georgian Bay, Ont.

The waters between Wiarton and Collingwood at the south end of Georgian Bay should offer excellent fishing in 1988. Lake trout hang near the stream mouths during April and May, and anglers cast from shore or troll with long lines. The summer fishing is slower, the lakers moving deep, but the action picks up again at the end of August and lasts through September. There's also a productive ice fishery. Though lakers do reproduce naturally here, stocking accounts for most of the catch. Steelhead fishing is good in spring and fall, off the stream mouths and in the lower reaches of the streams themselves. The steelhead average 5 to 10 pounds, but many around 15 pounds are taken; the Ontario record steelhead, a 29-pounder, came from this stretch of Georgian Bay. For chinooks, the best period is August through October: downriggers in deep water are productive until September, and then the fish move shallower and closer to the streams. Chinooks are growing more numerous in these waters; some are strays from the U.S., many are stocked by sportsmen's clubs, and there's also some natural reproduction.

Lake St. Clair, Ont./MI

This fertile body of water appended to the Great Lakes goes strangely unpublicized. Few anglers outside the region ever hear so much as a rumor of the excellent fishing on St. Clair. Averaging only 12 feet deep, it provides vast expanses of ideal habitat for smallmouth bass, walleyes, and muskies. Smallmouths in particular are abundant and only minimally beset by nimrods out of Grosse Pointe and Bloomfield Hills. Smallmouths run 2 to 3 pounds, with fair numbers over 5 pounds. Sand and gravel bars along the Ontario shore are especially productive; crankbaits work well, live crayfish and spottail shiners even better. Most walleyes this year will be from the strong year-classes of 1982 (about 3½ pounds) and 1984 (about 2½ pounds). The angling for muskies ranks with the best anywhere. Plenty of 15- to 18-pounders are taken; a popular method is downrigger trolling with plugs, often at high speed. The north end of the lake is best early in summer, the southeast later on. There's fine year-round angling for yellow perch, too.

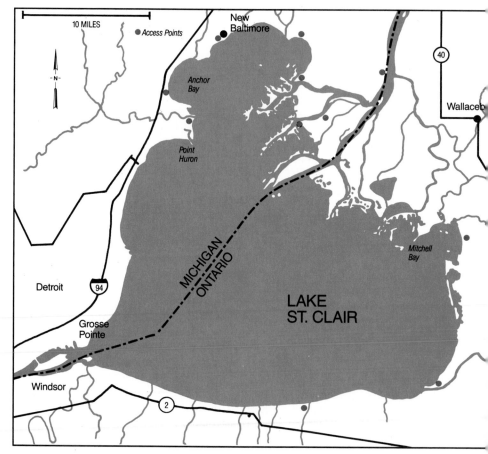

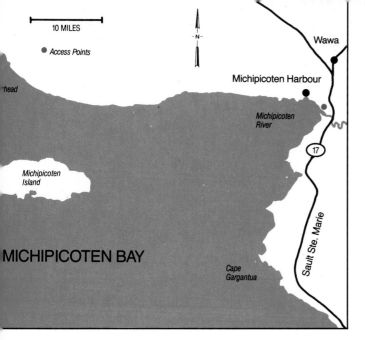

Michipicoten Bay, Ont.

No observers of boundaries, chinook salmon stocked in
the U.S. have been entering these waters on the Canadian
shore of Lake Superior for several years, even crashing
their way up the tributaries and spawning successfully.
The interlopers have steadily become more plentiful, a
trend that biologists expect to continue. The average
size of the fish has been increasing too; last year it was
slightly more than 15 pounds. June through September
is the productive season. Most salmon anglers here use
downriggers, trolling at depths of 40 to 120 feet. Lake
trout are also abundant; unlike the chinooks they're
stocked in these waters, and they reproduce naturally as
well. Surface fishing pays off in spring, deep trolling later
on. The area off the south side of Michipicoten Island
is a reliable producer. Most lakers here are in the 3- to
7-pound bracket. There's also a minor fishery for steelhead: few are encountered in the lake itself, but anglers
drifting spawn bags and yarn flies take fair numbers during the upstream spawning run in April and early May.

Door Peninsula, WI

Good news for anglers, and for all advocates of native
wild species: in the waters off this scenic peninsula, the
Wisconsin Department of Natural Resources has been
working to bring back the coaster brook trout. Coasters,
the native counterparts of the introduced steelhead and
salmon, were formerly abundant in the Great Lakes
region, living and feeding primarily in the lakes but
ascending tributaries to spawn. Coasters were all but
wiped out by the sea lamprey, then were forgotten in the
subsequent rush to manage other salmonids. But now
Wisconsin is stocking them heavily in bays along the
Door Peninsula. In 1988 coasters will provide good
angling in these waters, averaging 2 to 3 pounds, with
some 8-pounders possible. April and May are the prime
times to try. The species the peninsula is best known for
is not the brook trout but the brown, also most catchable
in the spring months. Browns run 3 to 5 pounds, but quite
a few 10-pounders are caught. And chinook salmon,
though smaller than in the past, still offer superb fishing from late May through August.

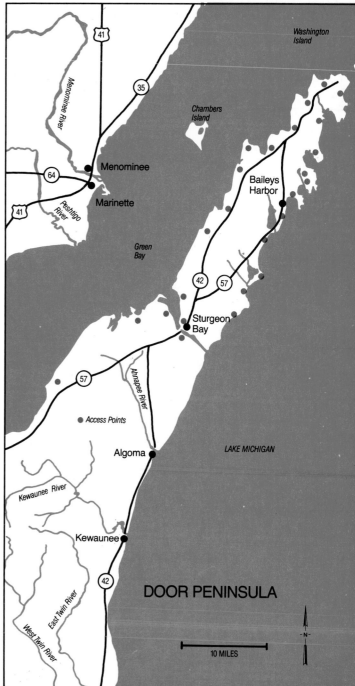

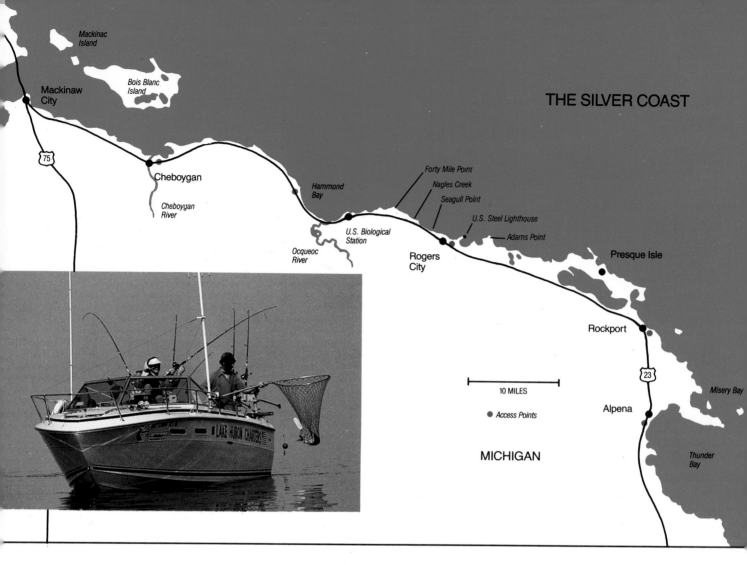

Mackinac Island

Bois Blanc Island

Mackinaw City

75

Cheboygan

Cheboygan River

Hammond Bay

Forty Mile Point

Nagles Creek

Seagull Point

U.S. Steel Lighthouse

Adams Point

U.S. Biological Station

Ocqueoc River

Rogers City

Presque Isle

Rockport

23

10 MILES

Access Points

Alpena

Misery Bay

MICHIGAN

Thunder Bay

1988 Hotspots: Silver Coast of Lake Huron

Tom Huggler

Maybe you've heard of the Gold Coast—the east side of Lake Michigan, from South Haven, Michigan, to Traverse City. The Gold Coast is both a haven for tourists and a playground for fishermen. And now comes the Silver Coast—a stretch of northern Lake Huron from Alpena, Michigan, to the Straits of Mackinac. It's the newest salmon hotspot on all the Great Lakes.

For anglers, the Silver Coast is aptly named. I can't think of it without seeing a silver-bright king salmon: Sagging deeply in the net, the twisting fish is swung aboard, the sun bouncing off its polished sides. Like a welder's flash, it hurts the eyes.

If you come to the Silver Coast, you might count more ore freighters than trolling boats, because northern Lake Huron lies waiting to be discovered by the salmon fleet. What's here for fishermen in 1988?

Consider the incentives: excellent trolling pastures with structure and deep water near shore; good launching facilities and accommodations; hordes of king salmon, thanks to aggressive planting by the Michigan Department of Natural Resources; plenty of other salmonids, including lake, brook, brown, and steelhead trout, as well as coho salmon; plus smallmouth bass and walleyes.

Along most of the Silver Coast's 80 miles, the 100-foot depth contour runs within a couple miles of shore. Ship-snagging reefs punctuate the area, providing structure for salmon and trout. Southwest winds prevail, so the waters are sheltered. These winds also push warm surface water offshore, and cool water welling up from the depths offers a prolonged period of low surface temperatures. A few years ago, surface temperatures between 43° and 65°F—ideal for fishing—were recorded from April 22 to July 6, August 10 to 21, and August 26 to November 24.

The hub of this new hotspot is Rogers City, midway between Alpena and Cheboygan. Swan Bay, nearby, is where the DNR has made massive salmon releases; 800,000 king salmon fingerlings were stocked in 1984, and the adults showed up in 1987. This year—1988—will see the second full-blown returns of these fish. And now the DNR has upped the annual releases of kings to 900,000.

There's more. Many salmon stocked elsewhere pass through the Rogers City area on their spawning migrations. From releases a decade ago, kings have established a natural run in the Ocqueoc River, which flows into Hammond Bay. In the Upper Peninsula, the DNR annually stocks kings in the St. Mary's and Carp rivers, and kings and cohos in Seymour Creek. In addition, hefty numbers of kings show up from Oscoda and Harrisville, south of Rogers City.

Nearly all the Silver Coast waters north of Rogers City are open to Indian gill-netting, so why the DNR emphasis on sport fishing here? Well, there are those ideal fishing conditions: shelter, deep water inshore, and cool surface temperatures. Further, the DNR wants to pull salmon-fishing pressure away from Harrisville and Oscoda. Plus, the sugar-sand beaches and relative solitude of the Silver Coast make it ripe for tourism. This is an area that needs—and wants—fishermen.

The third annual Rogers City Salmon Tournament will be held this year in late August. It's scheduled to coincide with the peak of offshore staging by salmon about to spawn. The fishing action, however, begins much earlier.

Trolling along the shorelines near Rogers City is productive in May and June. On a due-east heading from the harbor anglers troll past the U.S. Steel lighthouse, Adams Point, and then the Presque Isle lighthouse. Northwest of Rogers City lies Seagull Point, Nagles Creek at P. F. Hoeft State Park, Forty Mile Point, and the U.S. biological station at the entrance to Hammond Bay. Fishing can be good anywhere along these shorelines, out to bottom depths of 150 feet.

The action picks up strongly in July, as salmon begin to stage and move closer to shore. Waters along the 40- to 60-foot contours are productive, most trollers keying on the region from Presque Isle Harbor to Swan Bay. One hotspot is a reef a mile east of Adams Point that runs out 1½ miles into the lake. The salmon have no river to ascend in Swan Bay, so the fishing remains good there and along nearby shorelines of the main lake throughout September. Thanks to a good forage base of smelt,

emerald shiners, and alewives, the salmon average 15 to 20 pounds, with some egg-laden females reaching the 25-pound mark.

Lures trolled on downriggers, Dipsy Divers, and flat lines account for most catches, although a few anglers break out planer boards and outriggers when the salmon move into water less than 30 feet deep and the trolling traffic is light enough for such side-rigging. Hot spoons include G. W. Salmon Slammers, Finns, Silver Streaks, Northport Nailers, Flutter Chucks, and Stingers. In plugs, the hands-down favorites are J-Plugs. For all lures the preferred colors are silver, chartreuse, and green.

Besides the salmon, plenty of lake trout, steelhead, browns, and brook trout show up in boat coolers and on shore fishermen's stringers. For lake trout, the best bets are the waters off Forty Mile Point and Adams Point, where the DNR stocks yearlings annually. Both Rogers City and Hammond Bay receive annual stockings of steelhead and brown trout. If browns are the main drawing card for you, consider Thunder Bay at Alpena. And by wading or shore fishing you can score on steelhead in the Ocqueoc and Cheboygan rivers, and on brook trout in Presque Isle Harbor.

The Silver Coast also offers good fishing for smallmouth bass. Some productive spots are the Adams Point reef; the old Coast Guard pilings at the U.S. Biological Station on Hammond Bay; Misery, Huron, and Morris bays in the North Point region near Alpena; Zola Reef, along the northwest shore of Bois Blanc Island, near Cheboygan; and Duncan Bay (also good for pike) east of the island harbor. Smallmouth fishing is best from June through September. Successful anglers cast jigs and small spinners.

If walleyes are your game, look no farther than the Cheboygan River. There's good fishing from June through August, and some lunkers up to 10 pounds are caught. The one-mile stretch just below the dam is most productive. Current created by turbines at the power plant draws the walleyes up from Lake Huron. Nightcrawlers are effective, either trolled or drifted. So are twister-tail jigs cast from shore or boats.

Rogers City has a paved, two-lane launching ramp and a modern harbor. Hammond Bay and Cheboygan offer similar facilities. There's a new two-lane ramp at Rockport, and another at Alpena. The only other ramp is at Presque Isle Harbor, but it's not recommended for large boats.

Three good guides chartering out of Rogers City are Ted Planck, telephone (517) 732-2179; Phil Petz, 734-3855; and Bruce Grant, 734-7233. Details on lodging and other facilities are available from the Rogers City Chamber of Commerce, P.O. Box 55C, Rogers City, MI 49779; telephone (517) 734-2535.

Tom Huggler specializes in writing about the Great Lakes. His articles appear in Outdoor Life *and* Great Lakes Fisherman. *The most recent of his books is* The Cannon Guide to Downrigger Fishing.

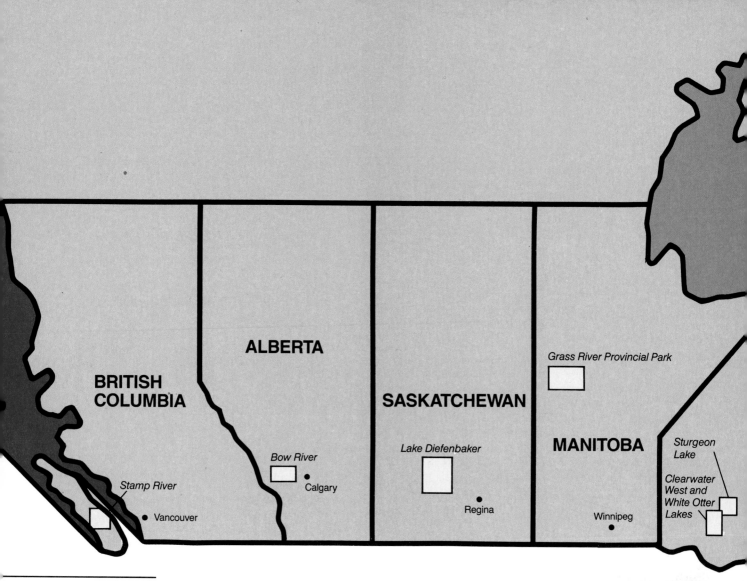

BRITISH COLUMBIA

ALBERTA

SASKATCHEWAN

MANITOBA

Grass River Provincial Park

Bow River

• Calgary

Stamp River

• Vancouver

Lake Diefenbaker

• Regina

• Winnipeg

Sturgeon Lake

Clearwater West and White Otter Lakes

1988 Hotspots:

Canada

T he adventure never really began until you reached the border. The Canadian customs men, you learned after a few years of these trips, were always friendlier and less formidable—less like hinterland versions of J. Edgar Hoover—than their U.S. counterparts would be on the way back. How long did you plan to sojourn in Her Majesty's wilderness? You weren't transporting any pistols, were you? And right on through the gate.

This might have been twenty or thirty years ago, but it seems much further back. A Canadian fishing trip was not so much a junket into another country, a separate topography, as a trip to an earlier and more primitive time. What Michigan or Wisconsin or northern New York had been to anglers a half century or so before, Canada still was. Those forests of spruce and fir lapped endlessly

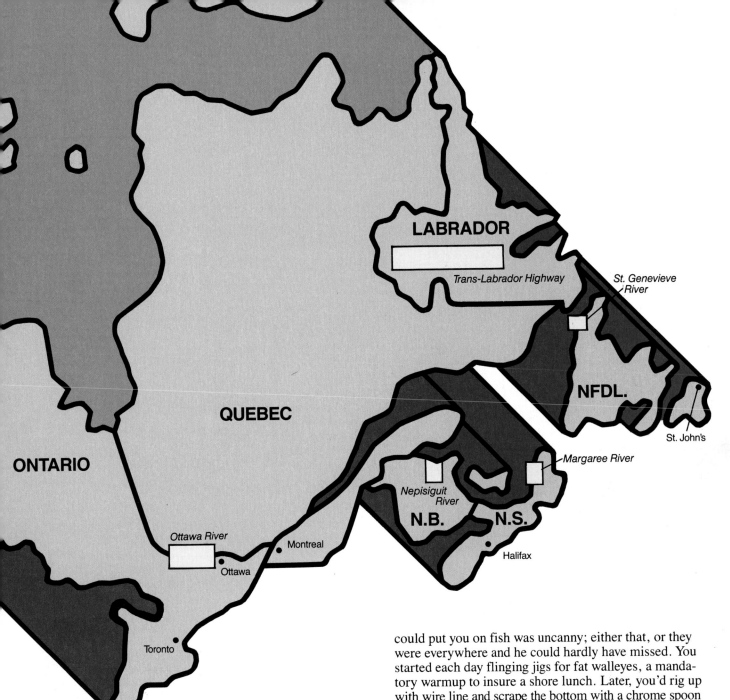

LABRADOR

Trans-Labrador Highway

St. Genevieve
River

QUEBEC

NFDL.

St. John's

Margaree River

Nepisiguit
River

N.B.

N.S.

ONTARIO

Ottawa River

Montreal

Ottawa

Halifax

Toronto

north, a green nearly black, fragrant with all the perfumes of the bush: resin, lantern fuel, fly-head cement.

One year, the lodge was a ramshackle log hive where you slept in a second-story room with a prickly hemp rope coiled under the bed and knotted to a bedpost, for escape out the window in case of fire. The owners bottled a volatile home brew in a room downstairs, and frequently in the night a cap would blow off and whack alarmingly against the floorboards mere inches from your sagging mattress. In the mornings the table held sticky tins of bitter marmalades and teas, their labels bearing grandiose British coats of arms and mystifying subtitles in French.

The boat they allotted you was a lapstrake Peterborough, your guide a fathomless, taciturn Cree. The way he

could put you on fish was uncanny; either that, or they were everywhere and he could hardly have missed. You started each day flinging jigs for fat walleyes, a mandatory warmup to insure a shore lunch. Later, you'd rig up with wire line and scrape the bottom with a chrome spoon as big as a Packard bumper—the Williams Wabler was a favorite—and eventually you'd get a heavy strike and winch up a serious candidate for taxidermy, a bilious laker that hadn't seen the light of day since back in the spring. Northerns would home in on a Pflueger Globe, a plug resembling those monstrous insects that used to appear on comic postcards depicting the effects of delirium tremens. The lure whirred through the bulrushes tossing up spray, and they'd crack it with the sound of a truck tire blowing out.

The great part is, it's all still up there, waiting. The lures have changed—a few of them, at least—and today your guide may rely less on his wits, more on his Lowrance. In all the essentials, though, Canada remains the earthly paradise that anglers to the south have always dreamed of.

You'll know you've arrived when they wave you through the gate.

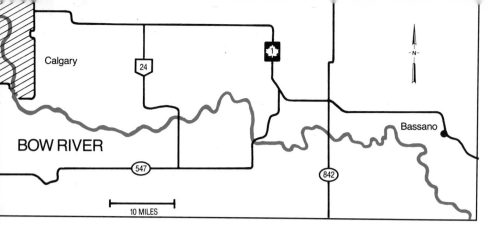

Bow River, Alta.

It's easy to draw wrong conclusions about the Bow, and many anglers have. The river is among the finest trout fisheries on the continent; there's no doubt about that. In a single day a good flyrodder might take dozens of hefty rainbows, extracting them from a nimbus of nonstop hatches. And it's true this extraordinary angling is a product of urban pollution. Treated sewage from the city of Calgary has fertilized a waterway that was unproductive in its natural state: far above Calgary, the stretch in Banff National Park is a milky turmoil of glacial debris, pristine but practically troutless. Still, there are days even on the productive downstream water when the angler must work hard for only a few; trout, after all, are trout. And whether the effluent proves a blessing in the long run remains to be seen. So now, not later, might be the best time for a trip on the Bow. Floating is the only practical way to fish; a dozen or so guide services operate from Calgary. Weighted nymphs and Muddlers work best during high water in June, hopper patterns and small dries from July through September.

Grass River Provincial Park, Man.

Water is everywhere in this wilderness park at the head of the Grass River drainage, with superb fishing for walleyes, pike, lake trout, and even rainbows. Good paved roads run through the park along its western and southern boundaries, but the only way to get around in the vast remainder is via water or air. Rental boats are available at lodges and in the settlement of Cranberry Portage, or you can trailer your own and launch at any of four scattered sites that give access to a time-warp network of unspoiled streams and lakes. Outboards are unrestricted, except on Amphipod and Webster lakes (the only rainbow water) where electrics-only is the rule. Four fly-in camps are located on remote waters unreachable by outboard. But surely the most adventuresome way to fish is by canoe: rent one at the Viking Lodge, or bring your own. You can embark from Cranberry Portage and paddle the length of the park, sampling all the major waters and, via portage, as many of the lesser ones as you like. Take-out is on the road near Snow Lake. Motels and drive-in campgrounds are least crowded in the late season, from mid-July on.

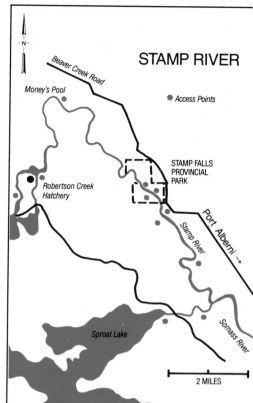

Stamp River, B.C.

If you visit Vancouver Island you'll probably want to sample a number of its famous steelhead rivers, rather than limit yourself to just one. Make a note: the Stamp should definitely be on your circuit. The runs are excellent, with 5- to 10-pound fish about average. Winter-run steelhead begin showing up in November; the fishing continues through the cold months, peaking in February. The summer run gets under way in late August and peaks in October. Fly fishing is the most demanding and exciting method. Zonkers, Skunks, and egg flies are effective anytime; big dries like the Irresistible often work well for summer-run fish. Another top method is drifting Spin-N-Glos or Gooey Bobs under cork or Dynk floats. The Stamp Falls Provincial Park offers campsites and good fishing access; farther upstream, there's access at Money's Pool just below the Ash River mouth, and at the Robertson Creek Fish Hatchery. The Stamp flows into the Somass River, which also has some good pools to fish. Steelhead caught in the Stamp may be wild or hatchery fish; only the hatchery trout, with clipped adipose fins, may be kept.

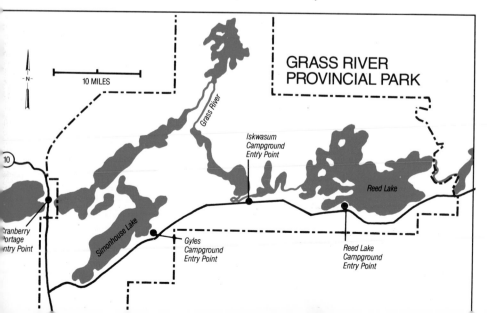

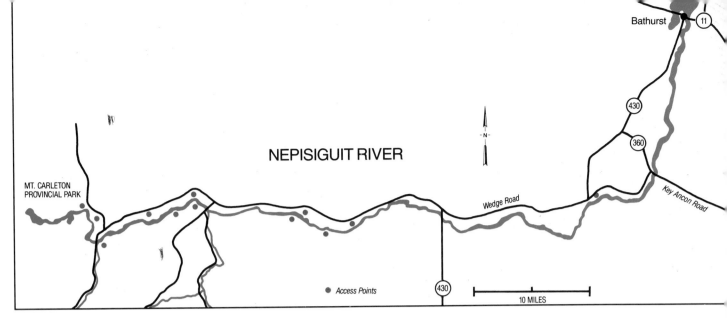

NEPISIGUIT RIVER

MT. CARLETON PROVINCIAL PARK

Wedge Road

Key Ancon Road

Bathurst

• Access Points

10 MILES

Nepisiguit River, N.B.

Anglers have helped rehabilitate this river, once dying
of mine pollution, chemical spills, and a ruthless commercial fishery. After the water was cleaned up in the
early 1970s, a group of sport fishermen formed the
Nepisiguit Salmon Association and went to work raising funds, building habitat, censusing young and adult
salmon, even stocking fish with government assistance.
From the low point in the late 1960s—everyone remembers a season when only a dozen or so salmon were
caught—the Nepisiguit has returned to enormous pro-

ductivity. Commercial netting was banned for good in
1985, and the runs are still getting better. The salmon
fishing takes place in the lower 18 miles, where there's
easy access to a winding staircase of pools. Salmon run
in June and again in late August and September, but many
are caught in midsummer. Salmon wet flies in size 6 are
popular; bushy dries, size 2 to 6, work well in July and
August. Nonresident salmon anglers must fish with a local
guide. The lower part of the river also has sea-run brook
trout; the upper part, 70 miles long, has resident brookies.

St. Genevieve River, Nfld.

The Atlantic salmon run in this abbre-
viated river near the northern tip of
the island has increased remarkably
since the 1970s and early '80s. To
fish here in those bad old days called
for a measure of faith the namesake
herself might never have summoned.
Stronger controls on fishing—both
sport and commercial—are credited
for the salmon revival. The season
is open three months, June through
August. In the early part, salmon are
sparse and anglers concentrate on the
resident brook trout in the river and
in Ten Mile Lake, which lies several
miles upstream. In July, the lower part
of the river loads up with salmon,
many being caught near the bridge
on Route 430. By early August, most
have moved to the falls about 3 miles
above the bridge; late August finds
them in the stretch above the falls.
Nonresident anglers are allowed to
fish a ½-mile stretch at the bridge on
their own, but must hire local guides
(two anglers per guide) to fish the
rest of the river. Both the river and
the lake are limited to fly fishing.
Bring standard salmon flies in sizes
6 to 10.

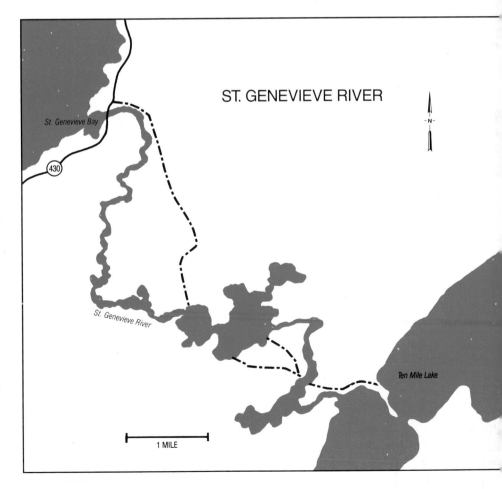

ST. GENEVIEVE RIVER

St. Genevieve Bay

430

St. Genevieve River

Ten Mile Lake

1 MILE

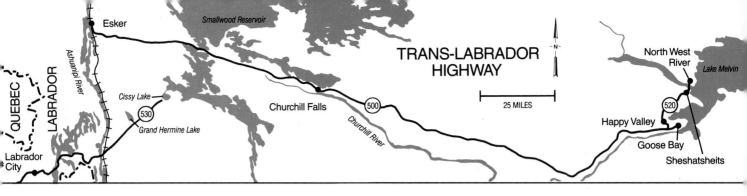

Trans-Labrador Highway, Nfld.

When completed, this gravel road will stretch 350 miles across the fish-filled Labrador wilderness, from Labrador City to Goose Bay. All but 50 miles are now in service, and you can bypass the gap by taking a weekly auto-train. A summer trip along the highway will take you to countless lakes and streams that until recently were accessible only by float plane, if at all. To reach the starting point at Labrador City, you drive the 360-mile route from Baie Comeau, Quebec, a road just opened last year. The Labrador City area has campgrounds, motels, and lots of good fishing: Grand Hermine Lake is great for lake trout, and the Ashuanipi River turns out trophy brook trout and landlocks. Farther east, the road will reach Cissy Lake this season, long a productive spot for fly-in fishing. The train, on the Quebec North Shore and Labrador Railroad, runs from Labrador City to Esker; reservations are required. East of Esker, Smallwood Reservoir has lakers, brookies, and pike, all big and abundant. The Churchill River holds oversize landlocks; Goose Bay offers sea-run brookies. A car-top boat or canoe is vital.

Margaree River, N.S.

Of all the top-rated salmon rivers in Nova Scotia, the Margaree has the longest open season—June 1 to October 15—and is the only one with runs both in summer and in fall. The angling has been on the upswing since the closing of the commercial salmon fishery in the mid-1980s, and since the enactment of stronger sport regulations. The daily limit is two salmon under 25 inches, none over. The Margaree flows through picturesque country, but nonresidents should take care not to stroll through streamside woods or croplands without hiring a guide as required by law. The waters themselves are all public, though, and unguided nonresidents are allowed to use public access sites and fish their way along the river as far as they want. Salmon are in the stream most of the season, but the runs peak from mid-June through early July, and throughout September and October. Ten- to twelve-pounders are common. The fishing is limited to flies only. There's also some excellent angling for brook trout, many of them sea-run fish reaching 2 to 3 pounds. The area has several lodges and campgrounds.

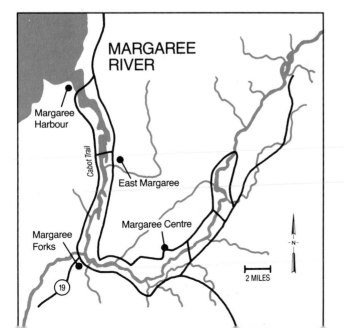

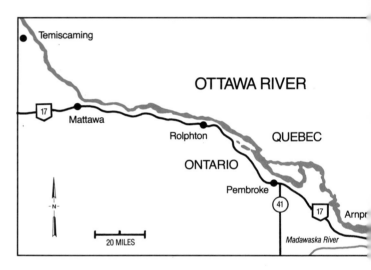

Ottawa River, Que./Ont.

This big river offers excellent fishing for a wide variety of fish, but pressure is remarkably light because most anglers concentrate on the many natural lakes nearby. Walleyes are the most abundant species, providing good angling all the way from the wide, domesticated water around Arnprior up to the thinner and wilder stretches above Temiscaming. They bite best in late May and June, around shoals and the mouths of tributaries where they've spawned. On summer evenings, one especially good spot is just below the coffer dam at Rolphton, where shore anglers often make quick limit catches when water is released. Pike are very abundant, and muskies somewhat less so, along the entire river as far up as the dam at Mattawa. Weedy bays and tributary mouths are productive; the Arnprior area, including the lower Madawaska River, produces many trophy muskies. Bass are plentiful along most of the river, both smallmouths and largemouths. Find them in shallow parts of the bays in spring; in deeper parts near the channel in summer. Brook trout are numerous in many Quebec tributaries above Rolphton. Most towns have boat ramps.

Sturgeon Lake, Ont.

First-rate angling for lake trout, without forking over like a sultan for a fly-in trip. Sturgeon is a big lake, 40 miles long, practically all of it prime habitat for lakers. And the best part is, you can drive right to it. In the spring, the trout average 4 to 6 pounds, and smack lures trolled or cast around shoals, islands, and shorelines adjacent to deep water, in almost any section of the lake. Popular spoons include Little Cleos, Five of Diamonds, and Williams Wablers; spinners tipped with minnows will do the job, too. By summer the usual size is up considerably—6 to 8 pounds—and you have to get down 60 to 100 feet where the ciscoes are under siege. Wire line, downriggers, and deep jigging will all pay off. Trollers favor Sutton spoons with sucker meat hung on the hooks. A dozen camps and resorts operate on Sturgeon, and boat rentals are available. Camping is restricted to commercial tent and trailer sites. Pike and walleyes, far less plentiful than lakers, are caught mostly in Nipigon Bay, Cobb Bay, and the Northeast Arm.

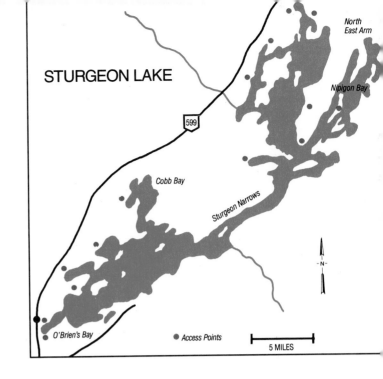

Lake Diefenbaker, Sask.

A double-headed monster of a reservoir, Diefenbaker forks at its deep end and boasts not just one dam but a pair. Though it's close to the province's three largest cities and it's loaded with walleyes, the fishing pressure is featherlight. Anglers would rather drive long hours on denture-rattling backroads to some boreal swamp famed mainly for its blackflies, than try out this prairie hotspot practically at their doorsteps. The lake is 130 miles long, all of it good for walleyes. Three- to five-pounders are common; the average size has been increasing because the tullibee population, prime forage, has exploded in the past few years. The best fishing comes in the spring on the countless sand-gravel points; 8- to 12-foot depths are productive, but when the water is roily the walleyes may venture into water less than 5 feet deep. In summer they're usually deeper, 15 to 20 feet. Jigs and Lindy rigs are popular, fished with nightcrawlers, leeches, or preserved minnows. Live minnows are banned. Diefenbaker also offers pike (Coteau Bay is a good spot), big saugers, perch, and lake trout. In the upper end of the lake, anglers take rainbows that drift down from the Bow River.

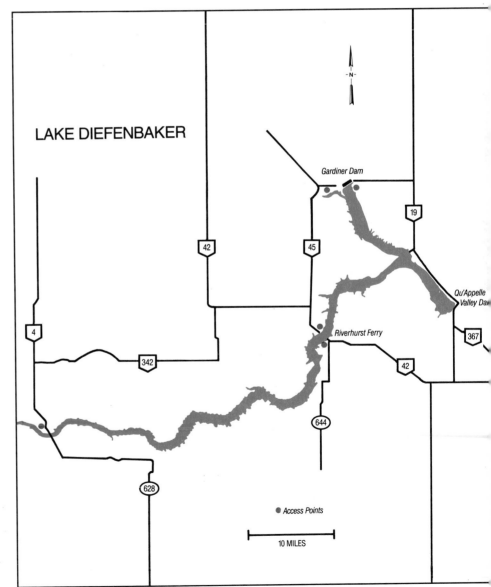

Clearwater West & White Otter Lakes

Butch Furtman

For ten years, Barry Brown served as a conservation officer for the Ontario Ministry of Natural Resources. His territory included some of southwest Ontario's prime fishing waters, and in time he became a walking encyclopedia on where to catch lake trout, walleyes, and smallmouth bass. So when Barry resigned in 1978 to go into the resort business, it was no accident that he and his wife, Janet, bought a resort on Clearwater West Lake near Atikokan, Ontario.

Clearwater West offered a rare combination of attractions: it had outstanding lake trout fishing, yet was easily accessible by road. And with only a 250-yard portage, you could also reach White Otter Lake, one of the region's premier waters for lakers and walleyes.

I'm always looking for a chance to fish at Clearwater West and White Otter, so when Hunting and Fishing Library director Dick Sternberg told me he needed to photograph some nice lake trout for his latest book, I recommended that we head for Barry's lodge. It was early February, not the best time to ice-fish for lakers (early January, right after the season opens, is usually tops), but I felt we could catch enough for the photos.

When we arrived, we decided to try White Otter first. We loaded our gear on sleds behind snowmobiles, and within 25 minutes were drilling holes on White Otter.

In winter, the super lake trout hangouts on White Otter are underwater extensions of islands adjacent to deep water. The most productive areas are 50 to 70 feet deep, with water at least 100 feet deep nearby.

After drilling several 10-inch holes over an underwater lip, we lowered ¾-ounce airplane jigs tipped with shiner minnows, and started jigging. I like to jig with a regular baitcasting rod and reel; the rod gives a better sweep than an ice rod and makes it much easier to set the hook. I usually jig on bottom for a minute or two, then reel up a few feet at a time until I find the trout.

The first laker struck about 15 feet off bottom. It wasn't a bone-rattling strike, just a light tap, typical of winter lake trout. I set the hook immediately and tied into a strong fish. Lake trout have a reputation as sluggish fighters, but you wouldn't know it in winter. This fish bulldogged its way to bottom and refused to give ground. I pulled as hard as my 8-pound mono would allow, and finally the fish started to tire. I worked its head into the hole and Dick gaffed it, a fat 7-pounder.

We caught a couple more lakers, then the action slowed, so we decided to do some exploring. Every spot we tried produced a fish or two. Late in the afternoon, we drilled on a long finger extending from an island. Within an hour, we took six lakers and lost several more. Final tally for the day: twelve trout from 4 to 9 pounds, and eight more hooked but not caught. Not bad, for the wrong time of winter.

Fishing like that is not unusual on White Otter. On Clearwater West, you may not catch quite as many trout but your chances for a trophy are better. In fact, one lucky angler landed a 40-pounder on Clearwater West in February 1987. It's the largest laker ever caught through the ice, anywhere.

Summer fishing on White Otter is great, too. After our successful ice-fishing trip, Dick and I decided to sample the angling the following July. Barry Brown, his brother Wayne, and Rod Whalley decided to join us to chase the White Otter lakers. We boated to the portage, carried our gear across, then transferred it to boats that Barry stows on White Otter. Barry had brought a "green box" sonar along so we could find the productive reefs. But when he opened it, he discovered that he'd forgotten the transducer. Dick was in favor of going back to get it.

"No problem," Barry said. "We don't need a depth finder anyway."

As we motored out onto the lake, I wondered how we would find the reefs and the right depths to fish. Soon Barry slowed the boat. "We should be pretty close to the reef. Let's try it."

We rigged up with ½-ounce Heddon Sonars, lowered them to the bottom, and began vertical-jigging. Within minutes Wayne yelled, "There's one," and set the hook. "He was at least 10 feet off bottom." While he fought his fish, we all raised our Sonars. Soon Dick was wrestling

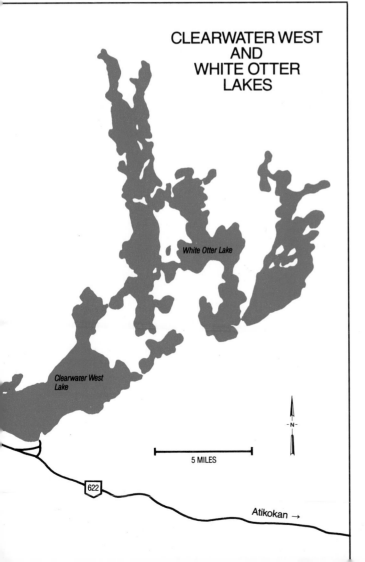

CLEARWATER WEST
AND
WHITE OTTER
LAKES

White Otter Lake

Clearwater West Lake

- N -

5 MILES

622

Atikokan →

a trout too, and so was Wayne. The fast action continued throughout the afternoon.

We were fishing blind for suspended lakers, yet managed to catch our fifteen-fish limit of 5- to 7-pounders by midafternoon. We finished off the day by catching a half dozen 3- to 4-pound walleyes in a shallow bay. They hit ¼-ounce yellow jigs tipped with ribbon leeches. On the run back to the portage, Dick remarked, "Think what we could have caught if we'd had a depth finder."

Back at the lodge, he asked Barry why fishing on White Otter was holding up so well when quite a few other lakes nearby were going downhill. Barry explained that the Ministry of Natural Resources had initiated special regulations to protect the lake from overharvest. White Otter doesn't open to fishing until June 16, a month after most other lakes in the area. Delaying the season protects the walleyes during their vulnerable post-spawn period, and protects lake trout when they're feeding actively in the shallows.

By the time the season opens, both walleyes and trout have scattered and moved deeper, so they're not so simple to catch. The regulations seem to be working well, both in terms of numbers of fish and average size. White Otter lakers average a solid 5 pounds, and the walleyes about 3 pounds. The lake also produces a surprising number of 7- to 8-pound walleyes.

For some unknown reason, Clearwater West does not support walleyes, but in recent years smallmouth bass have been showing up in increasing numbers. White Otter, by contrast, has no smallmouths.

White Otter and Clearwater West are not the only good fishing lakes in the area. Barry keeps boats on Gray Trout Lake, another first-rate spot for trophy lake trout just a few miles from Clearwater West. He also has boats on Kingfish Lake, known for its healthy population of walleyes. For smallmouth bass, a trip to Wasp Lake or the east end of Crowrock Lake usually produces the fastest action, with fish up to 4½ pounds.

In addition, the road from Atikokan (see map) to Clearwater West is now being extended northward, opening some virtually untapped fishing possibilities. By the spring of 1988 the road will open to travel all the way to Wapageisi Lake, 35 miles from Clearwater West. Anglers can drive to excellent fishing for lake trout, walleyes, and pike on such lakes as Islets, Beak, and Wapageisi.

Brown's Clearwater West Lodge (P.O. Box 1766A, Atikokan, Ont; phone 807-597-2884) is the only resort along the road. Cottages are available at reasonable rates, including several outpost cottages on remote beaches of Clearwater West; and there's a campground at the lodge for tents and RVs. Cook your own meals or eat at the lodge, American plan. The lodge rents boats and motors, and also offers guide service.

Butch Furtman is the host of the Sportsman's Notebook *television show in Duluth. He has worked as a guide in the Boundary Waters Canoe Area, and has written for* Outdoor Life *and other magazines.*

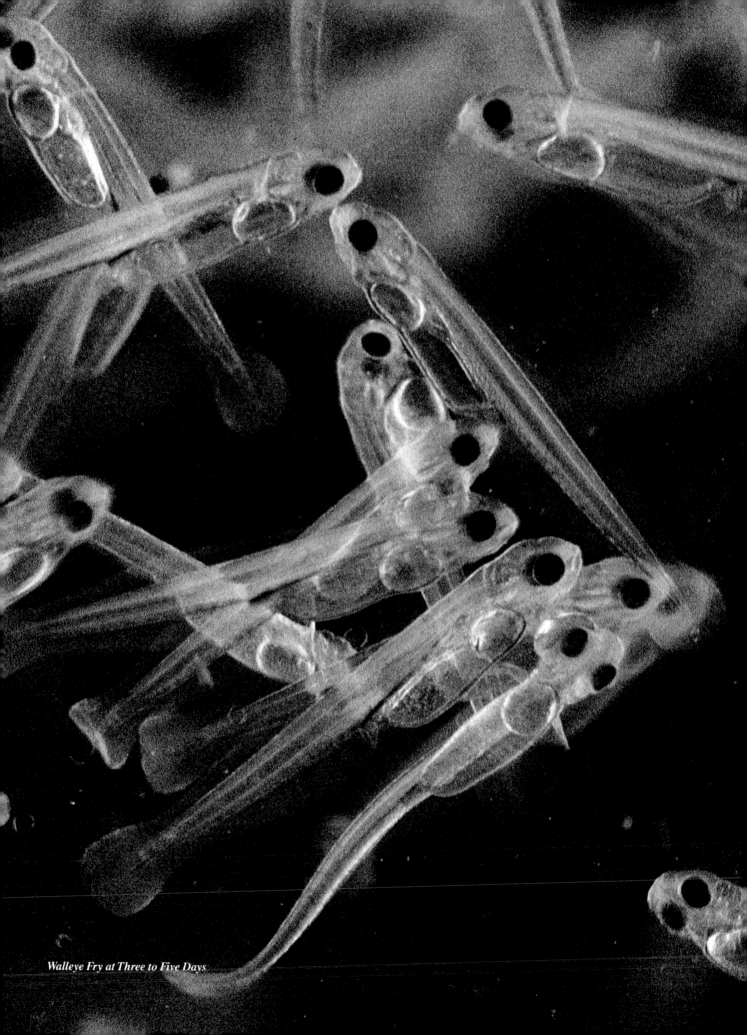

Walleye Fry at Three to Five Days

Fisheries Science

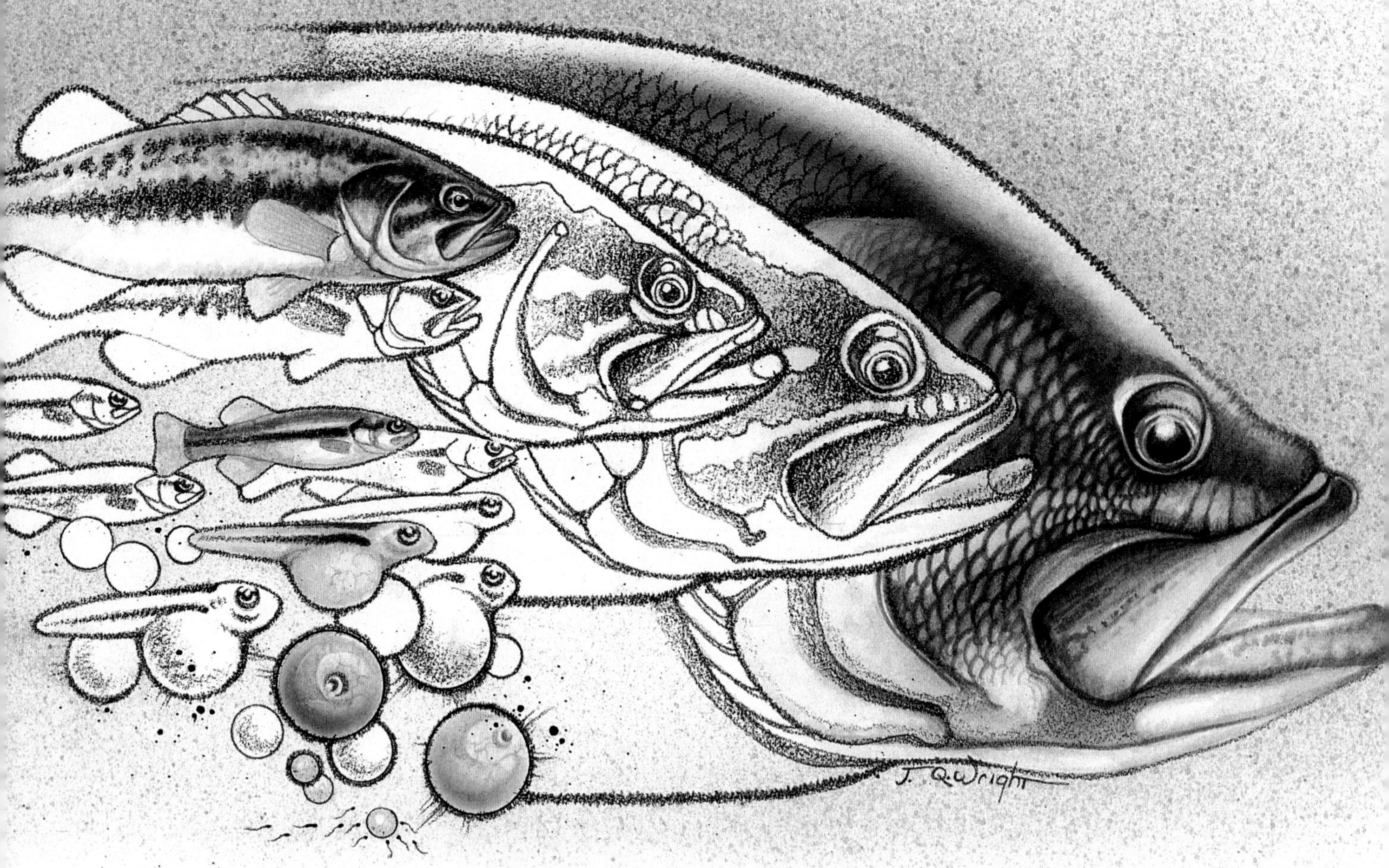

J. Q. Wright

Building the
Super Bass

Frank Sargeant

After more than fifty years, bass anglers and fishery managers have pretty well become convinced that Nature is not going to produce a fish to top George Perry's all-tackle world-record largemouth of 22 pounds 4 ounces. But there's growing hope that what Nature can't do, science can.

Texas has launched a full-scale attempt to produce bass that grow faster and attain larger ultimate sizes than its native fish, and that also are hardier in a wide variety of waters and climates. Its earliest effort, the importation of Florida-strain largemouths many years ago, has resulted in a remarkable increase in the state record. At this writing, the top fish is a 17 pound 10¾-ouncer taken in November 1986, which is still alive and growing in a hatchery at Tyler. But even that fish may be surpassed—and on a regular basis—if efforts now under way by research scientists in the Lone Star State bear the predicted fruits.

"We believe crossbreeding of stocks with maximum genetic variability is the key to producing fast-growing, vigorous bass," says Bill Rutledge, chief of fish hatcheries for the state. "Florida bass were stocked in California for the first time thirty years ago, and that stock has remained isolated long enough to develop slight genetic differences from the originals. Floridas were first stocked in Cuba seventy years ago, again plenty of time for variations to develop. Our program involves crossing these Cuba and California fish, as well as our natives, to turn out hybrids that feed more aggressively and grow faster than anything we've had before."

Hybrids typically grow faster than parent stocks and reach larger maximum sizes. Most of the string of new Texas records since 1980 have been hybrids. Before that, the state record had stood at 13 pounds 8 ounces for almost forty years, but since then the record has jumped five separate times. Rutledge hopes to continue the hybridization process in Texas, stocking more Floridas in waters where most of the bass appear to have northern largemouth characteristics, adding northern or native Texas bass where Floridas appear to be the primary stock.

Texas has also begun an aggressive catch-and-release program aimed at keeping more large bass spawning in its waters. And "Operation Share a Lone Star Lunker" encourages anglers to turn in live trophy bass for its hatchery spawning programs. Thus far, seven fish over 13 pounds have been donated, including that current state record.

"We don't know that these large fish will produce offspring that reach sizes larger than normal, but at least they've proven they have what it takes to get very big," says Rutledge. "It's possible they have some small variations in growth rate or feeding ability that caused them to get exceptionally big, and we might eventually be able to draw those traits out. But whether that happens or not, the public impact of fishermen turning in these trophies to continue spawning has been tremendous—it's a great promotion for release fishing."

Rutledge says part of the incentive for the program is that the anglers receive fiberglass replicas of their giant catches from the state. "We've found that the replicas are even more attractive than skin mounts and are more durable, plus the angler knows his fish is still alive and contributing to our stocking program."

Texas biologists have approached the development of larger average size from other angles, as well. They've begun cloning giant female bass—adding irradiated sperm to eggs so cells divide without the normal bisexual interaction of genes, thus creating genetic duplicates of the mother. They're also adding hormones and other chemicals to the brood water, in order to produce female bass only. Females normally grow far larger than males, so by stocking large numbers of females in a lake, biologists could increase the supply of trophy fish—provided the forage was adequate to support them.

And the state is looking at sterilizing bass as a way to generate some true giants that might knock off that long-standing 22-4 record. "Bass use a lot of their energy in reproduction," says researcher Nick Carter. "If you cut the reproductive cycle out of their lives, they'll grow much faster and should ultimately reach far larger sizes."

All this work is experimental at present, but once the new San Marcos Fish Hatchery goes on line in the fall of 1988, the state will be able to put many of its experiments into production. The facility is expected to turn out over three million largemouths yearly. And biologists now have the means to trace the progress of each bass they stock, in new PIT microchip tags injected into its body, giving it a ten-digit identity that can be read with electronic gear similar to the price scanners in your neighborhood grocery store. Biologists say the tags can't be lost and don't cause infections, making the study of individual growth patterns far more effective than ever before.

Texas doesn't have a monopoly on the development of super bass. In 1986, Oklahoma began work on "sex-change operations" for largemouths, producing females through the use of irradiated sperm, just as in Texas, then switching the females to males by feeding them hormone-laced food while the sex organs are developing. According to Dr. William Shelton, the result should be male bass with the greater size potential of female bass. These oversized males could be mated with large females, perhaps originating a strain of bigger-than-normal bass.

Alabama has been trying for many years to produce larger bass through line-breeding large Florida fish, and the progeny of these efforts have upped the state record to 14 pounds 11 ounces. The state had never produced a fish in the 14-pound class until 1976, when the Floridas had reached maturity.

Glenn Lau, the famed outdoor film maker and television producer, believes he already has the super strain of bass swimming in his hatchery near Ocala, Florida. Several years ago, Lau isolated large fish from northern Florida as a strain different in length and weight potential from the fish further south. He believes that a small area in the north-central part of the state, which historically has produced most Florida bass over 12 pounds, holds the only remaining stock of these great fish, and he has developed a hatchery there to preserve and propagate them.

Lau has predicted that his fish, bred only to others of their strain through several generations and fed only live fish diets, will attain growth rates unheard of elsewhere. There are skeptics in the scientific community, but Lau expects a fish from his stock will soon exceed the world record. In 1985, he told the world he could raise a 25-pounder in six years. He reported growth rates of as much as 1½ pounds in 53 days, some six times the normal rate for largemouths. Several three-year-old fish over 12 pounds are swimming in his grow-out ponds, and if he can maintain their growth rate, he clearly could produce a world-beater. In fact, Lau optimistically predicts he'll have no fewer than five fish over the 22-pound 4-ounce mark by 1990.

All this fooling with Mother Nature has not been welcomed by everyone in fisheries management. Dr. David Phillips of the Illinois Department of Natural Resources, among others, has expressed concern that stocking non-native fish strains will introduce undesirable genes, resulting in fish that may not survive local weather extremes or may not have resistance to local diseases or predators. Those involved in the genetic improvement of bass argue that their fish will strengthen stocks wherever they're released, but the opposite view may be worth a long look.

Whether the efforts under way spawn a fish that bumps George Perry from the top of the records probably won't make much difference to most of us. But one likely side effect will be lots more trophy bass across much of the nation—not a tough side effect to deal with.

Frank Sargeant is the outdoor editor of the Tampa Tribune. *His national magazine articles on fish and fishing have won numerous writing awards.*

Saving the Old West's Wild Trout

Ted Williams

"Trout," wrote Robert Traver in *Anatomy of a Fisherman*, "will not, indeed cannot, live except where beauty dwells." From his perspective this was true enough, for he never would have recognized as trout the beasts I was pursuing so relentlessly when I first read his words. It was the early 1960s, and what Traver was (and is) to Frenchman's Pond, I was to the Aberjona River.

If you do not know the Aberjona, I urge you to keep things that way. It is the ditched conduit that drains the world-famous toxic dumps of Woburn, Massachusetts. From its turbid flow, between patches of scum that could support the full weight of Norway rats, under cement bridges stained with pigeon and starling guano, in the silty outwash of storm sewers, I would extract "trout." There were, in the Aberjona River, only two types of trout—freshly stocked and dead.

At last a driver's license enabled me to migrate from the Aberjona to water where beauty did dwell—where the pigeons wore ruffs around their necks and dressed in royal ermine, where the rats were sleek and clean and swam among pond lilies, and where the starlings flashed red epaulets and rode cattails in a pine-scented breeze. But even there, beauty did not dwell in the trout.

The managers, for once precise and economical in their language, call stocked trout "the hatchery product." I like this. It says it all, and does not insult real trout—the wild, lovely creatures that make fishing something better and more important than shopping. In some ways, unleashing the hatchery product where beauty dwells strikes me as even more depraved than unleashing it where blight and ruin reign. But to fully appreciate wild trout one needs to have caught lots of the other kind.

I still angled for the hatchery product in 1970, when I went to work for the Massachusetts Division of Fisheries and Wildlife. Every season the trout I caught looked less and less like fish. Inbreeding gave rise to grotesque mutations: pinched caudal peduncles, twisted jaws, gill covers that didn't fit, eyes covered with bone. Cement pools blunted snouts, removed scales, rounded tails, and abraded fins. The dorsal—a trout's most beautiful fin—had no contact with the cement, but was nipped by pressing hordes to a withered, fleshy stump. So prevalent are withered dorsals among today's hatchery-reared salmonids that the deformity is used as a management tool where regulations require the public to distinguish between domestic and wild stock.

My first year on the job I visited the state's newest and biggest trout-rearing facility, and made the observation that a hatchery is the antithesis of a stream. When I strolled along the raceways I was appalled to see the fish scoot *toward* me in the hope of getting fed. A preference for live insects rather than processed "trout chow" precludes survival in such an environment. So does a preference for cover, shade, and solitude. The hatchery product, therefore, must be selected to be everything that real trout are not.

I complained to the managers about the physical appearance of the hatchery product, and they got puffy and defensive. I told them I liked at least to pretend that the trout I caught had some remote link with the natural world, and they fitted the hatchery product with tags that said "Make It in Massachusetts" and informed me that if I brought the tags to this or that store I could exchange them for prizes.

So I found myself pursuing the hatchery product with waning enthusiasm until, at last, I pursued it not at all. Now, I catch it only by mistake—when, for example, I wander too far downstream or when it snatches a deer-hair bug tossed for smallmouths. I begin each new search for trout by studying the state stocking list and inking from my topo maps all water it names. The trout I catch now are pretty small, but they are very beautiful. And they are real.

I had given up on the managers some years ago, but lately I sense an awakening among them, a sprouting of what the nineteenth-century outdoor writer George Bird Grinnell called "a refined taste in natural objects." The old guard is dying out and retiring, and suddenly there are new ideas. Here and there managers are rejecting the old shibboleth that "a trout is a trout."

In the East there isn't a lot for them to do, other than regulate fishing pressure. Here, in places where spawning habitat persists, the genes of native brook trout remain pure because rainbows don't breed with them, browns rarely breed with them, and domestic brookies are quickly culled by natural selection. The East's other native trout—the blueback and Sunapee—occur in a few remote Maine ponds, where the populations seem healthy. Basically, managers leave them alone.

The crisis is in the West, where many species and subspecies of native trout face extinction. Overgrazing, predatory logging, and diversion for irrigation have eliminated a lot of habitat, but the major threat has been the hatchery product. Domestic rainbows have been flung hither and yon. They have penetrated to the good water and wiped out native stocks by hybridizing with them—"genetic swamping," the managers call it. Elsewhere, naturalized browns and brook trout have displaced native western species.

Greenback Cutthroat Trout

The Bonneville cutthroat trout, *Salmo clarki utah*, thrived in glacial Lake Bonneville about nine thousand years ago. As this vast inland sea dried up, the Bonneville cutthroats retreated to the feeder streams where they evolved to fit the harsh environment of what is now Nevada, Idaho, Wyoming, and Utah. The species, once believed extinct, has been recommended for threatened status under the Endangered Species Act, which would severely restrict fishing. But the states and the U.S. Fish and Wildlife Service are resisting, and with good reason. They have removed the threat of extinction with an aggressive recovery plan.

I think the managers I've spoken with want to restore the Bonneville cutthroat not because it is big, strong and beautiful (although it is), but because it is part of a natural system, something that *belongs* to the West. Even from a purely business perspective, however, there is ample reason for the effort. Because the Bonneville cutthroat evolved in the range it now inhabits, it does better there than trout from, say, Germany or the coastal Northwest. Hardly astonishing, yet somehow this never dawned on those managers who, for example, polluted Utah's Bear Lake with hatchery rainbows. Survival was about zero, but the scrawny rainbows—assisted by scrawny browns and brook trout—eliminated the native Bonnevilles. Now that Utah has stanched the flow of put-and-take exotics and reintroduced the natives, fish are coming back in the 18- and 19-pound range.

Bruce Schmidt, Utah's fisheries chief, reckons he and his associates have doubled the number of streams in the state that support Bonnevilles, and have probably tripled the population. "Now," he says, "we're in the process of making a major change in management. In the next few years we'll increase the use of Bonneville trout, and decrease and possibly eliminate the use of introduced species."

Utah plans to seed Bonnevilles in its number-one trout fishery: 13,000-acre Strawberry Reservoir, currently overrun with rainbows, Yellowstone cutthroats, and hybrids of the two. The project—which will be the planet's biggest reclamation, requiring 1.3 million pounds of powdered rotenone—includes extensive habitat rehabilitation on 180 miles of tributaries, silted by cattle grazing to the point that they now are useless for spawning. Within ten years the Utah Division of Wildlife Resources expects significant natural recruitment.

In Nevada a similar cutthroat—the Lahontan, *Salmo clarki henshawi*—has a brighter future thanks to recent efforts by managers. The Lahontan is the state fish and a federal threatened species. One race, with an average spawning weight of 20 pounds, evolved in Pyramid Lake. Early in the century, the federal government announced it would divert a tributary of the lake, the Truckee River, to "reclaim" the unique habitat of the Nevada desert. The Paiute Indians, who depended on the Pyramid Lahontans for food, pointed out that the big fish spawned in the Truckee and that diversion would wipe them out. But Washington proclaimed it was concerned with "larger interests." The river was diverted in 1906, and the population eventually was lost. The managers came to the rescue with the hatchery product, but it did badly in the lake because trout other than Lahontans are not adapted to the extremely alkaline water.

Today, assisted by a federal hatchery, the Indians are raising Lahontans and managing the lake for sport fishing only. With inadequate flowage down the Truckee, the fish still cannot spawn, but they do very well on a put-grow-and-take basis, commonly reaching weights of 8 pounds. Whether they are the original Pyramid Lake strain is debatable, but what looks to be a pure population has recently been discovered high on a mountain in eastern Nevada, flung there by some forgotten Johnny Appleseed fish manager.

Another race of Lahontan, the Humboldt strain—native to the Humboldt River basin in northern Nevada—fares better. Viable populations have been found in more than sixty streams in the Humboldt watershed. Though the entire historical range is not known, management plans call for identifying it as closely as possible, poisoning out populations of exotic trout, erecting barrier dams to prevent reinfestation, and planting pure Lahontans.

In Colorado a similar strategy is under way to restore the greenback cutthroat, *Salmo clarki stomias*. Once classified as endangered, this striking gold-and-crimson fish was relisted to threatened in 1978 in order to facilitate transplanting. Currently it has been secured on twelve sites, and the managers are shooting for twenty.

U.S. Fish and Wildlife Service

Greenback Cutthroat Range: Hidden Valley Creek, Colorado

The Colorado Division of Wildlife anticipates delisting this subspecies about 1990, at which time streams will be opened to fishermen. A major obstacle, however, is the fishermen themselves. Philosophically, they seem as stunted as the brook trout currently infesting greenback range.

Even now you may angle for greenbacks on Hidden Valley Creek inside Rocky Mountain National Park, provided you don't kill them. The managers, however, urge that you do kill the alien brook trout which have surged back after rotenone and fyke nets failed to eliminate them. They are muscling out the greenbacks, but not because they are better adapted to the stream. They are more prolific and, as fall spawners, have a built-in size advantage, emerging from the eggs well before the spring-spawning cutthroats. When the division opened Hidden Valley Creek in 1982 to brook-trout killing and greenback releasing, Trout Unlimited members descended, catching 171 brook trout and, indoctrinated with no-kill-no-matter-what, *returning* 112 of these to the stream. It's been that way ever since.

Colorado kill-and-keep fishermen dislike the idea of managers cleaning out brook trout. They have nothing against greenbacks but don't cotton to the notion of waiting two or three years till the population establishes itself. A trout, they say, is a trout.

Still, Colorado managers are sanguine about the greenback's future. Wild fish, like wild anything, tend to do poorly in captivity. Because greenbacks prefer their water clean, their food alive, their sunlight muted, and their company scarce, it takes a lot of doing to rear them. "That's one of the reasons native stocks weren't used at first; the managers got impatient," explains Colorado aquatic specialist Dr. Jim Bennett, a member of the Greenback Trout Recovery Team. Hatchery production of greenbacks, however, is not impossible, and Colorado is learning a great deal about it. Currently, the state raises 100,000 a year, fertilizing eggs with wild milt to ensure what Bennett calls "genetic fresh air."

Cattle and exotic trout eliminated the Rio Grande cutthroat, *Salmo clarki virginalis*, from most of its historical range, but it still abides in forty or fifty tiny mountain rills mostly in New Mexico, a few in south-central Colorado. Sometimes these rills amount only to isolated pools, connected by underground seepage. Yet the native Rio Grandes do well and grow to startling size. The alien browns, squatting in the valleys, are descended from trout that took to sea—a large, diverse, highly competitive ecosystem demanding heavy recruitment. So they tend to overpopulate, stunting badly.

One would think that sportsmen—especially those who measure trout quality by trout size—would unite behind the New Mexico Game and Fish Department in its effort to restore Rio Grande cutthroats to their mainstream habitat. But they have not. Fisheries Management Project Leader Mike Hatch explains: "More often than not we find that a restoration site has great sporting appeal to some group. And if we were to put a barrier in and wipe out the exotics, we would carve into someone's sporting opportunity." Sometimes, he says, the resistance is "tremendous."

If, to the sporting public, a trout is a trout, how do you convince it that a cutthroat is not a cutthroat? All the cutthroat races are vaguely similar, after all; so why fret about the demise of some isolated population? One capable of asking the question is incapable of comprehending the answer. But there are in the West two full species of trout—neither rainbow nor cutthroat—that also are imperiled. These are the Gila trout, *Salmo gilae*, of New Mexico's Gila River drainage; and the Apache trout, *Salmo apache*, of Arizona's White Mountains.

It appears that the endangered Gila will shortly be relisted to threatened. By the early 1960s there were only five known populations, all inside the Gila National Forest. The recovery program, headed by the U.S. Fish and Wildlife Service, calls for "replicating" the five streams—that is, establishing new populations in similar habitat so the species will be less vulnerable to such disasters as forest fires and landslides. Work is progressing well, and it appears that the species will be available for limited angling by the end of the decade.

The Apache trout, relisted from endangered to threatened in 1975, may soon replace the ill-adapted rainbow in main-stream management throughout its native state of Arizona. The Fish and Wildlife Service has been collecting Apache eggs and taking them to the Williams Creek National Fish Hatchery, where the fry will be

reared to "catchable" size for stocking at lower elevations. And higher up in the mountains, where natural and manmade barriers can insulate Apache trout from rainbow contamination, managers are well on their way to establishing thirty self-sustaining populations.

So, all over the West, fish managers are waking up. But people who care about wild trout need to do more than just applaud; they need to push. Within the state fish and game agencies are information and education sections whose mission, as the name indicates, is to inform and educate. But somehow the student/teacher relationship gets flip-flopped.

The New Mexico Game and Fish Department, for instance, appears excessively concerned about whether the Gila trout will be "accepted" as a game species. "If the prognosis is good," it informed the Fish and Wildlife Service, "then we would be willing to consider expansion of the Gila trout into waters that would rate as good habitat. Should sportsmen get behind us to promote more Gila trout waters, the possibility would exist that considerable areas of such habitat in the historic range could be reoccupied."

Gila Trout

But the department is proceeding backwards. Instead of waiting to see where the sportsmen take it, it should lead the way. Its staffers are paid to understand and protect wild creatures. Management decisions ought to be based on their expertise and their ecological conscience—not on the demands of minority user groups, which all too often lack both.

"We like to proceed cautiously," explains a manager having trouble convincing sportsmen that stunted brown trout need to make way for Rio Grandes. "We're not here to ram anything down anyone's throat." Maybe not, but all his loyalty and all the loyalty of his associates ought to lie with the Rio Grande cutthroat. And if—after the rotenone and dead exotics have washed away—someone doesn't like it, the next step is to lay on the information and the education.

Ted Williams is a contributing editor of Audubon *and* Gray's Sporting Journal. *His book,* Don't Blame the Indians, *about the failure of the courts to protect wildlife from unreasonable native claims, has recently been published by GSJ Press.*

Where All the Stripers Gone?

Robert H. Boyle

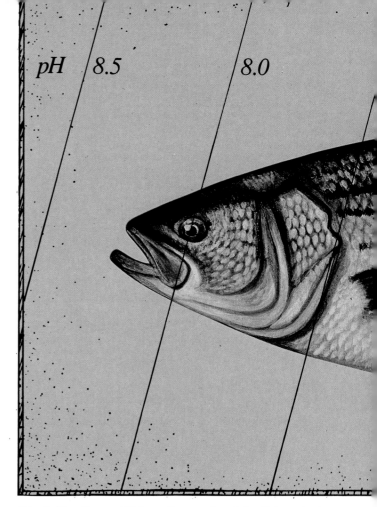

pH 8.5 8.0

It was the end of a not-so-perfect September day in 1983 on the eastern shore of the Chesapeake Bay. I had been fishing for striped bass with Jim Price, a charterboat captain from Oxford, Maryland, aboard his 20-foot Mako. We started in the morning off the mouth of the Choptank River and then went up into the river to fish the bridge abutments at Cambridge, where I took a striper and two white perch on jigs. We ended the day further up the Choptank at one of Jim's secret spots, but after eight hours of fishing I had caught only three stripers.

The fifth generation of his family to fish the Choptank for a living, Jim knew the river well, but was baffled by the increasing scarcity of stripers in recent years. Sexually mature stripers were still spawning, but not many young fish were found and the population was sinking out of sight. "Back in the sixties and early seventies," Jim said, "the Choptank was full of striped bass. In the fall you could run through 10 to 15 miles of breaking fish. Now we've got practically nothing."

The same held true for a number of other rivers on the Chesapeake—and also for coastal rivers from Nova Scotia down to North Carolina, and possibly even further south. The striped bass, the glamor gamefish of the Atlantic Coast, had fallen into a long-term decline. So had several other species normally common. At the time, no one knew why.

The striped bass spends most of its adult life in salt water but returns to freshwater rivers to spawn. Historically, tributaries of the Chesapeake produced the great majority of stripers that migrated along the coast from

North Carolina to Maine. One study of the fishery in its glory days estimated that Chesapeake rivers supplied 90.8 percent of the bass, the Hudson River in New York 6.5 percent, and the Roanoke River in North Carolina 2.7 percent.

Back in 1970, the coastal sport catch amounted to 73.3 million pounds, but a precipitous decline soon set in, and within a decade the catch dropped to little more than a million pounds a year. Senator John Chafee of Rhode Island was alarmed by the decline. He had read the book *Striper* by John N. Cole, which predicted the fish would eventually be done in by chemical contamination. In 1979, as a result of Chafee's concern, Congress authorized a $4 million emergency striped bass study.

My trip with Jim Price was not a day off, but business. *Sports Illustrated* had assigned me to do an article on the decline. The scientists working on the emergency study thought chemicals and overfishing might be responsible, but I was somewhat skeptical. Bass in the Hudson were far more contaminated by PCBs than the Chesapeake bass, yet the Hudson generally produced strong year-classes spring after spring. The scientists termed the high number of stripers in the Hudson an "apparent enigma," and attributed the abundance of juveniles to the closure of the commercial striper fishery in 1976 due to PCBs. But this overlooked the fact that the Hudson had an abundance of other species that were on the skids in Chesapeake rivers.

Take the American shad. In 1970 the Chesapeake catch amounted to 5 million pounds, but, like the striper, the

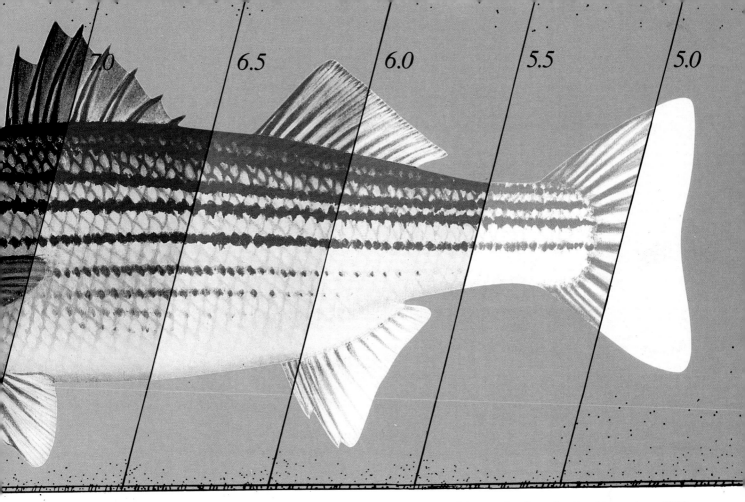

7.0   6.5   6.0   5.5   5.0

shad went into decline. By 1980 the catch had dropped by more than 80 percent, and Maryland imposed a ban on shad fishing. The ban remains in effect, but there is no sign that shad are making a comeback in the bay. While researching the striper decline, I asked Joe Boone, a biologist with the Maryland Department of Natural Resources, how the shad were doing. Joe had conducted annual surveys of the bay, looking for juvenile fish of various species. His answer was a shocker: "Our survey has failed to collect a single young shad in the vast nursery area of the upper Chesapeake Bay for ten consecutive years." By contrast, juvenile shad were all over the Hudson, even though commercial fishermen were catching perhaps a million pounds of spawning shad a year.

Similarly, blueback herring and alewives had slumped to record lows in the Chesapeake—spawning runs vanished from some streams—but these species were abundant in the Hudson. In 1983, their combined spawning population in the Hudson was estimated at 30 to 50 million. In 1987, it was 50 to 100 million.

Elsewhere along the coast, striped bass and shad were declining in North Carolina, especially in the Roanoke River. There were no hard numbers on the stripers, but shad landings in North Carolina had dropped by about 75 percent in a decade. Shad landings were also down in rivers of South Carolina, Virginia, and Georgia, though not as severely. Catch data from Florida were spotty, but indicated that shad were at very low levels. In Nova Scotia, striped bass were becoming a rarity in the Annapolis River. In fact the Annapolis had not had

any successful reproduction of striped bass since 1972, even though sexually mature fish, growing older and scarcer, were entering to spawn. In five years, puzzled biologists had managed to collect only two larval stripers. Yet young stripers were common in the Shubenacadie River less than 100 miles away.

In sum, it appeared there was something systemically different between the Hudson and the Shubenacadie on one hand, and the Chesapeake tributaries, the Roanoke, and the Annapolis on the other. Moreover, the decrease of spawning success in all the affected rivers had begun in the late 1960s and early '70s. Something had started happening to the young in those rivers at about the same time. What could that something be?

The article on striped bass was published in April 1984. In it I offered the hypothesis that acid pulses—sudden, temporary decreases in pH triggered by acid rainstorms or melting snow—were significantly responsible for the poor survival of striped bass eggs, larvae, and young in the affected rivers. Further, acid pulses could be adversely affecting the American shad, hickory shad, alewife, blueback herring, white perch, and yellow perch. The reason the Hudson and Shubenacadie continued to produce fish was that both were naturally buffered against acid pulses by limestone deposits.

As anyone who has kept an aquarium knows, water that becomes too acidic can kill fish, especially in their younger stages. Acidity is measured on the pH scale which runs from 0 to 14. The midpoint, 7, is neutral, with the numbers above increasingly alkaline and the numbers below increasingly acidic. The scale is logarithmic, so pH 4.6 is ten times more acidic than pH 5.6, and pH 3.6 is a hundred times more acidic than pH 5.6. Unpolluted rain has a pH of 5.6, because it combines with carbon dioxide naturally present in the atmosphere to form weak carbonic acid.

The acidity can be greatly increased by sulfur and nitrogen oxides emitted from coal- and oil-fired power plants, boilers, smelters, cars and trucks, and other sources of combustion. Aloft in the atmosphere, these oxides can transform into sulfuric acid and nitric acid. Later they fall to earth in the rain, perhaps hundreds of miles from their source. Where the soil contains readily available calcium, magnesium, or other carbonate minerals, a lake or stream can quickly buffer the acid, in much the same way an Alka-Seltzer tablet neutralizes an acid stomach. But in watersheds with little natural capacity for buffering, the effect can be devastating.

Decades of strong acids dropping from the sky have exhausted the buffering capacity of some waters in hard-rock regions. They have run out of Alka-Seltzer tablets, so to speak. This has happened to more than 200 lakes in the Adirondacks that have lost their fish life. This also has happened to many lakes and streams in New England, Pennsylvania, Ontario, Quebec, and Nova Scotia.

Because most of the damage was first discovered in poorly buffered high-elevation lakes and streams, acid-rain scientists, busy worrying about trout, did not think about striped bass or shad spawning in coastal rivers at or near sea level. And estuarine scientists did not pay attention to acid rain, because that was a problem up in the mountains, not down on the coast. Yet the coastal-plain soils in Maryland have little buffering capacity, and the rain that falls there is as acidic as any in the world. The pH ranges from 4.45 down to 3.5, fifteen to 110 times more acidic than normal. Several years ago, a rainstorm in Baltimore had a pH of 2.9, over 700 times more acidic than normal.

The article ran counter to the conventional wisdom of estuarine scientists. When asked about acid rain, they had maintained it could not affect the Chesapeake because any acid would immediately be neutralized by the brackish water in the bay. A $27 million, seven-year study of the Chesapeake, completed by the U.S. Environmental Protection Agency in 1983, did not even touch on the possibility of pH change induced by acid rain. It ignored the fact that freshwater tributaries are part of the bay ecosystem, that the declining fish spawned in streams subject to acid pulses, and that their eggs and larvae were, in Joe Boone's words, "long dead and gone" before they ever got into the bay.

As the article pointed out, a study in March and April 1983 on the headwaters of 23 streams feeding the Chesapeake showed that all experienced acid pulses. In the study, done for the Maryland DNR, the streams were sampled weekly, not daily. Even so, every stream dropped at least once to pH 5.8, fourteen of them fell to pH 5.5, and six suffered pH slumps lower than 4.9. Those drops

were extraordinarily sharp, but estuarine scientists on the Chesapeake dismissed the study as unimportant. One highly respected scientist—who, to his credit, later reversed his thinking—called it "bullshit."

In addition, investigators for the Maryland DNR found pH levels as low as 5.9 on the striped bass spawning grounds in the Choptank during the 1983 spawning season. This raised a minor blip on the mental radar screen of some scientists, but it soon vanished. An exception was Dr. Serge Doroshov, a striped bass authority at the University of California at Davis. "With those pH levels," he said, "I would speculate striped bass larvae wouldn't survive. They do best at a pH of 7.5 to 8.5. At Davis we raise them in water close to pH 8." Doroshov added that the larvae are extremely sensitive to sharp changes of pH even within the favorable range. He cited two instances where a sudden change of 1.0 or less caused 100 percent mortality.

The shad hit the fan when the article was published, and some scientists began to investigate the hypothesis. In my experience, federal and state agencies do not move swiftly to determine the truth or falsity of essentially simple propositions. Thus, no one so far has tracked an acid rainstorm that triggered an acid pulse that killed the fish in this or that coastal river. However, here are the major developments:

• In 1984, Lenwood Hall, an aquatic toxicologist at the Applied Physics Laboratory of the Johns Hopkins University, led a research team which found that larval striped bass placed in the Nanticoke River on the Chesapeake suffered excessive mortality rates. A total of 3,000 one-day-old larvae were put in chambers at three different stations in the spawning reach of the Nanticoke. Automatic samplers took water from the river every 15 minutes, and samples were analyzed for aluminum and other contaminants mobilized by acidity.

After four days, more than 90 percent of the larval stripers were dead, while control larvae in clean alkaline water in tanks on shore had only 25 percent mortality. The experiment was repeated with similar results. Afterward, Hall said: "The factors we feel are responsible are low pHs—approximately 6.3—plus high aluminum concentrations and very soft fresh water [indicating little buffering capacity]."

• The same year, Dr. Paul Mehrle at the National Fisheries Research Laboratory in Missouri found that ten-day-old striped bass suffered 100 percent mortality in water with a pH of 5.5. At pH 6.5, with small amounts of aluminum added to the water, mortality was 85 percent. Later studies at the lab indicated young striped bass remained sensitive to pH until 50 to 80 days old. Bass of this age died rapidly when exposed to pHs of 6.0 and below.

• In 1985, the Hudson River Foundation for Science and Environmental Research held a three-day conference on "Acidification and Anadromous Fish of Atlantic Estuaries." This was prompted by my article. In the conference summary, Dr. George R. Hendrey of the Brookhaven National Laboratory noted: "The experts

Checking pH on the Choptank River, Maryland.

agreed that the hypothesis that acid deposition is contributing to the loss of anadromous fish populations was … viable and important, and research dealing with this topic should be increased." Papers from the conference were published in *The Journal of Water, Air and Soil Pollution* in September 1987.

One of the papers, by Dr. Walton D. Watt of Canada's Department of Fisheries and Oceans, reported that severe acidification related to rain had lowered the pH of many rivers in Nova Scotia "to the point where their Atlantic salmon stocks have been destroyed or much diminished." Atlantic salmon are far more acid-tolerant than striped bass, but even salmon have their limit.

• In a 1986 report on striped bass in the Roanoke River, Dr. Roger A. Rulifson and his colleagues stated that excessive aluminum and pHs of 6.0 to 6.8 suggested "a potential problem for striped bass larvae."

• A paper soon to appear in *Transactions of the American Fisheries Society*, by Dr. Ronald J. Klauda and Robert E. Palmer, reports that blueback herring eggs exposed to a 24-hour pulse of pHs 5.5 to 5.6 and small amounts of aluminum had 48 percent mortality. Larvae suffered 100 percent mortality. Klauda and Palmer concluded that acid pulses following spring rainstorms "may be an important source of early life stage mortality for blueback herring" in Chesapeake Bay tributaries.

• For the past five years, Dr. Anthony Janicki of International Science and Technology, in Reston, Virginia, has been studying acid effects on Maryland coastal-plain streams. "Laboratory experiments with striped bass and blueback herring," he says, "suggest that acidic pulses could cause high mortality in the early life stages. Research is continuing with other anadromous fishes such as American shad and yellow perch. We're studying the extent of the problem all along the East Coast."

• Acid pulses also threaten fish in poorly buffered inland waters. They are blamed for the demise of white perch in Lake Matamuskeet, a 67-square-mile lake on the North Carolina coastal plain. And in South Carolina, acid pulses are suspected of causing a ten-year, 20 percent decline in the reproductive success of striped bass that run up from the Santee-Cooper Reservoir to spawn in the Congaree River. Plenty of eggs are produced, but the larvae don't survive.

Although the case against acid pulses hasn't been 100 percent proven in nature, only a fool would refuse to believe there's a problem of extraordinary magnitude, potential if not already under way, extending from Nova Scotia down to the southeastern states. If I had to pick a region at greatest risk, it would be the seaboard states from Maryland to Florida, particularly the coastal-plain streams. The mean pH of the rain now falling there ranges from 4.2 in Maryland to 4.6 in Florida. The Gulf Coast would be next, and the streams and lakes of the Appalachians from Virginia to Georgia and possibly Alabama.

Damage from acid rain has already been proven in the Northeast and in eastern Canada, and the problem is only going to worsen as long as we lack national legislation to control the emissions of sulfur and nitrogen oxides. Anglers should become involved with Trout Unlimited, the Izaak Walton League, and other organizations trying to get an acid-rain control bill passed by Congress. Too much is at stake to do otherwise.

Robert H. Boyle is a special contributor to Sports Illustrated. *His books include* Acid Rain, Bass, *and* The Hudson River: A Natural and Unnatural History. *He is president of the Hudson River Fishermen's Association, a conservation group working to protect the river.*

Nothing To Do But Eat

Joel M. Vance

When people have a psychological or physiological problem and resort to gluttony, it's called an eating disorder.

When fish do it, it's called management.

A normal fish eats to ready itself for its major genetic imperative: to reproduce itself. Take away its reproductive mandate and there's nothing left for it to do but eat.

And grow.

Enter a new wrinkle in fish management called *triploidy*—which is genetic jargon for slapping a physiological shock on fish eggs so the hatchlings wind up with half again as many chromosomes as a normal fish. That has the effect of sterilizing the fish—it can't reproduce.

Fish sterilization would seem to be counterproductive; angler logic says that the more fish produced, the more there are to catch. But in fisheries management, more is not necessarily better. When there are too many fish, they may become stunted or go out of control, eating what they aren't supposed to.

Further, many anglers today prefer trophy fish. They want size, not numbers. From this standpoint, the reason for producing triploid fish is that theoretically they should grow faster, since they waste no energy preparing for annual spawning.

In the case of salmon, triploids should grow far larger than normal fish which spawn and die in their third or fourth year. Think of it: a salmon that goes on and on past its natural lifespan, growing, eating, growing....

It's an angler's dream of heaven. Or is it?

Around the country, several triploid experiments are now under way. Michigan is trying to create a triploid chinook salmon of Godzillian proportions for the Great Lakes. Missouri has stocked triploid brown trout in a river where the species can't spawn successfully. Texas is working with largemouth bass. Idaho has introduced triploid rainbow-cutthroat hybrid trout to Henry's Lake, to fill an ecological niche not occupied by the native cutthroat population.

Triploidy is now a simple condition to induce, but it took a long time to develop the delicate formula of lab conditions and the timing necessary for unbalancing the chromosomal makeup of the eggs without killing them. "Fish spawn only once a year and if all the eggs die year after year, it gets pretty expensive," one biologist says.

One experiment resulted in 100 percent triploid fish, but most of the eggs died. Another saw acceptable survival of the eggs, but not many triploids.

Actually, there are several methods of creating triploid fish. The most popular is to dunk the eggs in water of a critical warm temperature for an equally critical length of time. Triploidy can also be induced by cold shock, pressure, or chemical shock.

There is no growth difference between a triploid and a normal diploid until the fish are sexually mature, usually at age two or three (four or five for salmon). That

pears that at least some triploid fish may grow *slower* than their diploid counterparts. The Illinois Natural History Survey studied grass carp intensively in the mid-1980s, and found that triploids of the species have a growth rate as much as 10 percent lower than that of diploids.

Until the 1990s, no one will know for certain if the triploid idea will actually benefit anglers.

stands to reason, because until then the habits of both are the same. It's only when the diploid diverts its energy to spawning and the triploid doesn't that the triploid jumps ahead in growth—or should, according to theory.

In practice, it may not work. The possibility exists that a salmon, for example, is programmed by nature to die in its fourth year whether it spawns or not. And it ap-

Some biologists think only Big Fish, and have no qualms about producing triploids. Others aren't so sure. "I'd hate to get people wanting these things when we may not be able to supply them," says one fish geneticist. "We may get some people screaming 'foul' and raising religious objections."

His concern is justified by events. In mid-1987, geneticists won approval to loose lab-altered bacteria designed to prevent frost damage in strawberries. The experiment seemed harmless enough, but it didn't happen without a court challenge by those who oppose any tampering with life processes.

Triploidy isn't really creating life—it's only addling the chromosomal pattern of a fish to make it sterile. But is that tampering with a life process? Well, is a vasectomy or a tubal ligation tampering with a life process?

It seems silly to defend a salmon's right to spawn when most people today acknowledge a human's right to become sterile. On the other hand, the human becomes sterile by his or her own choice; the salmon has its choice made for it.

For many years, seed and plant companies have addled plants genetically by irradiation. No one flinched when a biologist used irradiation to create a variety of soybean whose pods matured progressively, making it such a good quail food that it was called the Bobwhite Soybean. But what gives a beanstalk fewer rights than a chinook salmon?

Religious considerations aside, some people are vaguely uneasy about the goals of the triploid programs. One geneticist told me, "It's like selling our management, this emphasis on bigger is better. It's artificial somehow."

Another opponent felt that triploid fish probably will be like big, dumb cows in a feedlot, waiting for the truck to come and haul them to the slaughterhouse. But there's no evidence that a triploid fish is any dumber (or smarter) than its normal diploid counterpart. The genetic alterations are made to its reproductive system, not to what passes for a brain in a fish.

There are some, however, who believe it's desirable to create bigger fish quicker, regardless of the method. After all, biologists search constantly for better fish food, for better habitat, for regulations designed to bring the fish in a given population to their optimum numbers and individual size.

What it boils down to is that genetic diddling with fish is new enough that those inclined to rush in and try everything are counterbalanced by those who feel the wrath of God gathering, like a distant thunderstorm.

For anglers, there are some strictly practical questions as well. What about the poor guy who holds a world record, earned by hooking and landing a naturally spawned fish, then suddenly finds himself in second place when someone trundles in a lard-ass laboratory product? It's something to think about. Should a lab-created record fish have an asterisk after its weight, like Roger Maris's season home-run record?

"Triploid fish do occur naturally, though it's rare," a biologist told me. No one would argue with an angler who caught a lumbering eunuch of a fish produced after some natural heat shock to the egg. It would be a "natural" fish.

Remember the old Frankenstein movies where the obsessed doctor harnessed the power of lightning to bring life to his grisly assemblage of graveyard relics? That was considered perverted, but what if some corpse en route to his final rest got zapped by a lightning bolt and suddenly sat up and said, "Hey, why is everyone lookin' so bad?" Would he be a monster?

No one would know a triploid fish if it came to net or gaff because there is no visible indicator of triploidy. It takes incredibly sophisticated laboratory techniques to identify triploid fish, and even those are not surefire.

Elwood Harry, the president of the International Game Fish Association, the major fish record-keeping organization, says: "Under normal policy, it would be desirable for us to maintain separate categories for triploids, but considering the type of information and quality of photographs that we receive, it's questionable whether we could establish separate categories. Accordingly, at this stage of their development, they'll be recognized just like any other of their species."

A photograph wouldn't tell anyone anything. There are four methods of sorting out the chromosome count, and three of them probably are impractical or impossible under most circumstances.

One involves a "chromosome squash," in which a section of liver or gonad is prepared on a slide and the chromosomes counted. But it involves injecting a chemical into a live fish to induce a situation called metaphase where chromosomes are easy to count. It isn't a likely test for a record fish, which almost invariably is dead meat before it becomes a media object.

Two other methods, flow cytometry and the use of a Coulter Counter, measure the mass of cell nucleuses. A triploid fish has about 50 percent more nuclear mass than a diploid, since it has half again as many chromosomes. But both methods rely on fresh blood, which rarely is available. "By the time I see record fish," says a fish geneticist, "they're already at the taxidermy shop."

The most practical method is electrophoresis, which involves electrically charging a fish sample in a gel dish to separate the proteins, then staining it to make the protein pattern visible. If the species is known and the stain has a pattern about half again as dense as it should be, it must be a triploid.

The test is not a sure shot, though. A geneticist I talked to was super-cautious as to whether electrophoresis could identify a triploid often enough to be workable. Trout triploids are especially hard to determine.

So it seems that while labs perhaps can create triploid trophies, they can't really identify their prodigals upon return.

Michigan is now stocking sterile chinook salmon in the Great Lakes. Michigan State University and the Michigan Department of Natural Resources are cooperating in the experiment, which began in 1985. Eggs were heat-shocked at 28.5°C (the decimal indicates how critical temperature is) for ten minutes after they were fertilized; then they were cooled slowly. Survival was low, though all the survivors were triploids. So, Michigan still is working out a way to insure both triploidy and survival.

Michigan stocked about 45,000 triploid chinook salmon in Lakes Huron and Michigan in 1986, and 140,000 there and in Lake Superior in 1987. It will be 1991 before there are any conclusive results. A conclusive result would be some angler dragging in a 60-pound chinook, when the average is about 20 pounds.

The current Lake Michigan record is 46 pounds 1 ounce, and the Great Lakes record (from Lake Ontario) is 47 pounds. But chinooks obviously can grow larger: the world record is a 97-pound 4-ounce fish caught in Alaska's Kenai River in 1985. A commercial fisherman once took a 126-pounder.

Wisconsin is stocking sterile salmon in the Great Lakes, too, but is not involved with triploidy. It is sterilizing hatched salmon with a synthetic steroid, methyltestosterone. But the result should be the same: fish that have no urge to spawn, and instead spend their energies in growing.

Missouri's experiment is with brown trout. Because of fluctuating water levels and temperatures, browns can rarely spawn successfully in Missouri streams. "Why not let the energy they would expend in spawning go instead into growth?" asks Spence Turner, state Department of Conservation trout biologist. "Since triploids do occur rarely in nature, we're not really changing anything, just augmenting it."

Religious considerations aside, some people are vaguely uneasy about the goals of the triploid programs. One geneticist says, ''It's like selling our management, this emphasis on bigger is better. It's artificial somehow.''

Texas has several fast-grow experiments with the largemouth bass, the bread-and-butter freshwater fish. One of these is triploidy. The world-record 22-pound 4-ounce largemouth was caught in Georgia more than fifty years ago, and eager anglers in Texas and elsewhere have been shooting at it ever since—and pressuring biologists to come up with bigger bass. (See "Building the Super Bass," on page 128.)

The problem that Idaho faces at Henry's Lake is to manage a small lake with a worldwide reputation for trophy trout. Hordes of anglers come there expecting to do battle with big fish.

Each year Idaho stocks the lake with 300,000 hybrid rainbow-cutthroat fingerlings, sterilized by triploidy, and these now provide about a fifth of the fishery and a quarter of all the fish over 20 inches. The hybrids grow faster than normal, and triploidy guarantees they won't crossbreed with the native cutthroats, which the state wants to preserve in as pure a strain as possible.

While most of these experiments are intended to produce heftier stringers, another use of triploidy is to control an exotic and only partly welcome fish, the grass carp or white amur.

Americans have an insatiable desire to import biological goodies from other countries, and with rare exceptions the result is bad. Because somebody wanted us to enjoy all the birds that Shakespeare wrote about, we now have the starling. Gypsy moths were supposed to spin silk stockings for Miss America. The common carp was hailed as "the coming fish" back in the 1880s when it first was stocked.

Once you get past the ringnecked pheasant, you've just about exhausted the list of successful exotics. Grass carp are the latest alien biological time bomb.

Grass carp first came to the United States in 1963, imported from Malaysia for study by both Auburn University and the U.S. Fish and Wildlife Service. The fish eat aquatic vegetation, and the idea of a nonchemical weed control is environmentally attractive.

But no one has figured out how to train a grass carp to eat only target weeds, and to quit eating once the desired amount of vegetation is gone. And it has proved impossible to keep the fish from escaping into waters where they not only weren't wanted, but also could proliferate to pest proportions.

By 1970, grass carp had been loosed in the waters of Arkansas. Private importers spread them widely around the country through the 1970s, and now they have spawned and are established in many major watersheds.

Triploidy is used on grass carp not to create trophies, but to make them sterile so they cannot reproduce and possibly become aquatic pests on the order of their common-carp cousins. Illinois, for one, requires any grass carp sold there to be triploids.

The bottom line where triploids are concerned is an oft-repeated truism: Nature abhors a vacuum.

And yet, where a vacuum exists, perhaps there's a reason. It's difficult to see how a fish unable to reproduce could pose a threat—but it was difficult for those who imported starlings or gypsy moths to see any problems either.

Tomorrow's super fish could be a trophy created in a lab, just as challenging and tough to catch as a wild-spawned fish. Or it could be a Frankenfish, a monster loose in the countryside. Whatever its fate, we won't know until the next decade.

Joel M. Vance works as an information specialist for the Missouri Department of Conservation. He has written three books, including a collection of essays, Confessions of an Outdoor Maladroit. *His articles appear in* Audubon, National Wildlife, *and* Missouri Conservationist.

Midnight on Grosvenor Lake, Alaska

On the Water

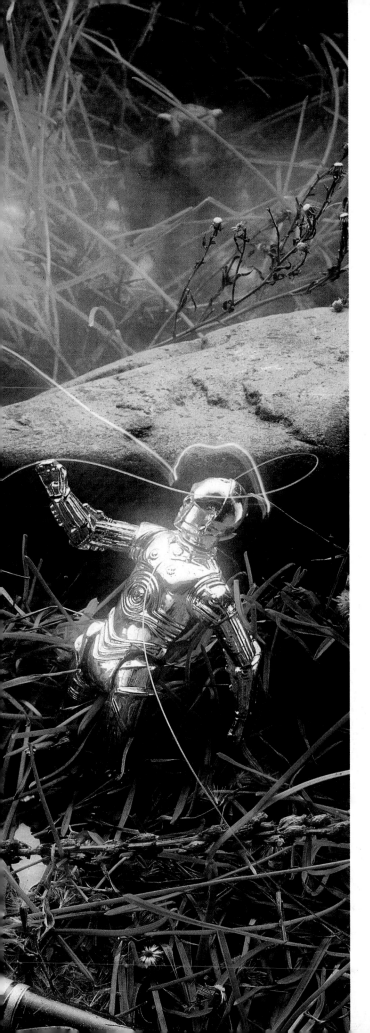

Fathers and Sons

William Hjortsberg

Norman Rockwell country: a father and his son going fishing. The old man smokes a briar pipe and has a twinkle in his eyes. He's a fly fisherman, his sheepskin hatband bright as a bejeweled diadem with Royal Coachmen. Canvas chest waders make him larger than life. His tapered split-bamboo rod seems the most magic of wands to the grinning freckle-faced kid coyly hiding a can of worms behind his back. Subscribers to the old *Saturday Evening Post* sighed in effusions of false nostalgia, pinning the cover over garage workbenches across America.

Life doesn't always imitate art. My father was a fly fisherman back in that innocent age after World War II, a time as distant as Rockwell's magazine covers, now curling and fading like ancient papyri. Fishing tackle did not yet spin and even Eagle Claw manufactured bamboo rods. Utilitarian objects; no one dreamed they would one day be the collectibles of millionaires.

I remember my father after a weekend's fishing, drying his braided line to prevent the ravages of mildew: long yellow strands festooned across the stone wall at the bottom of the rock garden. There were silkworm-gut leaders from Abercrombie & Fitch which had to be soaked overnight to make them pliable. I still have my father's leather "Common Sense" leader book with the flannel pads he moistened to keep his leaders damp. I also have his three-piece, 8-foot 6-inch Granger Special. I never fish with it now, because once in high school I loaned it to a friend who was a nephew of the legendary Carl Hubbell and he snapped both tips, cracking it like a whip. My father's split-willow creel with the leather hasp shaped like a fish was lost with the house overlooking Woodland Brook.

The legacy I prize most is his antique silver-mounted Karalian sheath knife. I was not allowed to touch this treasure as a boy, and broke off the point playing mumblety-peg the day after my father died. For years, I kept my secret shame hidden at the bottom of a drawer. In college, I ground a new blade for it at the metal shop. Today I use it only as a letter opener.

Many mementos of my father the fisherman remain, but very few memories of actually fishing with him. Not that I blame the old man. After a long week in his restaurant in Manhattan, up until 4 a.m. playing host to a pack of New York drunks, all he wanted was the solitude of the trout stream. He didn't want some little kid who couldn't tell a blood knot from a blood worm tagging along and pestering him.

I learned this years later from my mother—part of her endless diatribe against a ghost whose main affront was that she could no longer rebuke him in person. "I always had to make excuses … keep you busy so he could sneak off and go fishing." But I blamed her. Fishing was my father's refuge from endless nagging. Once, promised to be included, I hurried to cancel a date with a friend. When I got back, my father was already gone. The sense of betrayal lingers forty years later.

This is not to say that I never fished with my father. He took me to the Ashokan Reservoir several times. Using a rowboat that a friend kept chained among the pines, we trolled for bass with crawfish and hellgrammites. At five, I caught a three-pound smallmouth, and stories of it nearly pulling me out of the boat were retold at dinner parties for years. When we didn't have the boat, my father cast fat wooden plugs from the rocky shore. I never mastered the timing. Terminal backlash restricted me to dunking worms for bluegills and sunfish. Not much adventure in this, and I soon abandoned my rod and hunted newts in the leaf-choked coves. Whole towns and graveyards lay under the surface of the Ashokan, New York City's water supply. I dreamed of giant bass lurking deep in submerged cellars and open tombs.

After hooking my first rising trout, I knew that my father's love of solitude was forever part of me.

My father never took me trout fishing. A gang of us roamed the tributaries of the Esopus with fly rods and worms. Prime memories include tickling the bellies of brook trout, my friend Spinner taking them barehanded from under the rocks. Once, Billy Sickler and I caught a four-pound brown in a rushing creek not four feet across. It bent Billy's rod double, thrashing from pool to pool until I waded in and hauled the flapping brute to shore.

I started fly fishing in graduate school on a tiny stream ten minutes from the New Haven Green. Armed with my father's truncated 8-foot 3½-inch Granger, his "Common Sense" leader book, and a collection of his flies tied in the early forties, I began matching hatches that drifted in ephemeral gossamer clouds from among discarded double-ply radials and rusted hot-water heaters. After hooking my first rising trout, I knew that my father's love of solitude was forever part of me. I fish with him often now, alone on the rivers of Montana, and wish he'd showed me how to tie a nail knot or timed my first awkward backcasts.

We seek to remedy the omissions of childhood in the lives of our own children. I began urging my boys to be

fishermen at a time when they were still more interested in playing with G.I. Joes. Mitch was the first to take any real interest in fishing. When he was eight, I gave him a spinning outfit, deciding it was more important to actually catch fish than be frustrated by difficult techniques in the name of a theoretical purity.

A friend who had recently moved to a house on the Yellowstone was hosting a Sunday barbeque and I took the boys along. Max, age six, came loaded with toy trucks and tiny plastic Star Wars "people." Mitch, hoping for lunkers, brought fishing outfits for both of them. Along the way, I stopped at the Wan-I-Gan and bought a cardboard ice-cream container squirming with night crawlers.

The party was in full swing. Antelope steaks sizzled on the grill. The soft popping of beer cans punctuated the spring afternoon. I wandered off from the boasting and laughter to see how the boys were doing. Earlier, I had set them up on a cutbank below the house. I showed them how to bait their hooks and let the current carry the wriggling worms under the eroded bank, where a curling wave of topsoil and range grass shaded the water.

Now a couple hours had passed and only Mitch still fished. He thought he'd felt some good hits. Determination is born of optimism. I knew he dreamed of lunkers: mysterious, solitary, holding deep beneath the world of air. Easy understanding his obsession. My own imagination was haunted by memories of the Ashokan Reservoir and behemoth bass hunting among watery graveyard grottos.

Max's rod was cast aside. He manuevered R2-D2 through the grass, his dreams captured by droids and starfighters.

I sat on the bank offering inane encouragement. It was a slow afternoon. What for the angler is intense, fraught with expectation, is for the spectator a study in tedium. The only thing more boring than watching someone else fish is watching him sleep. I began to wish for some Star Wars "people" of my own.

Max and I returned to the party, leaving Mitch alone on the river. A heavy dose of solitude for a youngster. Either Mitch would like it and be a fisherman forever, or he would renounce the noble pastime on the spot and search out more gregarious sport. In truth, I expected to see him soon, trudging in for a burger. Dusk gathered. No Mitch. An impromptu search party set off from the merrymaking. Mitch met us halfway, a nine-inch cutthroat dangling from the monofilament clutched in his hand. His grin was brighter than a sunrise. Becky Fonda had the wit to produce a mini flash camera and capture the moment for scrapbook eternity: a young boy and his first trout. Even Max was impressed.

Nature has a way of embellishing fishing's long silences with perfect epiphanies: a solitary mink looking up in astonishment from the bank where it paused to drink; a bald eagle struggling to the shore with a whitefish clutched in its talons; an angry beaver, its domain invaded, slapping the still surface of the pond over and over with its spatulate tail. Mitch's triumph was marked with just such Marlin Perkins magic. Heading back, we encountered a mother raccoon and six cubs in a line behind her.

Catching that first fish did the trick. Mitch was hooked. Now I found myself in a predicament, the reverse of my father's quest for solitude: wading a stream, fishermen go separate ways. My johnboat was the solution. Manning the oars, I kept an eye on each young angler, offering sage advice as I passed out sandwiches and soda pop. The boys graduated from worms to spoons and spinners. They tied their own clinch knots and knew all about swivels, clips, and sinkers.

They even caught a few fish. At least Mitch did. Max's heart wasn't really in it. Discouraged by bee stings and the loss of snagged lures, he would quit, complaining that nothing was biting. Only a miracle would serve to turn him into a fisherman. Football and skateboards were his passion. Worthy activities, but not likely to appease the ghost of a fly-fishing grandfather.

Most miracles require sleight of hand. A friend owned some backwoods property just over the ridge from my place on the Boulder. He had set up a hunting camp on one of a series of small lakes. Six years earlier, he had stocked the largest with cutthroat fry. The survivors now were four pounds or better. Unable to spawn, they were living out the seasons trapped in the lake, growing bigger and bigger. Miracles in the making.

It was an easy hike. We strapped on our packs at the cabin door and headed straight up Baker Draw. There was no need for a map. An hour later we crossed the ridge and spotted the lakes set out like silver dinner plates on the plateau below. Morris had built a pole corral and hung a wall tent in an aspen grove close to the shore of the largest lake. Our superlite high-tech backpacking gear seemed suddenly superfluous. Cast-iron skillets and a grill rested by the campfire cook pit. Split kindling and logs were stacked nearby. There were a chainsaw and gas, several old mattresses inside the tent, assorted tools and fishing gear, even a canoe. I searched without luck for a forgotten six-pack. One can only expect so much from miracles.

We camped three days on the lake, seduced by the easy rhythms of the vagabond life. The line between camping and merely loafing is tenuous at best. The boys spent most of their time in the canoe, drifting and paddling. When the wind wasn't blowing, usually in early morning and along toward evening, the continual rises of big cruising trout patterned the still surface of the lake like a sporadic rainfall. We fished from the canoe without success. Mainly, the boys wandered the shore with their spinning rods, intrigued by the possibilities of a fishing hole that held nothing but lunkers.

Mitch caught the first. His joyous yelping sent me scrambling from the breakfast fire to the lakeshore. He had a big one on, the five-foot rod pumping like a

dowser's wand above a hidden spring. His excitement was contagious, and it was all I could do to make my manic shouts comprehensible. Mitch remembered to keep his rod tip up and held the cutthroat away from a Sargasso snarl of algae and weeds. He brought the fish in, and I snapped a few pictures before we carefully unhooked the spinner and eased the big trout back into the water.

Discouraged by bee stings and the loss of snagged lures, Max would quit, complaining that nothing was biting. Only a miracle would serve to turn him into a fisherman.

The sight of Mitch holding a four-pound cutthroat made something click for Max. He set out with his rod, circling the lake. It was his turn for determination. By suppertime, he was a bit crestfallen. In spite of several encouraging strikes, he hadn't hooked a fish. I reminded him that the mornings were often best, and he wolfed his Rice-A-Roni wishing it were breakfast.

Max was up at dawn. I was scouring the skillet with sand when I heard his eager shouting. It was a time of miracles. He had one on and the energy transmitted from the furious struggle raced up the taut line, through the bowed rod, and into his imagination like a jolt of electricity. By the time I reached him, the fight was nearly over. The big cutthroat thrashed in the shallows. Max slid him expertly onto the gravel bank as if he'd been doing it all his life.

There are moments you know you'll remember forever: bits of time frozen in memory like butterflies trapped in amber. I looked at Max, smiling at me over the heaving fish, and I saw in his eyes that we would share this for the rest of our lives. Reality intruded when I couldn't free the treble hook from the trout's tongue. There was no way, short of surgery, to remove the lure without fatally wounding the fish. So I thumped it hard against a rock and photographed Max holding up his trophy.

Perhaps it was a fitting sacrifice. The big fish live on in the boys' personal mythologies, epic creatures keeping alive the promise of adventure and the unknown. Mystery, miracles, and magic belong to them now. We fish together without encouragement from me. Instead, their enthusiasm serves as inspiration.

A couple months ago, Max asked if he could have a fly rod for his birthday. Somewhere, high on that celestial trout stream meandering through eternity, my father's spirit must be beaming like the ultimate Norman Rockwell cover, his smile brighter than a thousand rainbows.

William Hjortsberg has written four novels, including Gray Matters *and* Falling Angel, *and numerous screenplays. His fishing essays have appeared in* Esquire *and* Sports Illustrated. *He has lived—and fished—in New York, California, the Virgin Islands, Costa Rica, Spain, and Montana.*

On the Water:

Not Exactly a Boy

Mason Smith

I have a brand-new wife and I say to her, All right, this spring I'm going to fish for brook trout.

For brook trout, like a kid.

As for the prospects, there's acid rain. But there's also that day we had last spring, a year ago:

The day we took the red canoe, the Morris, that I had recanvassed right in the living space of the camp, between my writing table and my bed, at Lake Ozonia. Took it to Lake Lila, and went looking for brook trout up Shingle Shanty Brook.

The day, that is, before the day when I was to stop writing on the book, go sailing with Liz, and somewhere out there, propose.

The brook was an interminable series of hard bends, and we were going upstream against high water that caught the bow and drove us against the brush. We had to learn when to switch sides, when to use draw strokes, how to cut close to the sandbanks on the insides. There were some people behind us in a metal canoe. Liz couldn't take her shirt off.

We pushed on hard, hoping to outdistance them. But then, the way the brook folds back on itself, there they would be again, going the opposite way just behind a

screen of alders. We crossed Whitney's line without knowing it, or Brandreth Park's, whoever's. We were already trespassing if we touched bottom, skinning and squirming our way through beaver works.

We hadn't seen a fish, and I wanted to see a brook trout, and Liz wanted lunch alfresco, sandwiches and beer and no shirt. We ought to see a fish, I thought—see one startle from under a bank, catch the light right and see its colors clear to the bottom.

So anyway, lunch, the next good place. But just there in front of a good place, one rose. Then another. So we drove the canoe into the grasses on the inside of the bend. She popped the Saranacs, and I, shin-deep in the cool grassy muck, caught two trout. I showed them to her, and then the people in the tin canoe came up.

They were ADKers. Adirondack Mountain Club. So were we, but kept it to ourselves. They asked about the boundary but didn't care. Who owns this? C. V. Whitney, big deal. It's navigable water. So they banged on through the hole I was fishing.

Liz lay back on the cooler, her ankles on the sheer, expedition hat over her eyes, green bottle on sternum, the sun white on her skin. I couldn't raise anything more in that bend, so I put on a Muddler, too big a one, and walked carefully around the curve, upstream. To cast, I had to keep to the edge of the grass, and here there was no bar, the edge was undercut. It gave, I went halfway in, but the cool water felt good. Waist-deep, I got the line working and shot it up there, where the stream was crossing right to left and crowding under one overhanging bunch of withe-rod and berry bush.

And a marvelous brook trout, two pounds or maybe three, came out a foot high, arched, and looked down at the Muddler.

I saw all the colors, red, white, and black, and the blue-ringed spots.

And the fly came back light. I'd taken it away from him.

I called back to Lizzie, whose eyes stayed closed while she murmured her pleasure. I cast again and let the fly do the same thing. Nothing happened. Again and nothing. On the third float the trout sailed up, carmine, shining, suspended. I left the fly for him this time and when he disappeared I pricked him, but I knew by the infinitesimal snap that I'd paid for my laziness, not biting back the leader when I'd put the Muddler on.

He was there, though. I'm a bad fisherman this way. I make much of a fish's being there.

Because you don't always know, any more, whether they are there. Or not.

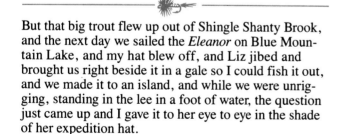

I have spent the year since then on a boat-building scheme that is supposed to take up the slack of *Volunteers* not being done and published and paid for. Boat number three is now in a sportsmen's and outdoor show in the Long Lake Town Hall where we had our reception in September. Right in the middle of the room where we were contra-dancing, this boat that was supposed to be a nice fat book.

One of the other exhibitors has some old rods and plugs and pamphlets, and one of the pamphlets, published in 1876, tells about the restocking of the Fulton Chain Lakes. The brook trout were practically fished out of the Fulton Chain a hundred ten years ago.

At the Adirondack Museum where she works, Liz has done an exhibit on acid rain: Map of Adirondacks. Pins of different colors to show the damage. The map is all pins. Yellow pins, pH 6 to 7, mayflies can no longer reproduce successfully. Orange pins, pH 5 to 6, reproductive failure in some trout, bass, walleyes. Red pins, pH 4 to 5, a range at the lower end of which only the stubbornest organisms survive. Caddis not among them, brook trout not among them.

Long Lake, where we live, sixteen miles long, a wide part of the Raquette River, has an orange pin stuck in the middle of it.

But that big trout flew up out of Shingle Shanty Brook, and the next day we sailed the *Eleanor* on Blue Mountain Lake, and my hat blew off, and Liz jibed and brought us right beside it in a gale so I could fish it out, and we made it to an island, and while we were unrigging, standing in the lee in a foot of water, the question just came up and I gave it to her eye to eye in the shade of her expedition hat.

And then we ate a picnic of all kinds of sea things, herring, clams, anchovies, sardines.

We rented a house across the head of Long Lake from Owl's Head Pond Outlet. Owl's Head Pond: west slope, no pin, unless we are to generalize from all those other west-slope pins.

I think, I'm going to fish again like a boy. Fish local, fish for brook trout, be part of the food chain myself.

Back when I started fishing, not exactly a boy, I fished barefoot for brook trout. That was what trout meant, the pretty ones, pretty as a flag. Then I went away; and before I came back from the Navy the river was all stocked browns and rainbows. I went on to fishing browns and rainbows which I had read about but did not like to see in brook trout water. I still do not really care about those fish so much. In Wyoming I do, for some reason, but home I don't.

My great-uncle George Everett knew a banker who lived by a brook. The banker let Uncle George put up a little sign by the white cement bridge. Uncle George was a Cornell professor but he spelled *No Fishing* with the *s* backwards and no *g*. He advised me to crawl the last fifty feet whenever I approached the brook. He thought he was a devil to fish with two flies at once and put a little piece of worm on the hooks.

Up the brook past what used to be pastures were mixed woods where you felt far from any road. Uncle George used to say, "You know Old Mister Brook Trout won't live just anywhere."

Then with my first father-in-law I'd fish brookies in Quebec Brook, on Madawaska Club. We fished them in the rapids during a certain few days early in the season, and then later in the spring holes where they would gather. Thurm was losing his visual acuity and was a modest man, but he would admit, "There was a time when, if a trout rose, well sir, he was pret' near mine."

Except in fiction, I've written about brook trout only once before, and that was telling about Bill Flick's work on the Ross and Rockefeller parks, up north of St. Regis Mountain. Bill worked for Cornell University studying the brookies in dozens of ponds. One night we put a canoe on Black Pond, where he kept the brood stock of the Assinica and Temiscamie strains, from up near Hudson's Bay. These big fish were cruising for midges in late evening, and we would pick one, maybe by the size of the dorsal, and bring a wingless fly in front of it and be on, and play the fish to the Old Town for a look, to see which kind it was—the Temiscamies much brighter colored—before we let it go.

The hybrid vigor of the cross between Assinicas and the hatchery stock was the success story then, fifteen years ago. Now I read in *Adirondack Life*, our pretty regional magazine, a rehash of my old *Sports Illustrated* article about Bill and his colleagues' brook trout work. Not a rehash, Liz corrects me: an article on the same subject. The big deal now is a new "chow" for the hatchery trout that makes them more acid-resistant. Bill Flick has retired to fish for brown trout in Montana and his colleagues are working on a hellgrammite "chow."

Good luck.

In the Adirondacks there are a lot of fishermen who seriously attack the brook trout in the ponds the moment the ice goes out. On the way to the boat shop in Tupper Lake early in the morning, I see half a dozen vehicles parked along the beach in Long Lake: Jeeps, Broncos, Isuzu Troopers, and so on. The Helmses have had their pontoon planes serviced and are flying people out, strapping canoes to the struts and taking them straight to remote ponds on state land, anywhere except designated wilderness.

I think it does not matter how much you have to do or spend, to see and hold in your hand fresh from the water a beautiful fish that is not from California or Germany and will come from the bottom *zingo*, bang anything bright, fight all over the place, look great, taste good, not even seem like a thing dying when you kill it. In one of the pure, refreshing places it still lives in.

Myself, I have in mind going across the head-the-lake to Owl's Head Pond Outlet and wading up that to the pond, with a paddle, in case there's a tin canoe up there that some fisherman has left for himself illegally and some righteous hunter has not shot full of holes.

Also, fishing the Raquette River between our house and Buttermilk Falls, where Tom Donnelly caught a three-pound brook trout one spring on a frozen smelt and rushed it down to Hoss's Country Corner to have it weighed.

And of course, we have to go back to Shingle Shanty Brook.

I'm feeling very good. To have gotten through a winter and got the boat developed, and now to be starting out on another of those paddling-day highs up the brook with Lizzie after eight months of the dangerous new life.

We get up when we want to, have a real breakfast, load the red canoe. We drive up toward Tupper Lake, turn off toward Horseshoe Pond, go six miles on dirt, and are on the carry to Lake Lila by 9:00. It's a short carry, half a mile. We paddle out from the beach, trailing an antique pre-Mepps Mepps imitation with orange feathers. Two miles, I suppose, to the brook, around the major point, into the major bay.

You feel high here because the hills are lower west of the central Adirondacks, sky bigger, and it's a broad, open, varied lake. Shingle Shanty Brook comes out of the lowest, flattest part of the shore, southeast. We pole over the bar and up the brook and are alone. The few fishermen out today are all fishing lakers in the lake. No one has been up here this year, we figure, because a deer, drinking, is dumfounded. Every so often bittern startle from beside us in the not-yet-green grasses of a bend, and merganser pairs swim ahead accelerating and take off.

It's not so warm for Liz's paganism. She paddles from the bow, pulling me. I try stuff, not expecting much at first.

Anyway, it won't be what happens or doesn't happen, I tell myself. Not far up the meanders, one shows himself at the Muddler or at something else, and Liz holds the

canoe on a mudbank while I go back onshore and catch him. Brook trout. Keepable, but there'll be more. This is ideal, this is going to be good.

I don't catch many, though, and they're small. I put them back.

On one stretch we find a sky full of large fork-tailed spinners. They're Hendricksons, a surprise this early in May; and I think, My oh my, Shingle Shanty Brook has massed Hendricksons. But these are spinners. Wait until a hatch, this will be a scene. I have one Red Quill, one only, but it doesn't matter, these are wild, wild trout. When a hatch comes off here, imagine what a scene.

I'm electric with that, and it gets warmer further up, and we cross the Whitney line, see old palings on the bottom. The brook is deep willow-bordered bends, scoured-out turns, clean sand and gravel, mudbanks on the inside and undercut grassbanks on the outside, with cool flowing water and occasionally a gathering enough to murmur but no riffles or rapids. Is it true, I wonder, that brook trout go into the rapids of whatever stream in black-fly time, to wash off? Wash off the slime of winter, as I guess?

"You're the fisherman," she says, and takes off her shirt.

And we have beers and sandwiches and I fish on up ahead on foot, climbing through the alders while she dozes in the boat, in privacy. And then she comes along and catches up with me not catching much, and we go up and try the place where the ADKers came through and right behind the banging boat the big one flew up.

But the place is very different now, the water lower, and the big fish is down deep, waiting for the Hendricksons.

If that isn't too brown-trout a thing to say.

I tell Liz that I could make a good lyrical story out of this day alone, that I wouldn't have much respect for myself if I couldn't.

I say, "You don't want too much about fish in a fish story."

"Well," she says, "there wouldn't be too much about fish."

Muskrats and a belted kingfisher on the way out, and a great blue heron lifting off as we pole over the bar onto the wide lake, and the wind up, against us, and the sun ahead low, and a nice bit of teamwork to do to get home.

"Nothing wrong with the fishing but the fisherman," I say, happy. "Any good worm guy would have cleaned up on that creek."

Mason Smith builds wooden row-and-sail boats at his Adirondack Good-Boat Co. in Tupper Lake, New York. He has written outdoor articles for Sports Illustrated, Gray's Sporting Journal, *and* Outside. *His first novel was* Everybody Knows and Nobody Cares.

Judge, He Was Delicious

Vance & Philip Bourjaily

I n early May last year, I wrote to my grown son, Philip, from Harpswell, Maine:

DEAR PHILIP: This is a long way from my little red house in Baton Rouge, in the vicinity of which fresh-water fishermen sit at anchor watching bobbers, beneath which dangle split-shot and hooks baited with crickets. When a six-inch bream is caught, there is satisfaction, if not exhilaration. Uncatchable mullet flip exuberantly in and out of the water, and inedible gar rise to the surface to sun themselves. There are said to be good bass lurking around the cypress knees, which I don't doubt, but the exciting fishing is in the salt water of the Gulf, an hour away, for redfish, snapper, and speckled trout, and for big-game fish farther out.

Here in Maine, fresh water is something else. John came by yesterday to eat a decent number of lobsters,

and invited me to join him and Art on what sounds like a rather scary fishing trip for landlocked salmon. The West Branch of the Penobscot, where they're going, is a river that draws more whitewater nuts than fishermen. Those who wade do so most cautiously. John and Art are taking a canoe, with a small motor, a big anchor, and John's considerable experience from his own white-water feats.

"Love to go," I said, with my best weasel smile. "But don't worry about making room for me in the boat. I'll just fish from shore." I believe John chuckled.

We didn't talk much about the fish, of which I know nothing. Tomorrow I shall do some angling at the Bowdoin College library, though I'm aware of the ancient wisdom that says you can fill your creel with facts but you can't *sauté* them *amandine*. LOVE, DAD.

DEAR DAD: Glad you're going on a fishing trip; you haven't done enough of that in the last several years. But why you would leave the safety of your polluted, gator- and cottonmouth-infested Louisiana bayous to go fishing with John, of all people, is beyond me. Remember, it was John's rapid-shooting partners who waited until he was safely aboard the plane home before they fell to their knees and kissed the runway, chorusing: "He's gone, he's gone, and we're still alive."

The last time you and I went fishing with John — and it must have been fifteen years ago — he took us on a whirlwind tour of northeast New Hampshire, during which I fell into three of a possible four rivers in the space of three days. The biggest and baddest of these was the Androscoggin, which John admitted was "pretty rough," although he promised it held trout "as big as

your leg." I don't recall seeing too many leg-sized trout as I bounced around the bottom, but it certainly was wet and cold down there.

Incidentally, the Androscoggin meets the Atlantic right near Harpswell. If you get a chance, you might check with the Coast Guard and see if they picked up any of my stuff. LOVE, PHILIP.

DEAR PHILIP: My best fishing buddies in the dark waters of the Bowdoin Library were Byron Dalrymple, Derek Mills, W. B. Scott, and a man with the perfect name, Anthony Netboy. From their works the following is cheerfully plagiarized:

Landlocked salmon are a nonmigratory form of *Salmo salar*, the Atlantic salmon. People used to think there were two distinct kinds of landlocks—the Sebago and the ouananiche—and each kind was classified as a separate subspecies of the Atlantic. Today we've decided such distinctions were oversubtle; all Atlantic salmon, migratory or no, are now tossed into the same taxonomic pot.

Exactly how landlocks get landlocked is open to question. Some may have been trapped in fresh water when their river systems were rearranged by glaciation. Others, however, have a clear shot to the sea but don't take it. The closest that men ever came to establishing Atlantic salmon in the Pacific was in Lake Te Anou in New Zealand. The fish crossed them up. They had access to the ocean, but chose freshwater life and were doing fine until the introduction of brown and rainbow trout; the salmon are very scarce now.

In Lake Ontario, which, in 1835, had an enormous population of landlocks, they aren't just scarce, they're extinct. On the Canadian side, it's claimed that someone once landed a 44-pounder. Our North American landlocks, living principally in Maine and eastern Canada, have analogues in Sweden, Norway, Yugoslavia, and Russia. If you happen to be fishing in Sweden, just ask the folks around Lake Vanern what's the hot fly for *blanklax*.

Lake Sebago, Maine, is where the unofficial U.S. record was caught, back in 1907. It went 22 pounds 8 ounces, and I'm not at all sure I want one anywhere near that size on my line two weeks from now, dragging John's canoe towards the rapids. That name "ouananiche," by the way, is an Indian word meaning "he drowns you in white water and laughs like crazy."

Sea-run Atlantic salmon are fished for on their spawning run, when they aren't feeding, and no one understands why they take flies at all. But landlocks are easier to catch, because they're fished for while feeding; my authors say they readily take flies, spinning lures, and various trolled baits, probably including live goats. When they can't get goat, smelt is their favorite food—landlocked smelt, actually—so that streamer flies like the Grey Ghost are recommended.

I'm advised that the best fishing is just after ice-out and again in September, neither of which corresponds to late May. I'm also advised that landlocked salmon hunt their food in rough water, as if I needed to be reminded.

But my next fishing place will be L. L. Bean, which should be relatively safe, and a lot of fun. I'm to meet Art there on the way to the river. LOVE, DAD.

DEAR DAD: You think a visit to L. L. Bean is safe? Ask the next guy you see sleeping on a park bench under a pile of old Herter's catalogues. Chances are the last thing he remembers is going into Bean's tackle department to buy some leaders. Just thinking about the place makes me want to spend money I don't have. If you see anything I might need, like a couple of popping bugs or a sixteen-foot bass boat with a chart recorder and a really big outboard, go ahead and put it on my Visa.

Since you're determined to go through with this trip, let me add to what you told me everything I now know about landlocked salmon.

The main thing I've found is that they don't get nearly as much press as their more adventurous sea-run brothers. In *The Salmon*, however, J. W. Jones does devote a few paragraphs to theorizing why landlocks get that way. He draws on the observations of a guy named Ward who studied the phenomenon when a power dam in Washington created Lake Shannon and a new population of landlocked sockeyes. The salmon tried to find a way downstream, but were turned back, not by the dam itself but by low water and warm temperatures. The fish retreated to the cold depths of the lake where they lost the urge to migrate. Jones thinks the same explanation would hold true for natural lakes.

Having reported that, I realize I've done nothing to advance your practical (how-to-catch) knowledge of the landlocked salmon. All I can really do is wish you good luck. And do be careful. APPREHENSIVELY, PHILIP.

DEAR PHILIP: You were right, except that Art was already waiting when I got to L. L. Bean, which is probably all that kept me off the park benches. Being observed prevents a true shopping frenzy from developing. Even so, having been away from fly fishing for ten years, I was grabbing stuff with both hands and with my eyes closed—flies, fly boxes, tools, waders, shoes, and a new reel and line for my old bamboo Orvis. The rod was treated as a curious antique by the salesmen, who kept calling one another over to see it.

On the five-hour drive from Freeport to the river, I learned more from Art about our fish. They look like seafaring salmon in the development stage called "grilse," when they come in after the first year at sea. Landlocks aren't as great a table fish, Art feels, but then he doesn't think any freshwater fish matches up with those from salt; I suspect he's never eaten walleyes. Anyway, landlocked salmon flesh is white, not pink; the minimum keeper is fourteen inches, and spinning gear is used as commonly (and legally) as the fly rod.

Got my first look at the river from the car ten miles before we reached camp. It looked reassuringly smooth. Got my second look a minute later, and it was still smooth enough but a yellow raft full of guys in wetsuits and crash helmets went tearing past at just a little less than the speed of light. The road, as well as the campsite where we found John's pop-up, is owned by a paper company. Huge trucks loaded with logs careen by from time to time as an added hazard, and there is a metal barrel on wheels near our spot with "DANGER: BEAR TRAP" lettered on the side.

On the camper was a note: "Am at the Holbrook, looking for supper. John." Art had his rod case out of the trunk while I was still reading this. I barely had time to notice that, while the place is quite primitive—no electricity or telephones—the woods are rather open. There's birch and a variety of evergreens, but not much underbrush. Holbrook is the name of one of the pools we'll be fishing. This evening John and Art ferried me 150 yards across it. The current was even stronger than I'd imagined, and the rapids above and below the pool even noisier. Each paddle stroke John took from the stern, and each one he instructed Art to make in the bow, was calculated and precise; seeing them work got rid of some of my tension.

Still, I was happy to have my feet under me while I tried to recover a fly-casting technique which was never more than five on a scale of ten, nor was I back up to three when, watching my Adams drift past on the surface, suddenly I had a fish. It was a beautiful little ten-inch brook trout, and catching it delighted me more than I'd anticipated, until I realized this was because the rest of my tension about the river was gone.

Hell, I loved this river. The constant roar of the rapids which started twenty yards below me was great. The pull of the current against my new waders was invigorating. I'm ready for salmon, and ready for bed. Will write again when I get back to the coast. LOVE, DAD.

———————————— 🪰 ————————————

DEAR PHILIP: The second morning I caught a salmon. I'd walked a mile up the bank, enjoying the spray and the smell of balsam, casting now and then, till I reached a pool called the Little Eddy, which is big enough to hold a couple of kidney-shaped football fields, and very deep. There's a rock ledge that goes sixty yards up the north edge, from which I could cast and cover maybe two percent of the water, but fish were rising within range.

A small hatch was on, and I scooped up one of the fluttering creatures it consisted of, something with brown wings and a white body. Naturally, the closest I could come from my L. L. Bean collection had white wings and a brown body. I decided not to use it. John had given me a generous number of flies he'd tied for the trip, among them an Atlantic salmon fly called a Bomber. It looks like a bit of horse dung tied to a size 8 hook. "Salmon like it dry," John had said. "They don't like

it wet." It was close to the wing color of the insect I'd looked at.

I kept it dry, and on the fourth cast a fish hit and dove that made my recent brook trout seem insincere. "Landlocked salmon are strong fish," Art had told me, but I was amazed to see, from the first of many leaps, that my fish wasn't more than seven inches long. I put him back, and many more like him in the next four days.

The biggest salmon I caught came, as the books had predicted, out of the roughest water I fished. Again, it was off a rock ledge, at a pool called the Big Eddy, and I was using the Bomber again, mostly because it was big enough to see when cast directly into the rapids. This fish hooked himself and ran in that fast water so strongly I was sure I'd lose him, fishing at my mentors' advice with a 2-pound-test tippet on my leader.

The tackle held, and I beached my fish on the rocks. He looked enormous.

Just then Art came along with his canvas Orvis creel, which has a ruler printed on it. We measured, and I had a fifteen-incher, and Art a couple more. But at camp we compared Art's creel ruler with a metal one John keeps, and found that the canvas had shrunk greatly during the years, the ruler with it; my fish was thirteen inches now.

So in five days of fishing long hours, I didn't catch a legal landlocked salmon, but I sure did eat one. Judge, he was delicious.

John had caught four legal fish, Art two. They were disappointed, and it didn't help to notice that the guy at the next campsite had so many big salmon he was smoking the excess ones. We introduced ourselves, of course, and inquired about his method. "Well," he said, "I tie these," and the thing he held out for us to see looked more like a cigarette than a trout fly—a long, white cylinder of clipped deer hair with red stripes down each side, nothing like my now-bedraggled Grey Ghosts but clearly far more resembling a smelt in the view of a fish.

If I can't find a Rapala or something that looks like that next time, there'll be nothing for it but to buy, well, let's see: fly-tying kit, plenty of deer hair, extra-long hooks, white lacquer, illustrated book on smelt .... Have I survived the river only to be borne by treacherous currents back into the jaws of L. L. Bean? LOVE, DAD.

———————————— 🪰 ————————————

DEAR DAD: I see that I have failed utterly in trying to be a stabilizing influence from afar. Obviously I'll have to go along with you next time. Get two of everything at Bean's. LOVE, PHILIP.

Vance Bourjaily has written nine novels; his sporting essays have appeared in The New Yorker *and* Esquire, *and in his books* Country Matters *and* The Unnatural Enemy. *He directs the M.F.A. Program in Creative Writing at Louisiana State University. Philip Bourjaily works at the Museum of Natural History at the University of Iowa, and has written for* Sports Afield *and other national outdoor magazines.*

On the Water:

A Kind of
Atonement
Geoffrey Norman

It was the fat middle part of a late November day: the Saturday following Thanksgiving. The big deer drive had ended an hour or so earlier, and men were out in the swamps trying to round up the last hard-going dogs and dragging in the few deer that had been killed.

None of the deer were mine. As usual, I'd drawn a marginal stand and seen only a few panicked does, their eyes bulging and their mouths foaming with the strain of staying ahead of the dogs. I was twelve years old and this was only the fifth or sixth drive I had been on, but already I had begun to wonder if I'd ever learn to like it or, more to the point, ever get to shoot at a buck.

I had wandered away from the camp, where the hunters who had killed deer were being bloodied and those who had missed were having their shirttails cut off and everyone was having a big time talking about what they had—and had not—seen in the woods that morning.

Later—much later—I learned how to enjoy the role of unsuccessful deer hunter, but that's another story. For now, I was a mightily discouraged boy.

A narrow, sullen little creek flowed through the bottomland where the drive had been held, and one of its bends swung within a hundred yards or so of the clubhouse. I came to that point and stood there watching the water for a while. An old juniper skiff was tied, not very snugly, to a stump on the bank. But the boat wasn't going anywhere. It was half beached and half sunk, with evil-looking water standing halfway to the gunnels. For some reason, I decided to bail the boat. Maybe I'd had so much practice bailing boats it just came automatically.

The job took about twenty minutes, and when I'd finished I walked back to the camp to hunt up my uncle and see if he had any fishing tackle in the trunk of his car. He did, and a few minutes later I was in the skiff, heading downstream and off into the side channels and the little ponds that had backed up behind the many beaver dams running like forgotten parapets through the swamp. As I went, I was casting a little yellow spinner ahead of me into likely-looking places.

I worked the brush piles and the deep cutbanks and the scattered gum trees that seemed to grow out of the

I snatched back on the rod and drove the hook into the fish's jaw. He came out of the water right away, looking like tarnished bronze in the dapple light. He shook his head to free the hook and then landed back on the surface of the water with a loud smack. In that instant, all my disappointments vanished.

That fish weighed about two pounds. I lifted him into the skiff by his pugnacious lower lip and used my bootlace for a stringer. A few minutes later, a cast to the rim of an old beaver house produced another fish a little smaller. Within an hour, there were six bass on my rawhide bootlace. Two or three others had thrown the hook.

I was prepared to stay all day—to sleep over, in the cabin, and fish out the weekend before I had to go back to school. But I heard my name called out through the woods, the same way the names of the dogs had been shouted a few hours earlier.

I paddled back to the landing, reluctant to quit but eager to show off my catch. I looked at it as a kind of atonement.

When I held up my stringer, the men on the bank made like they were impressed—and I suppose they were. Not quite as impressed as they would have been if I'd shot an eight-point, blue-backed swamp buck, but enough to redeem the day for me.

"Hell, I didn't think there was any fish in that old ditch," one of them said with the sound of approval in his voice.

shallow water itself. I could still hear the men talking and laughing back at camp, where the beer had been broken out and the rituals of the skinning and butchering and inspired lying proceeded in my absence.

I was still feeling sorry for myself when the first largemouth came out from under a fallen bay tree. The fish was mad, hungry, or both. I saw the flash two feet from the point where he mugged the little yellow spinner.

"That one fish there," said another, "he might go four pounds."

"You know, I believe I'll bring *my* rod along on the next hunt."

"You're going to have to get here mighty early," another man said, "to beat me to that skiff."

Twelve years old and I'd showed them something. It was a wonderful feeling.

The sensations of triumph didn't last long, but the lesson of that day stays with me. Whenever I'm in the South for any reason, I treat the bass as a target of opportunity, a fish to be taken on a quick raid rather than by a massive expedition.

So as I move around, I keep my eyes open, looking for water. My rule of thumb is: If there's enough water to support a growth of lily pads, then there's probably enough to hold some bass. Which means that there's enough to provide me with some sport.

That same rule was a terrific aid to a young boy with a passion for fishing. I couldn't drive off to the acknowledged first-rate bass waters in my car. I didn't have a car—not even a driver's license. But I did have a bicycle and young legs. I could get around even if my range wasn't all that great. I drew my borders close and took advantage of everything within them.

Which included, among other things, a nice-looking hazard on the seventeenth hole of the local golf course. It was actually a small cypress swamp that had been "improved" by bulldozers and culverts to challenge the golfers, but it had that dark, tannin-stained look that makes me think of bass. I first noticed it when I was caddying to make enough money to pay for all the fishing tackle I used. I studied it while my golfer studied his approach. I knew that it had to hold fish.

So that evening, while there was still some light but long after the last foursome had finished the course, I went back and gave the pond a try. It was alive with fish and they were absolute junkies for a crippled minnow.

Before I left for the night, I ran my landing net through the muck on the bottom of the pond. Several drags brought up a dozen or so lost Titleists and Maxflis. That night, after I cleaned my fish, I washed the golf balls in Clorox. The next day, I sold them at the golf course for half what a new ball would cost, and put the money straight into my tackle fund.

That little pond was good to me for a long time. In my memory, it is always glowing with orange, late-evening light, since I never fished there during the day when the golfers were out. One of them might have been a bass fisherman as well, and come poaching on my pond.

I found several other ponds in those years, some of them so small they were nothing more than sloughs. Also some creeks which were small and brushy enough that older, more mobile fishermen passed them by. But those creeks had their open waters, especially where the beaver had thrown up one of their many dams.

I caught a lot of fish in beaver ponds, and now and then I would shoot some of the beaver for the bounty the landowners paid on them. But it always felt like a kind of betrayal when I did that, so after a while I quit.

My affair with small, marginal waters lasted until about the time I got my driver's license. After that, I had things other than fishing on my mind. Then, there was a long time away from the South, first in military service and later during a career that took me to the big cities of the North. By the time I started spending any serious time in the South again, bass fishing had been transmogrified into something I barely recognized.

It was now done on waters that were not just large but huge, vast, almost epic. These bodies of water were called "impoundments" and were created when the Army Corps of Engineers put one of its dams across a river. The Corps was filled with dam builders as energetic as any beaver that ever lived, and while I never heard of a bounty on them, some people I know would probably consider it a good idea.

But that is another matter.

What the impoundments did, other than hindering the natural flow of the rivers and burying a lot of fine bottomland, was create a whole new breed of bass fishermen who believed in the expeditionary style. Where I had gotten around by juniper skiff and a sculling oar, they required fiberglass speedboats covered with metal-fleck paint and powered by engines that would push them across the water at speeds that would have gotten them arrested on dry land. The boats had more in common with the cars Buddy Baker and Richard Petty were driving up at Darlington than with my little flat-bottomed skiffs.

Bass boats came equipped with depth finders to read "structure" on the bottom. Also with electric motors to move the boats slowly when the fisherman was actually fishing, and electric winches to raise and lower the anchor so he wouldn't get tired from too much work.

I treat the bass as a target of opportunity, a fish to be taken on a quick raid rather than by a massive expedition.

The men who rode these bass boats and fished out of them wore bright jumpsuits with patches sewed on them—in close imitation, again, of the way Richard Petty and Cayle Yarborough dressed for work. On weekends, the bass fishermen gathered at one impoundment or another and fished against each other in tournaments. Before long, there was a "circuit." And a magazine devoted to it. Television shows featuring the men who won on it.

I knew this was not for me. Just the same, I welcomed it. There was prosperity and leisure in the South now, and you couldn't be against that unless you'd never been around to see the other thing. But if Southerners were going to enjoy their leisure by fishing, far better to have them out on the impoundments in their metal-fleck boats, than crowded onto the little ponds and creeks where I did my fishing. When I went back, I had those to myself just like the old days.

Meanwhile, I had learned some new tricks up north—on smallmouth, actually. I'd learned about fly fishing for bass, and when I went back south I carried a five-piece glass rod in a case I'd made out of PVC pipe. It fit in my carry-on luggage, though I had to show one or two security people that I wasn't carrying a mortar onto the plane. I used that rod in Birmingham on a business trip, not twenty minutes from downtown, and caught a couple of fat bass and almost stepped on a fatter moccasin. So much for the New South.

On another trip, in the spring when the dogwoods were in bloom and the attentions of golfers everywhere were focused on Augusta and the Masters, I was hunting turkeys with a friend in the Black Belt of Alabama, so named for its rich, alluvial soil.

I was no better with turkeys than I had been with deer all those years earlier, but I was better by far at handling disappointment. Also, I had the little rod in the PVC case, packed away in my duffel. After a morning of talking to a gobbler who answered but wouldn't come in, I knew I could rescue the day if I could just find a little water.

Well, yes, my host said, there was a little pond, if you wanted to dignify it with the name. More like a duck marsh, really. The beaver had thrown up a dam and backed up some water. He could show me how to get there in the four-wheel. Seemed like he'd left some kind of boat down there when they were building the duck blind. Never got around to pulling it out.

Fat city, I thought, and asked for directions. Two of us went down there. A dozen green-winged teal got off the water when we parked. The water looked dark, still, and shallow. A very undistinguished pond.

"Just right," I said.

"If you say so." My partner wasn't sure I knew what I was talking about. He'd seen me hunt turkeys.

I bailed the skiff—this seemed like old times—and rigged the fly rod. We pushed off.

I sculled. We both fished small green popping bugs. The day was warm and the air was fragrant with all the rich scents of spring.

My partner put his bug up against a rotting stump in about three feet of water. I held the boat steady and watched as the rings spread and died. He gave the bug a twitch and it disappeared in a surge of foam.

"Bingo."

The line came tight, the rod took a bend, and the bass cleared the water.

We stayed out there until the sun began to drop. By then we were on our second circuit of the pond. We had caught, and released, perhaps a dozen fish between us. We'd seen several snapping turtles, a snake or two, and an ungainly blue heron which came in late when the frogs had started chanting, to do a little fishing of his own.

The air changed slightly and took on the fragrance of pine. An owl hooted somewhere off in the hardwoods.

"You suppose this pond has a name?" my partner said.

"I doubt it."

"That's good."

"Why do you say that?"

"Well, this way, maybe nobody will find out."

"Maybe," I said. "But don't worry about it. There's lots more where this one came from."

Geoffrey Norman is a contributing editor of Esquire *and* Outside *magazines. His books include* Alabama Showdown, *about college football;* The Ultimate Fishing Book; The Orvis Book of Upland Bird Shooting; *and a novel,* Midnight Water.

Where to Write for More Information on 1988 Fishing Hotspots

State Agencies

Alabama Game and Fish Division
64 N. Union St.
Montgomery, AL 36130

Alaska Department of Commerce and
 Economic Development
Division of Tourism
P.O. Box E
Juneau, AK 99811

Arizona Game and Fish Department
Information and Education Branch
2222 W. Greenway Rd.
Phoenix, AZ 85023

Arkansas Game and Fish Commission
#2 Natural Resources Dr.
Little Rock, AR 72205

California Fish and Game Commission
1416 Ninth St.
Box 944209
Sacramento, CA 94244-2090

Colorado Division of Wildlife
6060 N. Broadway
Denver, CO 80216

Connecticut Bureau of Fisheries
165 Capitol Ave.
Hartford, CT 06106

Florida Game and Freshwater Fish Commission
620 S. Meridian St.
Tallahassee, FL 32301

Georgia Department of Natural Resources
Game and Fish Division
Fisheries Management Section
205 Butler St. SE
East Tower, Suite 1358
Atlanta, GA 30334

Idaho Department of Fish and Game
Information and Education Bureau
600 S. Walnut, Box 25
Boise, ID 83707

Illinois Department of Conservation
Division of Fisheries
600 N. Grand Ave. W.
Springfield, IL 62706

Indiana Department of Natural Resources
Division of Fish and Wildlife
607 State Office Building
Indianapolis, IN 46204-2267

Iowa Department of Natural Resources
Wallace State Office Building
Des Moines, IA 50319-0034

Kansas Department of Wildlife and Parks
R.R. 2, P.O. Box 54A
Pratt, KS 67124

Kentucky Department of Fish and Wildlife
#1 Game Farm Rd.
Frankfort, KY 40601

Louisiana Department of Wildlife
 and Fisheries
Information and Education Division
2156 Wooddale Blvd., Suite 900
Baton Rouge, LA 70806

Maine Department of Inland Fisheries
 and Wildlife
Attn: Public Information
Station #41
284 State St.
Augusta, ME 04333

State of Michigan
Department of Natural Resources
Fisheries Division
Box 30028
Lansing, MI 48909

Minnesota Department of Natural Resources
Box 12, 500 Lafayette Rd.
St. Paul, MN 55155

Mississippi Department of Wildlife
 Conservation
P.O. Box 451
Jackson, MS 39205

Missouri Department of Conservation
P.O. Box 180
Jefferson City, MO 65102

Montana Department of Fish, Wildlife
 and Parks
Conservation Education Division
1420 E. Sixth St.
Helena, MT 59620

Nebraska Game and Parks Commission
P.O. Box 30370
Lincoln, NE 68503

Nevada Department of Wildlife
1100 Valley Rd.
Reno, NV 89520

New Mexico Department of Game and Fish
State Capitol, Villagra Building
Santa Fe, NM 87503

New York Department of Environmental
 Conservation
Bureau of Fisheries
50 Wolf Rd.
Albany, NY 12233

North Carolina Wildlife Resources Commission
512 N. Salisbury St.
Raleigh, NC 27611

North Dakota Game and Fish Department
100 N. Bismarck Expressway
Bismarck, ND 58501-5095

Ohio Department of Natural Resources
Division of Wildlife
Fountain Square, Building C-4
Columbus, OH 43224

Oklahoma Department of Wildlife Conservation
1801 N. Lincoln St.
P.O. Box 53465
Oklahoma City, OK 73152

Pennsylvania Fish Commission
P.O. Box 1673
Harrisburg, PA 17105-1673

South Carolina Wildlife Department
P.O. Box 167
Columbia, SC 29202

South Dakota Department of Gamefish
 and Parks
445 E. Capitol St.
Pierre, SD 57501

Tennessee Wildlife Resources Agency
Information Section
P.O. Box 40747
Nashville, TN 37204

Texas Parks and Wildlife Department
4200 Smith School Rd.
Austin, TX 78744

Utah Division of Wildlife Resources
1596 W. North Temple
Salt Lake City, UT 84116

Vermont Agency of Natural Resources
Department of Fish and Wildlife
103 S. Main St., 10 South
Waterbury, VT 05676

Virginia Department of Game and Inland
 Fisheries
P.O. Box 11104
Richmond, VA 23230-1104

Washington Department of Wildlife
Fish Management Division
600 N. Capitol Way
Olympia, WA 98504

West Virginia Department of Natural Resources
Wildlife Department
1800 Washington St. E.
Charleston, WV 25305

Wisconsin Department of Natural Resources
Box 7921
Madison, WS 53707

Wyoming Game and Fish Department
5400 Bishop Blvd.
Cheyenne, WY 82002

Tribal Agencies

Pyramid Lake Paiute Tribe
Pyramid Lake Fisheries
Star Route
Sutcliffe, NV 89510

Wind River Indian Reservation
Shoshone and Arapahoe Tribes
Fish and Game Department
P.O. Box 217
Fort Washakie, WY 82514

Provincial Agencies

Alberta Forestry, Lands and Wildlife
Fish and Wildlife Division
Main Floor, North Tower
Petroleum Plaza
9945 108th St.
Edmonton, Alberta T5K 2G6

British Columbia Recreational Fishing Program
Ministry of Environment and Parks
2569 Kenworth Rd.
Nanaimo, British Columbia V9T 4P7

Travel Manitoba
Department 6002
Winnipeg, Manitoba R3C 3H8

New Brunswick Fish and Wildlife Branch
Department of Natural Resources and Energy
P.O. Box 6000
Fredericton, New Brunswick E3B 5H1

Newfoundland and Labrador Department of
 Development and Tourism
P.O. Box 2016
St. John's, Newfoundland A1C 5R8

Nova Scotia Department of Tourism
P.O. Box 130
Halifax, Nova Scotia B3J 2M7

Ontario Ministry of Tourism and Recreation
7th Floor, 77 Bloor St. W.
Toronto, Ontario M7A 2R9

Quebec Ministry of Tourism
C.P. 20 000
Quebec, Quebec G1K 7X2

Saskatchewan Department of Tourism and
 Small Business
2103 11th Ave.
Regina, Saskatchewan S4P 3V7